SONIC MODERNITY

Edinburgh Critical Studies in Modernist Culture
Series Editors: Tim Armstrong and Rebecca Beasley

Forthcoming Series Volumes:

*Modernism and Magic: Experiments with Spiritualism,
Theosophy and the Occult*, Leigh Wilson

*Sonic Modernity: Representing Sound in Literature, Culture and
the Arts*, Sam Halliday

Modernism and the Frankfurt School, Tyrus Miller

Late Modernism, Laura Salisbury

Modernism, Space and the City, Andrew Thacker

Modernism and the Idea of Everyday Life, Leena Kore-Schroder

SONIC MODERNITY

Representing Sound in Literature, Culture and the Arts

Sam Halliday

EDINBURGH
University Press

For Matilde

© Sam Halliday, 2013

Edinburgh University Press Ltd
22 George Square, Edinburgh EH8 9LF

www.euppublishing.com

Typeset in Sabon and Gill Sans
by Servis Filmsetting Ltd, Stockport, Cheshire, and
printed and bound in Great Britain by
CPI Group (UK) Ltd, Croydon CR0 4YY

A CIP record for this book is available from the British Library

ISBN 978 0 7486 2761 5 (hardback)
ISBN 978 0 7486 3256 5 (webready PDF)
ISBN 978 0 7486 7852 5 (epub)
ISBN 978 0 7486 7853 2 (Amazon ebook)

The right of Sam Halliday
to be identified as author of this work
has been asserted in accordance with
the Copyright, Designs and Patents Act 1988.

CONTENTS

List of illustrations   vi
Series Editors' Preface   vii
Acknowledgements   viii

Introduction: The Sonic Cultures of Modernity   1

1   Theorising Sound and Hearing   20

2   Sound and Social Life   52

3   Seeing Sound   89

4   Modernising Music   124

5   The Art of Listening   157

Bibliography   183
Index   203

LIST OF ILLUSTRATIONS

2.1 Diagram from Hadley Cantril and Gordon W. Allport, *The Psychology of Radio* (1935)   68

3.1 Page from Stéphane Mallarmé, 'Un Coup de Dés Jamais N'Abolira Le Hasard' (1897)   94

3.2 Pages from Guillaume Apollinaire, 'Lettre-Océan' (1914)   95

3.3 Gino Severini, *Cannoni in Azione* (1915)   98

3.4 Image from *Man with a Movie Camera* (dir. Dziga Vertov, 1929, USSR)   100

3.5 Woodcut from Persifor Frazer, Jr, 'Some Microscopical Observations of the Phonograph Record' (1878)   105

SERIES EDITORS' PREFACE

This series of monographs on selected topics in modernism is designed to reflect and extend the range of new work in modernist studies. The studies in the series aim for a breadth of scope and for an expanded sense of the canon of modernism, rather than focusing on individual authors. Literary texts will be considered in terms of contexts including recent cultural histories (modernism and magic; sonic modernity; media studies) and topics of theoretical interest (the everyday; postmodernism; the Frankfurt School); but the series will also re-consider more familiar routes into modernism (modernism and gender; sexuality; politics). The works published will be attentive to the various cultural, intellectual and historical contexts of British, American and European modernisms, and to inter-disciplinary possibilities within modernism, including performance and the visual and plastic arts.

ACKNOWLEDGMENTS

My first thanks go to Tim Armstrong and Becky Beasley, who invited me to write this book (Tim also suggested the title, generously sharing one of his own). Secondly, I would like to thank students and colleagues at Queen Mary, University of London, including Michèle Barrett, Julia Boffey, Mark Currie, Markman Ellis, Rachael Gilmour, Paul Hamilton, Suzanne Hobson, Catherine Maxwell, Chris Reid and Bill Schwarz. Another kind of debt is owed to Douglas Kahn, John M. Picker, Jonathan Sterne, Emily Thompson, and other scholars who have done much to energise the study of sound in recent years. Geoff Chew showed great generosity and patience, as well as expertise, in reading a draft of my fourth chapter. This book was written in London, and is both circumstantially and substantially informed by that city's parks, rivers and canals, galleries, museums, libraries and cinemas. Giacomo Halliday, my son, was born part-way through writing of the book, and has provided companionship ever since. But this book can only be dedicated to Giacomo's mother, Matilde Nardelli, whom I usually accompanied to all those galleries, museums and so on. Many of what good ideas this book may have I owe to her; the mistakes, of course, are all my own.

Figure 3.1 Page from Stéphane Mallarmé, *Un Coup de dés jamais n'abolira le hasard: Poème* (Paris: Gallimard, 1914), © The British Library Board

Figure 3.2 Pages from Guillaume Apollinaire, 'Lettre-Océan' (1914), *Calligrammes: Poèmes de la paix et de la guerre (1913–1916)* (Paris: Mercure de France, 1918), © The British Library Board

Figure 3.3 Gino Severini, *Cannoni in Azione* (1915), reproduced in black and white, © Archivio Fotografico Mart, il Museo di Arte Moderna e Contemporanea di Trento e Roverto / © ADAGP, Paris and DACS, London 2012

Excerpts from Mina Loy, *The Lost Lunar Baedeker*, reprinted by permission of Roger L. Conover.

Excerpts from *The Complete Poems of Hart Crane*, edited by Marc Simon. Copyright © 1933, 1958, 1966 by Liveright Publishing Corporation. Copyright © 1986 by Marc Simon. Used by permission of Liveright Publishing Corporation.

Excerpts from 'Blues Fantasy' from *The Collected Poems of Langston Hughes*, edited by Arnold Rampersad with David Roessel, associate editor. Copyright © 1994 by the Estate of Langston Hughes. Used by Permission of Alfred A. Knopf, a division of Random House, Inc. , and David Higham Associates Inc.

Excerpts from H. D. (Hilda Doolittle) from *Collected Poems, 1912–1944*. Copyright © 1982 by the Estate of Hilda Doolittle. Reprinted by permission of New Directions Publishing Corp and Carcanet Press Limited.

INTRODUCTION: THE SONIC CULTURES OF MODERNITY

What is 'modern' about sound, and what is the significance of sound for modernism? How is sound represented in literature, and the other arts? A perfect way to begin answering these questions comes via a feature film, a minor classic, Marcel L'Herbier's *L'Inhumaine* (1924).

The plot revolves around a famous and enchanting singer, Claire Lescot, played by Georgette Leblanc. Because of her coquettish and unfeeling manipulation of men's affections, she is known as 'the inhuman'; hence the film's title. However, her own affections are eventually engaged by Einar Norsen (played by Jacques Catelain), an engineer whose love for the singer is bound up with his invention of a thrilling and portentous machine. With this machine, Lescot's voice can be transmitted across the world, much as real-life radio in the early 1920s was starting to broadcast the voices of broadcasters across Europe and North America. However, unlike its real-life equivalent, Norsen's device also allows Lescot to *see* her audiences, as they listen. In the scene where the invention is unveiled, a series of moving images is displayed upon a screen as Lescot sings, much as in television – a word which itself appears on an intertitle, as part of Norsen's explanatory dialogue. Each set of images represents a part of Lescot's global fan base. And so, we, the film's audience, along with Lescot, come to see a group of Arab men sitting around a loudspeaker, somewhere in the Middle East (here, as in the following shots, people's location and ethnicity is signified by props and clothing). Then, we see another group of men, crowded around a loudspeaker on a street in western Europe. And most remarkably, we see a woman, apparently in Africa, listening raptly to Lescot's voice coming out of a loudspeaker. As she listens, this woman's lips part, first in appreciation, then astonishment. She picks the speaker up and holds it to her ear. And then, she looks *behind* the speaker, apparently in an attempt to 'see' where the sound is coming from. The woman, we hereby gather, is unacquainted with a possibility that western cinema audiences at the time of *L'Inhumaine*'s making were familiar with: that of sounds being broadcast over distance, sometimes great, and made present in the visible absence of their sources. This is a possibility that, in 1924, may apparently still provoke astonishment in those unused to it. So it is that, as the sequence ends, the woman calls to a person or persons off-screen, in words that are not directly represented but which we can readily infer: 'what a lovely voice!', she must be saying, 'but where's the singer?'

Implicit in this sequence is a series of predicates and assumptions about the nature and appeal of sound; together, they tell us much about the significance of sound in modern life. For a start, the episode helps document the excitement surrounding sound technologies in the early twentieth century, particularly, in this case, radio, of which Norsen's invention appears as an extension. (Elsewhere in the film, we see two other important sound technologies, the gramophone and the telephone.) In its depiction of the African woman, moreover, the film suggests that though these technologies increasingly span the globe, they presently serve to differentiate, as well as interconnect, the world's various populations. For while sound transfixes everyone, it seems, it is only in industrialised western countries that people have got used to its being manipulated in ways that make its wide-scale geographical dissemination regular, predictable and operationally transparent. But perhaps the most striking thing about the film for us is that all this is represented visually. Like almost all films of its era, *L'Inhumaine* is a 'silent' film, lacking a pre-recorded, synchronised soundtrack, either of spoken dialogue or music. (The first commercially successful film to feature such a soundtrack, *The Jazz Singer*, appeared in 1927.) The only dialogue directly rendered in the film appears in written form, as inter-titles, while music can accompany the film only if grafted on afterwards, as it were, with a pianist or band playing along at any given screening. And though such accompaniment was in fact the norm for most screenings of most films throughout the 'silent' era, this does not change the fact that *L'Inhumaine* itself is soundless. So it is that, though L'Herbier's film is 'about' sound, in all sorts of ways, it does not feature sound directly, and is not *made* of sound at all. By necessity, as much as aesthetic choice, it represents sound indirectly: mainly by considering sound's causes and effects, and by considering the social and technical conditions surrounding sound's production.

For all these reasons, *L'Inhumaine* exemplifies a cardinal thesis of this book: that sound in modernism, in whatever art form, is irreducible to sound alone. Sound, instead, is best conceived as a configuration, with 'real' sound at its centre, to be sure, but other sense phenomena, such as touch and vision, rarely at more than one or two removes on its periphery. To fully grasp the significance of sound in modern culture, it follows, we must consider visual cultures of sound and verbal cultures of sound, and see all of these in dialogue with 'sounded' cultures of sound, more self-evidently made out of sound itself. Claire Lescot's art form, music, may initially appear exempt from this injunction, but this in fact is not the case, for as *L'Inhumaine* begins to suggest, and as we shall further see throughout this book, it was entangled in the same trans-sensory matrix of concerns as literature, painting, cinema and other art forms, just as it was frequently represented by these other art forms, and variously described and theorised, painted and sculpted, photographed and filmed. This is made obvious, indeed, by Norsen's invention, which makes the act of listening into an object of visual representation – a spectacle worth watching. And we need only add that this is just as true of Lescot's making music as it is of those who listen to it. Within the same sequence, after all, her singing is itself a spectacle for us, as a cinema audience, to see.

The 'visuality' of listening is, indeed, underlined by two other music-related sequences in the film – which also serve to indicate how music, no less than any sound technology, comes to be implicated in the constellation of urges, affects, arguments and institutions that help constitute 'the modern'. In an early scene, a dinner party at Lescot's house is entertained by a group of musicians. From their instruments, which include saxophones and drums (which can be seen, but of course not heard), we know they are playing jazz, then enjoying an unprecedented vogue in France, where the film is set, and itself one of the period's most potent symbols of aesthetic and social innovation.[1] The second sequence begins as Lescot is about to perform what an advertisement calls 'Musique Moderne Française'. As she takes the stage, a section of the audience begin to boo – at this point in the film, she has been implicated in Norsen's apparent suicide – though other sections of the audience applaud once she starts singing. This is the moment of the film where Lescot's talents are meant to elicit the cinema audience's sympathy – though in the on-screen audience, in fact, the two factions continue arguing. But in addition to its narrative function, the sequence has a further, documentary significance transcending the film in which it appears and helping to illuminate the entire cultural milieu of which *L'Inhumaine* is part.[2] To secure footage for the scene, L'Herbier installed cameras at a real-life performance at the Théâtre des Champs-Élysées in Paris, hoping that a riot would take place. The appearance of George Antheil (1900–1959), an American composer and pianist whose work had already prompted a riot in Berlin, ensured that it would. In his memoir, *Bad Boy of Music* (1945), Antheil recalls some of the luminaries in attendance:

> I remember Man Ray punching somebody in the nose in the front row. Marcel Duchamp was arguing loudly with somebody else in the second row. In a box near by [*sic*] Erik Satie was shouting, 'What precision! What precision!' and applauding. The spotlight was turned on the audience by some wag upstairs. It struck James Joyce full in the face, hurting his sensitive eyes. [. . .] In the gallery the police came in and arrested the surrealists who, liking the music, were punching everybody who objected.[3]

Though some of the details here may be fanciful, the names Antheil gives offer a fair indication of the Parisian avant-garde in which he would soon play a part. And these were not the only such people supposedly in attendance: just prior to the account given above, Antheil also names Picasso, Igor Stravinsky (whose *The Rite of Spring* had provoked a similar riot when premiered at the same theatre some ten years earlier), Sergei Diaghilev (whose Russian Ballet had staged that premier of *The Rite*) and the English writer Ford Madox Ford.[4]

It is another writer, however, not mentioned here (though he appears prominently elsewhere in Antheil's memoir) that best explains why Antheil's music might have caused such consternation. For Ezra Pound, who wrote a tract on Antheil in 1924, the composer's music represents 'a scaling of eye-balls, a castigating or purging of aural cortices'; an experience more akin to medicine than entertainment.[5] That Pound meant this as an expression of approval is indicative of his relentless campaign for uncompromising innovation in every art form: a campaign that also saw him promote the causes of painters and sculptors, as well as many fellow writers. This, then, is a further sign of how thoroughly entwined the sound-based and apparently non-sound-based art forms were throughout the modernist period. And what of Joyce, another author who *is* mentioned in Antheil's list of audience members at the Champs-Élysées concert, and a figure whose own career may equally well be taken as a sign of music's complex entanglement with literature, and vice versa? Before settling down to writing, Joyce at one point hoped to be a professional singer.[6] His first book is entitled *Chamber Music* (1907) and features poems which were set to music by composers almost forty times while he was alive (others have followed since his death).[7] During the 1920s, he collaborated with Antheil himself on an abortive project to adapt an episode from his novel *Ulysses* (1922) as an opera.[8] And according to at least one critical study, Joyce's entire *oeuvre* is marked by sustained engagement with the aesthetic theory and topical preoccupations of perhaps the most important figure in nineteenth-century opera – and one of the most influential figures in any art form – Richard Wagner.[9]

We may turn to this aesthetic theory, indeed, for a final introductory indi-cation of the present book's own topical concerns. In his essay 'Beethoven' (1870), Wagner claims the existence of a *'sound-world* beside the *light-world'*, parallel to that of vision, and bearing 'the same relation to the visible world as dreaming to waking'.[10] The analogy continues: 'As the world of dreams can only come to vision through a special operation of the brain, so Music enters our consciousness through a kindred operation.'[11] Listening to music, then, is rather like a dream we have while waking, transporting us outside the world our 'normal' senses know. Just what this might mean for the musician or com-poser need not detain us at this point, but the postulation of a 'sound-world' might. For what if we were to extrapolate from Wagner's account, and say that such a world contained *all* sounds, not just musical ones – including those of, say, nature or a city? What if this world could be shown as changing over time, or even as specific to a given period: not in the sense of being unique to that period, perhaps, in every detail, but of having a distinctive and, at least in some respects, unprecedented character? And what if this world could be shown to be decisively inflected by the appearance of new technologies and the elaboration of new scientific concepts; the emergence of new topographies and habitations, together with correspondingly new types of relationship and institution; and the accumulated insights and deliberations of writers, artists, and other intellectuals for whom the senses were both incessantly receptive of new subject matter and worthy of analysis in their own right? The wager of this book is that these hypotheses can be confirmed, and that the questions they are couched in can be answered in the affirmative. For I do think such a thing as 'sonic modernity' exists, and that it can be delineated with a fair degree of specificity and detail. I will say more about this 'modernity', and its parameters, later in this introduction; for now, let us consider how it is that we come to perceive sounds in the first place.

THE EAR IN HISTORY: SOME THEORY

In recent years, there have been many scholarly accounts of sound in modern culture, often based on premises comparable to those just sketched above. Some of these, such as Emily Thompson's *The Soundscape of Modernity: Architectural Acoustics and the Culture of Listening in America, 1900–1933* (2002) and John M. Picker's *Victorian Soundscapes* (2003) take their lead from R. Murray Schaefer's conception of the 'soundscape' (as formulated in *The Tuning of the World*, 1977), a para-Wagnerian term aimed at appre-hending all sounds occurring in a given time and place as a totality.[12] Other studies, such as Jonathan Sterne's *The Audible Past: Cultural Origins of Sound Reproduction* (2003) regard sound both as an object studied during the Enlightenment and as an investigative lever of that very movement, as well as something subsequently processed, parsed and packaged by technologies.[13]

Most of these texts owe a spiritual, if not substantial debt to Walter Benjamin's ground-clearing suggestion that '[d]uring long periods of history, the mode of human sense perception changes with humanity's entire mode of existence'.[14] For all these writers, then, sound is subject to specific modes of production and dissemination that inform sound's experience and understanding, in ways that feed back upon sound's production and dissemination in turn. Both sound and hearing are historical.

Once this is granted, the way is open for considering how hearing might relate to other senses, equally historical. For Benjamin's friend and some-time colleague Theodor Adorno, the senses 'all have a *different* history', and thus 'end up poles apart from each other, as a consequence of the growing reification of reality as well as of the division of labour'.[15] According to this argument, the rise of industrial capitalism, along with economic specialisation, and the consequent narrowing of each person's practical and social interests, means that the senses have lost whatever unity they may once have (but in Adorno's view, have probably never) had. The 'reification' of reality – that is, the 'thing'-like appearance reality assumes under such conditions – is in this respect a function of the 'false' objectivity sense data have when they do not function as part of an ensemble. The triumph of commodity exchange – subjecting every human product to a single calculus of monetary value, regardless of its intrinsic worth and specificity – moreover means that sense perception becomes infected with the same market-oriented motives as every other behavioural element of economic life. It is significant that Adorno mounts this argument while critiquing none other than Wagner, whose own distinction between a 'sound-world' and a 'light-world' might otherwise appear congenial to this very view. For it is Adorno's passionate belief that Wagner obfuscates rather than reveals the conditions under which visual and acoustic 'worlds' are differentiated, presenting their socio-historic split without sufficiently accounting for its very socio-historicity.

In his *Composing for the Films* (1947), written with Hanns Eisler, Adorno offers what amounts to an elaboration of some of these views:

> The human ear has not adapted itself to the bourgeois rational and, ultimately, highly industrialised order as readily as the eye, which has become accustomed to conceiving reality as made up of separate things, commodities, objects that can be modified by practical activity. Ordinary listening, as compared to seeing, is 'archaic'; it has not kept pace with technological progress. One might say that to react with the ear, which is fundamentally a passive organ in contrast to the swiftly, actively selecting eye, is in a sense not in keeping with the present advanced industrial age and its cultural anthropology.

> For this reason acoustical perception preserves comparably more traits of long bygone, pre-individualistic collectivities than optical perception.[16]

Though Wagner is not the target here, the sense of vision is – though admittedly, only insofar as this is fingered as the 'bourgeois' sense par excellence. This qualifies Benjamin's original claim about the senses, reminding us that their histories are neither monolithic nor necessarily 'in sync', one thing always leading to, or proceeding in parallel with, another. But what it also raises is the intriguing possibility that hearing might open up a kind of front against bourgeois culture from within, activating social impulses the dominant order otherwise suppresses. Hearing, then, is oppositional, insofar as it implies a form of politics. And it is critical, having the ability to undercut or query the evidence provided by the other senses.

At this point, it is worth pausing to wonder if all features of this argument are equally compelling. For a start, the distinction between 'passive' ear and 'active' eye, while possibly valid in some instances, seems unlikely to cover all cases in which the two senses might be engaged. Surely there are cases when the ear may be proactive and the eye sluggish, while there are others where both sense organs are either more or less active or passive at the same time? Similarly, it may be that hearing is not always as 'archaic' as Adorno and Eisler seem to imply – at least insofar as, in their account, this denotes insensitivity to technological change. For does not the evidence we have assembled so far, especially from *L'Inhumaine*, make clear that sound technologies, with their direct effect upon the ear, are part and parcel of this very process? Finally, the very notion that the senses are definitively and progressively differentiated from each other might be qualified – even if it is not ultimately rejected. For might there not be ways, no less 'historic' than Adorno and Eisler indicate, in which the senses are encouraged to converge?

It is as a partial corrective to Adorno and Eisler's argument, then, that we may now turn to Marcel Proust's *In Search of Lost Time* (1913–27), perhaps not coincidentally amongst the very greatest 'bourgeois' artworks. In the remarks on the senses that stud this novel, hearing and seeing are certainly distinguished but rarely seen as tending in opposite directions; rather, they are more often seen as co-operative and complementary.[17] Take the special sort of 'gaze' which, the narrator claims, 'is not merely the messenger of the eyes, but at whose window all the senses assemble and lean out'.[18] A similar gaze is later turned upon young girls, the eyes thus becoming 'delegates from our other senses' (vol. 2, p. 546). These senses

> follow, one after another, in search of the various charms, fragrant, tactile, savorous, which they thus enjoy even without the aid of hands and lips; and able, thanks to the arts of transposition, the genius for synthesis in which desire excels, to reconstruct beneath the hue of cheeks or

bosom the feel, the taste, the contact that is forbidden them [. . .]. (vol. 2, p. 546)

If it is sexual desire that knits the senses here, these senses must nonetheless possess some innate predisposition to be 'synthesised'. And in the novel's second paragraph, it is made clear that hearing can perform a similar office, with respect to vision, as that performed by vision here, with respect to taste and touch. Lying in bed at night, the narrator recalls:

> I could hear the whistling of trains, which, now nearer and now further off, punctuating the distance like the note of a bird in a forest, showed me in perspective the deserted countryside through which a traveller is hurrying towards the nearby station. (vol. 1, pp. 1–2)

'[T]raveller[s]' and a locale are *seen* through hearing.

Faced with such evidence, it is clear that people in the modern period were not collectively condemned to experience their senses as, as Adorno puts it, 'poles apart'. Proust's fundamental point, though, is not that the senses always blend and interchange in this way, any more than it is that they never become detached, but that both sorts of experience form part of a standing repertoire of possibilities. Immediately prior to the 'delegate[d]' senses passage, the narrator notes that in contrast to young girls, many other types of person 'exist for us only on a flat, one-dimensional surface, because we are conscious of them only through visual perception restricted to its own limits' (vol. 2, p. 546). This well may be taken as confirming rather than undercutting Adorno's point about how the senses' isolation contributes to the 'reification of reality'. And are there not be experiences that more or less inevitably leave one or other sense isolated, without either the means, or possibly even the wish, to 'synthesise' with others? Compare what Proust says about watching a person at close quarters above with his following account of hearing a similarly well-known person speaking on the telephone: 'one discovers on the telephone the inflexions of a voice which one fails to perceive so long as it is not dissociated from a face in which one objectivises its expression' (vol. 5, p. 603). And now compare both passages with a more famous episode, again involving the telephone, where the narrator is in conversation with his grandmother:

> suddenly I heard that voice which I mistakenly thought I knew so well; for always until then, every time that my grandmother had talked to me, I had been accustomed to follow what she said on the open score of her face, in which the eyes figured so largely; but her voice itself I was hearing this afternoon for the first time. And because that voice appeared to me to have altered in its proportions from the moment that it was a whole, and reached me thus alone and without the accompaniments of her face

and features, I discovered for the first time how sweet that voice was [. . .]. (vol. 3, p. 149)

Desire may synthesise what it likes, but certain experiences are ineluctable: in these two cases, paramount among these is the experience of recognising qualities within a person's voice *because* it is transmitted by the telephone. In Proust's gloss on telephony, then, it is clear that the device not only separates vision from audition, but in doing so, makes each of these senses somehow more themselves: in the case of vision, by retroactively purifying visual impressions of all things not truly visual (though it is not spelled out, it is clear that when perceiving his grandmother now, the narrator can better identify those things about her which are truly facial, truly visible); and hearing, because once 'freed' from visual supplementation, the ear can literally sense what it could not otherwise, as if its range or subtlety were heightened. And in a way, perhaps, it *has* been heightened, in much the same way that blind people are sometimes said to 'compensate' for their loss of sight by becoming more adept at discriminating with their remaining senses (we shall consider versions of this claim above in Chapter 5). To quote another line by Walter Benjamin: 'technology has subjected the human sensorium to a complex kind of training'.[19]

REPRESENTING SOUND IN LITERATURE

By now, it is becoming clear that two contrasting principles are at stake. On one hand, we have claims suggesting that the senses are prised apart by new technologies, and by the broader-scale historic shifts in which these technologies are embedded. On the other hand, it appears that, in certain circumstances at least, the senses operate as part of an ensemble, sometimes even interchanging functions. That Proust should, in effect, appear on both sides of this argument suggests that that these principles are not as irreconcilable as they might at first appear, and may even, in fact, be symptomatic of the same historic crisis. For Wagner, this is, above all, the crisis registered by *art*; which accordingly, should try to heal the sensory, as much as social splits which he – no less than Adorno, in so many other respects his adversary – sees as endemic to modernity. Commenting on the decline of Greek tragedy (for him the highest form of art to date) Wagner writes: 'As the Spirit of *Community* split itself along a thousand lines of egoistic cleavage, so was the great united work of Tragedy disintegrated into its individual factors.'[20] The history of art since Greek tragedy's decline has thus been one of mutual isolation, with each of these 'factors' (listed here as 'rhetoric, sculpture, painting, music, &c') condemned 'in lonely self-sufficiency to pursue its own development'.[21] How then should one remedy this situation? By means of the *Gesamtkunstwerk*, or 'Total Work of Art', which Wagner's own musical dramas aspire to realise, and which attempts to reintegrate each now-sundered art form into a single, all-sufficient whole. The rationale behind this is set out in Wagner's key essay, 'The Art-Work of the Future' (1849); notice here how his theory of the senses is imbricated with a theory of each artistic medium, and how each of these is rooted in an underlying human 'faculty':

> Each separate faculty of man is limited by bounds; but his united, agreed, and reciprocally helping faculties [. . .] combine to form the self-completing, unbounded, universal faculty of men. Thus too has every *artistic* faculty of man its natural bounds, since man has not *one only Sense* but separate *Senses*; while every faculty springs from its special sense, and therefore each single faculty must find its bounds in the confines of its correlated sense. But the boundaries of the separate senses are also their joint meeting-points, those points at which they melt in one another and each agrees with each: and exactly so do the faculties that are derived from them touch one another and agree. Their confines, therefore, are removed by this agreement; but only those that love each other can agree, and 'to love' means: to acknowledge the other, and at like time to know one's self. Thus Knowledge through Love is Freedom; and the freedom of man's faculties is – *All-faculty*.
>
> Only the Art which answers to this 'all-faculty' of man is, therefore *free* [. . .].[22]

Because man is an 'All'-containing being (at least when social and political circumstances allow it), the art 'he' makes should properly be integrated too. Thus, the fact that each 'artistic faculty' grows out of a specific sense – painting, for example, grows out of sight, just as music grows out of hearing, and so on – should not distract us from the fact that deep down, all such faculties are complementary: again, 'the boundaries of the separate senses *are also their joint meeting-points*.' In other words, Wagner's understanding of the senses and his prescriptions for future artworks are strictly homologous, the 'total' work of art being simply that which maximally stimulates each of the senses, ensuring that each of these converge upon on a single summit of appreciation. The 'light-world' and the 'sound-world' which, we may remember, are said to underpin all art, may remain theoretically distinct. But experientially, Wagner's pledge is that he can put his audiences squarely in the midst of both at once.

This programme for, and theory of, the arts was, to say the least, enormously influential in Wagner's lifetime, and continued to be so long into the modernist era and beyond.[23] This is not to say that it was universally accepted – indeed, it represents just one of many reasons why Wagner provoked as much hostility as admiration, as he continues to do to this day – but that it provides a touchstone, whether cited admiringly or otherwise, for most serious reflections on art ever since. What then might this mean for literature, a medium not generally thought of as having any special affinity with other art forms, and thus, it might be thought, inherently unsuited to providing the kind of multisensory experience Wagner seeks? More generally, we might ask: what has literature got to do with sound itself, given that in most contexts, at least in western culture (especially since the rise of print culture, and widespread literacy) it is generally read in silence, on the page?[24]

To address these questions, I want first to turn to a literary representation of music, the art over which Wagner's influence was greatest (notwithstanding his ambitions of omnipotence). In the first line of the first poem of Joyce's *Chamber Music*, 'Strings in the earth and air' are identified as a source of music.[25] This is an allusion to a specific philosophical or cosmological claim, according to which celestial bodies emit a form of music as they move, inaudible to human ears: the so-called 'music of the spheres' hypothesis, usually attributed to the ancient Greek philosopher Pythagoras (c. 570 – c. 495 BC). Through this allusion, Joyce frees the concept, 'music', from any need to be audible to be effective. In the poem's second stanza, meanwhile, music is associated with riverside trysting and with 'Love', again sidestepping the specific issue of music's audibility (p. 13). Thus is music connected to desire and the sensibilities more generally. Finally, the poem's third stanza attends to the ways listening and performance by musicians condition and are conditioned by the body. (These musicians play, the poem specifies, with 'head to the music bent', p. 13.) In sum, the poem, while acknowledging 'music's' literal meanings, moves beyond these to consider music's metaphorical, figurative and pragmatic dimensions. Although Joyce welcomed the attempts of composers to set his poems to 'real' music, we might therefore consider that such efforts rather miss the point.[26] For what his poem surely shows is that one form of art, in this case poetry, can meaningfully think about another without thereby needing that other to 'complete' it.

Joyce's poem, while hardly without parallel in earlier writing, is indicative of the particularly strenuous efforts modernists made to unsettle distinctions between the audible and inaudible. In doing so, they also sought to bring all sounds, not just music, into the domain of language. Take the following description of a crowd assembling at a pageant from Virginia Woolf's *Between the Acts* (1941):

> Feet crunched the gravel. Voices chattered. The inner voice, the other voice was saying: How can we deny that this brave music, wafted from the bushes, is expressive of some inner harmony? 'When we wake' (some were thinking) 'the day breaks us with its hard mallet blows'. 'The office' (some were thinking) 'compels disparity. Scattered, shattered, hither thither summoned by the bell. 'Ping-ping-ping' – that's the phone [. . .].'[27]

Here, even more systematically than in Joyce's poem, the audible and inaudible are juxtaposed – with the overall effect that it becomes very hard to see where one ends and the other begins. Clearly, those thoughts that liken daybreak to 'mallet blows' evoke a sound, but do so soundlessly, presumably somewhere in the recesses of the thinkers' sensible (but not directly sensing) heads. Perhaps this is a sound people have actually heard in the morning, but it is explicitly here invoked more metaphorically, by way of an analogy. The 'crunch' of the gravel and 'chatter' of their voices, meanwhile, really are part of the present scene, as is the music coming from the bushes – though in the latter's case, again, this turns figurative, expressing 'inner', non-acoustic 'harmony'. The 'ping-ping-ping' of a telephone, by contrast, is identified as an unwelcome signature of modern life. In sum, Woolf conceives a 'total' or inclusive 'sound-world' where the sonic and the non-sonic, and the musical and non-musical, occupy a common space: a space, moreover, that is as much social as it is geophysical, as much conceptual as it is sensory, and as much imaginary, or subjective, as it is 'real'.

How, then, do these aesthetic strategies compare with Wagner's programme for a 'total' work of art? Clearly, neither Joyce's nor Woolf's text arrives at absolute identity with the sounds that they refer to, even if they might want to (which is by no means certain). Both in principle and in fact there remains an irreducible gap between evoking, say, a piece of music and actually hearing that music itself. Similarly, neither writer indicates that Wagner's argument would be 'better' treated as a theory of literature than as a programme for opera – if for no other reason than that this would misinterpret one of Wagner's central points, according to which (as we have seen) no artistic medium can absorb or substitute for any other, but should rather aim only at those effects which the sense organs corresponding to them are best able to perceive. But what these examples do show is that literature – like film, as in the case of *L'Inhumaine* – is especially well suited for revealing sound's 'configured' quality, which is, again, sound's imbrication in the non- or trans-acoustic. Correlatively, literature is especially well suited for revealing such para-sonic factors as sound's social connotations, its relationships with other senses, and – perhaps most importantly of all – the qualitative dimension that means certain sounds are actually of interest to people, things they actively seek out or shun. Consider one last example, from Dorothy Richardson's epic novel-cycle *Pilgrimage* (1915–67); here, a billiard ball has just been struck: 'the faint thundering roll of the single ball, the click of the concussion, the gentle angular explosion of pieces into a new relation and the breaking of the varying triangle as the ball rolled to its hidden destination, held by all the eyes in the room until its rumbling pilgrimage ended out of sight in a soft thud.'[28] Not only does this superb description give a vivid sense of what is seen and heard, but it also enfolds the reader, as it were, in the same attentive web as the auditory and visual sensations of the persons represented. The players and spectators invoked here are, above all, *interested* in what is going on in front of them; without this interest, we might speculate, it is highly unlikely that the game they are witnessing would sponsor such detailed and highly differentiated sense impressions. This, then, is the work of Adorno and Eisler's 'active' eye – but also of an active ear: an ear thoroughly penetrated by volition and curiosity, and able on that basis to make the finest of discriminations.

DEFINING 'MODERN' SOUND; OR, MARVIN GAYE AS THEORIST OF MODERNITY

In each of the chapters that follow, the central topics broached so far will be addressed in greater detail: in Chapter 1, by making a more detailed survey than has been possible so far of ways in which sound is theorised and appreciated from classical antiquity onwards, focusing especially on the latter part of the nineteenth and the first half of the twentieth centuries; in Chapter 2, by considering ways in which sound helps articulate and differentiate forms and objects of social interaction; in Chapter 3, by showing the many attempts at 'seeing,' or visually representing sounds that punctuate the history (and prehistory) of modernism; in Chapter 4, by considering self-conscious attempts by musicians and related commentators at 'modernising' music; and in Chapter 5, by treating listening – and failing to do so – as historical and philosophical, as well as aesthetic problems. But before any of this can be done, we must first consider how 'sonic' and 'modernity', the two words of this book's title, fit together. Are there truly 'modern' sounds, qualitatively distinct from their pre- (and maybe post-) modern counterparts? Three recently influential ways of answering this question affirmatively may be singled out for consideration here, on the grounds that they both seek to show what such sounds are like, and consider such sounds' historical conditions of emergence. These are Pierre Schaeffer's concept of the 'acousmatic'; James Lastra's account of the historic advent of sound's capture and retention; and Douglas Kahn's category of 'all sound'.

To begin with 'the acousmatic', this sadly rather un-euphonic term was first applied to a pedagogical method of Pythagoras, who would speak to his disciples from behind a curtain, ensuring that his words were heard, though he could not be seen.[29] In Schaeffer's more extended usage, the term refers to any sound heard without accompanying visual impressions of its cause or source, and thus, correspondingly, to 'the perceptive reality of sound as such, as distinguished from the modes of its production and transmission'.[30] Though historically aspecific (insofar as anyone in any period may, say, speak from behind a curtain) the late nineteenth and early twentieth centuries saw a pronounced rise and 'normalisation' of acousmatic listening, principally through the diffusion of technologies such as the telephone, gramophone and radio, whose 'bracketing' of sounds from visible sources is more or less intrinsic to their use. This, we should recall, is precisely the experience of those listening to radio in *L'Inhumaine*, and the one whose relative novelty, amongst other things, is represented by the African woman's astonishment when she hears Lescot's transmitted voice. (It is also, of course, the experience of Proust's narrator at the telephone – whose awareness of previously unnoticed features in other people's voices, moreover, exemplifies the consciousness of sound *as such* that Schaeffer has in mind.) We need not say that all acousmatic sounds are 'modern', then, or that all 'modern' sounds are acousmatic, to agree that acousmatic sound and listening are indeed important signatures of modern life.

The rise of acousmatic sound technology is also, in large part, responsible for the historic breakthrough represented by sound's capture and retention – though the latter is also linked to scientific developments, occurring as early as the first years of the nineteenth century. In 1802, the German physicist E. F. F. Chladni showed how sound vibrations would produce clearly visible patterns in piles of sand when passed through underlying metal plates.[31] As James Lastra writes, the resulting images 'were widely recognized as having inaugurated a new era in sound representation', both because they produced a record of the sounds that had occasioned them, and because they did so 'through the agency of the phenomenon itself rather than the investigator'.[32] Taken together, these two principles suggested not only that sound might be 'stored' for future reference, but also that if the resultant record could somehow be *re*-sounded, the resultant sound would reproduce the original as it had 'really' been, without a listener's interpretation. Both possibilities, it seemed, were realised by a series of technologies appearing later in the century: the phonograph (patented in 1878), the graphophone (patented in 1886) and, perhaps most crucially, the gramophone (patented in 1887, in production from 1894), which ultimately revolutionised the way in which a whole variety of sounds circulated and provoked pleasure or desire. As well as their documentary function, Lastra adds that such technologies brought permanence and repeatability to what had once been 'evanescent and singular' – a shift in sound's relationship to time which allowed the latter's passing to be captured and, so to speak, re-released *as* passing.[33] (Jacques Attali calls this the ability to 'stockpile time'.[34]) Hereafter, even non-recorded sounds might take on something of the quality of sound recordings: witness William Faulkner's *As I Lay Dying* (1930) – a novel which climaxes with the acquisition of a graphophone – where the 'clattering reverberations' of wooden planks being moved about on trestles are said to cease 'without departing, as if any movement might dislodge them from the immediate air in reverberant repetition'.[35]

It is with an eye to both of these historic shifts – to the rise of acousmatic listening on one hand, and the emergence of indiscriminate, non-interpretative sound storage technologies on the other – that Kahn proposes 'all sound' as a rubric for the modern experience of sound.[36] In this, seemingly the most sweeping of the three accounts of modern sound we are considering, the phonograph is again located at an historic threshold, serving as a paradigm for 'phonographic' modes of consciousness, able to operate independently of their model, even if no corresponding apparatus is in use. Precisely because it is not, in fact, conscious of sounds, as human beings are – it does not 'listen to' or 'hear', but only stores and reproduces whatever sonic objects it encounters – the phonograph treats all sounds equally, irrespective of aesthetic or affective 'rank'. Accidental or intrusive sounds are thus raised to a position of fundamental parity with the intended and sought out, resulting in a sonorous democracy where musical and 'noisy', natural and man-made, significant and senseless, and all other kinds of sounds have equal claims upon the listener. A literary example once more helps demonstrate this point; here is Leopold Bloom, contemplating a printing shop in Joyce's *Ulysses*:

> The nethermost deck of the first machine jogged forward its flyboard with sllt the first batch of quirefolded papers. Sllt. Almost human the way it sllt to call attention. Doing its level best to speak. That door too sllt creaking, asking to be shut. Everything speaks in its own way. Sllt.[37]

Although the 'sllt' here is a disruptive presence, tampering with the syntax of Joyce's sentences, it is also welcomed, savoured in the palate of Bloom's mind. And though the door's 'creak' asserts its rights, as it were, against 'sllt' sounds made by the machine, the two also complement each other, colleagues in an animistic orchestra. Once noticed, all sounds contribute to the allure of sonic life.

Of course, it would be possible, given such evidence, to say that 'modern' sounds are simply those made by all 'modern' things, including typesetting machines – and, of course, phonographs themselves. With this in mind, the present book might content itself with simply surveying as many as possible of these 'modern' sounds and things. But whilst there may be some merit in that method, care must be taken not to absolutise the distinction between modern and pre-modern, or suggest that only modern sounds feature in or even help define the modern 'sound-world'. For in fact, modern and pre-modern sounds always, necessarily, exist in a dialectical relationship. Take a famous case from Henry David Thoreau's *Walden* (1854), where a train's presence in the sonic landscape is likened to the 'scream of a hawk'.[38] What at first seems a straightforward attempt to contrast the modern and pre-modern, by highlighting their difference from one another (immediately prior to this point, Thoreau has anatomised the quieter sounds audible to him at his bucolic pond-side cabin), turns out on closer inspection to weave the two together, the train's noise being 'naturalised' by virtue of its likeness to a bird call. Similarly, Woolf writes, in *The Waves* (1931), that the 'growl' of motor traffic 'might be any uproar – forest trees or the roar of wild beasts'.[39] The modern is inscribed within the ahistoric or primordial.

It is the difficulties inherent in trying to separate the modern from the pre-modern that lead us, finally, to a definition of modernity itself that is as supple and open-ended as possible. And in this, we are assisted by someone who can only appear as an unlikely figure in this context: the American soul singer Marvin Gaye. In Gaye's great album *What's Going On* (1972), a sustained attempt is made to define Gaye's present and his nation's state in terms of *crisis*, a general imperilment of life and well-being whose causes are simultaneously ecological, economic, social, political and spiritual. In the last of the album's nine songs, 'Inner City Blues', some of the more specific afflictions this precipitates are listed more or less systematically; these include urban poverty, the rising cost of living, involvement of one's countrymen in overseas wars, increased crime and possibly lethal violence by the police. For any twenty-first century listener, this list may appear uncannily familiar. But to perceive this uncanniness in its true light, one should look to this *familiarity's familiarity* – the fact that in the thirty-six-odd years since Gaye's record was released (notwithstanding the specific circumstances behind each item of the list's appearance in this context) almost anyone, in any number of countries, could have produced a similar, or even identical, list, and applied it their own specific time and place, with equally good reason. Thus, anyone coming to Gaye's record for the first time at any point since its original release may experience the strange sensation that Gaye is singing 'about them', giving voice to their own sense of historical exceptionality. This does not mean that Gaye was 'wrong' to identify his own period as one of crisis; rather, it means that the feeling of living in exceptional times is an outstretched one, that this feeling is chronic rather than transient, and that it thus remains the same, in a sense, paradoxically, however much the temporally specific developments provoking it may change. In fact, the understanding of one's present as a time of intense and perhaps unprecedented crisis is a keynote of the discourse of modernity from at least the early nineteenth century onwards.[40] Gaye's voicing of this understanding long after the major dramas of modernity have supposedly unfolded (these would include industrialisation, and all the other associated developments we have seen Adorno allude to) indicates that a state of exception has, so to speak, become the norm. The point to take from Gaye's example, then, is that feelings of living on modernity's front line enjoy a degree of trans-historic currency, linking people despite the passage of historic time, as well as because of it. Modernity, in this sense, is not historically specific, but a quality of 'now-ness' that may, potentially at least, appear at any time.

There is, however, another important sense in which modernity is of course historically specific – if only because use of the concept more or less implies some form of periodisation, however qualified. For the purposes of this book, then, let us say that modernity begins at some point in the eighteenth century, reaches self-conscious maturity around the middle of the nineteenth century with the writings of Wagner and others, becomes central to the work of modern*ist* writers and artists such as Proust, Joyce, Woolf, Richardson, L'Herbier and Antheil, and leads up to the present moment, where it either terminates in or coincides with post- or 'late' modernity. Though this study focuses on modernism and the early twentieth century, I do not accept that modernists are, by virtue of their modernism, better able to evoke the special flavour of modernity than their non-modernist predecessors, or that non-modernists working at the same time as modernists are not capable of significant insights into modernity in their own right. Modernism is central to the story this book tells, but not co-extensive with it. The sonic cultures we shall consider in coming chapters are diverse and complex things; let us then maintain as broad as possible an approach in trying to hear them.

NOTES

1. On jazz as a signifier for modernity in France, see Bernard Gendron, *Between Montmartre and the Mudd Club: Popular Music and the Avant-Garde* (Chicago: University of Chicago Press, 2002).
2. For more on what follows in this paragraph, see Standish D. Lawder, *The Cubist Cinema* (New York: New York University Press, 1975), ch. 6.
3. George Antheil, *Bad Boy of Music* (London: Hurst and Blackett, [1945] 1947), pp. 12–13.
4. Antheil, *Bad Boy of Music*, p. 12.
5. Ezra Pound, *Antheil, and the Treatise on Harmony* (Chicago: Pascal Covici, [1924] 1927), p. 44.
6. Richard Ellmann, *James Joyce*, new and revised edn (New York: Oxford University Press, 1982), pp. 150–2.
7. Myra T. Russel, '*Chamber Music*: Words and Music Lovingly Coupled', in Sebastian D. G. Knowles (ed.), *Bronze by Gold: The Music of Joyce* (New York: Garland, 1999), pp. 57–90; p. 58 cited.
8. Paul Martin, '"Mr Bloom and the Cyclops": Joyce and Antheil's Unfinished "Opéra Mécanique"', in Sebastian D. G. Knowles (ed.), *Bronze by Gold: The Music of Joyce* (New York: Garland, 1999), pp. 91–106.
9. Timothy Martin, *Joyce and Wagner: A Study of Influence* (Cambridge: Cambridge University Press, 1991).
10. Richard Wagner, 'Beethoven' (1870), in *Richard Wagner's Prose Works*, translated by William Ashton Ellis, 8 vols (London: Kegan Paul, Trench, Trübner, 1892–99), vol. 5, pp. 57–126; p. 68 cited; emphasis in original.
11. Wagner, 'Beethoven', p. 68.
12. Emily Thompson, *The Soundscape of Modernity: Architectural Acoustics and the Culture of Listening, 1900–1933* (Cambridge, MA: MIT Press, 2002); John M. Picker, *Victorian Soundscapes* (New York: Oxford University Press, 2003); R. Murray Schaefer, *The Tuning of the World* (New York: Alfred A. Knopf, 1977).
13. Jonathan Sterne, *The Audible Past: Cultural Origins of Sound Reproduction* (Durham, NC: Duke University Press, 2003).
14. Walter Benjamin, 'The Work of Art in the Age of Mechanical Reproduction' (1936), in *Illuminations*, edited and with an introduction by Hannah Arendt, translated by Harry Zohn (London: Fontana Press for HarperCollins, 1992), pp. 211–44; p. 216 cited.

15. Theodor Adorno, *In Search of Wagner*, translated by Rodney Livingstone, with a new preface by Slavoj Žižek (London: Verso, [1952] 2005), p. 91; emphasis added.
16. Theodor Adorno and Hanns Eisler, *Composing for the Films*, with an introduction by Graham McCann (London: Athlone Press, [1947] 1994), pp. 20–1.
17. I dissent here from the view of Sara Danius, whose otherwise unimpeachable account of the senses in Proust's novel stresses vision and audition's progressive differentiation: *The Senses of Modernism: Technology, Perception, and Aesthetics* (Ithaca, NY: Cornell University Press, 2002), especially pp. 11–17; ch. 3.
18. Marcel Proust, *In Search of Lost Time*, translated by C. K. Scott Moncrieff and Terence Kilmartin, revised by D. J. Enright, 6 vols (London: Vintage, [1913–17] 1996), vol. 1, p. 168. Subsequent references to this edition are given in the text.
19. Walter Benjamin, 'On Some Motifs in Baudelaire', in *Illuminations*, pp. 152–96; p. 171 cited.
20. Richard Wagner, 'Art and Revolution' (1849), in *Richard Wagner's Prose Works*, vol. 1, pp. 21–65; p. 35 cited; emphasis in original.
21. Wagner, 'Art and Revolution', p. 52.
22. Richard Wagner, 'The Art-Work of the Future', in *Richard Wagner's Prose Works*, vol. 1, pp. 67–213; p. 97 cited; emphases in original.
23. The most recent detailed study of this influence is Juliet Koss, *Modernism After Wagner* (Minneapolis: University of Minnesota Press, 2010).
24. On the auditory substrate of such 'silent' reading, however, see Garrett Stewart, *Literature and the Phonotext* (Berkeley: University of California Press, 1990).
25. James Joyce, *Chamber Music* (1907), in *Poems and Shorter Writings*, edited by Richard Ellmann, A. Walton Litz and John Whittier-Ferguson (London: Faber and Faber, 1991), p. 13. Subsequent references to this edition are given in the text.
26. Russel, '*Chamber Music*', p. 58.
27. Virginia Woolf, *Between the Acts*, edited by Stella McNichol, with an introduction and notes by Gillian Beer (Harmondsworth: Penguin, [1941] 2000), p. 73.
28. Dorothy Richardson, *Pilgrimage*, 4 vols (London: Virago, [1915–67] 2002), vol. 1, pp. 434–5.
29. Pierre Schaeffer, 'Acousmatics' (1966), translated by Daniel W. Smith, in Christoph Cox and Daniel Warner (eds), *Audio Culture: Readings in Modern Music* (New York: Continuum, 2006), pp. 76–81.
30. Schaeffer, 'Acousmatics', p. 77.
31. Perhaps the most thorough and illuminating English-language account of Chladni is Myles W. Jackson's *Harmonious Triads: Physicists, Musicians, and Instrument Makers in Nineteenth-Century Germany* (Cambridge, MA: MIT Press, 2006), ch. 2.
32. James Lastra, *Sound Technology and the American Cinema: Perception, Representation, Modernity* (New York: Columbia University Press, 2000), p. 42.
33. Lastra, *Sound Technology and the American Cinema*, p. 46.
34. Jacques Attali, *Noise: The Political Economy of Music*, translated by Brian Massumi, with a foreword by Fredric Jameson and an afterword by Susan McClary (Minneapolis: University of Minnesota Press, [1977] 1985), p. 101.
35. William Faulkner, *As I Lay Dying: The Corrected Text* (New York: Vintage Books, [1930] 1987), p. 67.
36. Douglas Kahn, *Noise, Water, Meat: A History of Sound in the Arts* (Cambridge, MA: MIT Press, 1999), p. 9; emphasis removed.
37. James Joyce, *Ulysses: The 1922 Text*, edited with an introduction and notes by Jeri Johnson (Oxford: Oxford University Press, 1993), p. 117.
38. Henry David Thoreau, *Walden*, edited with an introduction and notes by Stephen Fender (Oxford: Oxford University Press, [1854] 1999), p. 106.

39. Virginia Woolf, *The Waves* (Harmondsworth: Penguin, [1931] 1964), p. 97.
40. The classic study of this 'keynote' is, of course, Marshall Berman, *All That Is Solid Melts Into Air: The Experience of Modernity* (London: Verso, 1983).

Chapter 1

THEORISING SOUND AND HEARING

This chapter surveys philosophical and aesthetic accounts of sound and hearing from antiquity to the first half of the twentieth century. It makes no claims for comprehensiveness but rather focuses on theories of particular relevance to literary and other artistic modernism. To do this, the chapter takes a very quick look at the ancient and early Christian periods, moves swiftly to the late eighteenth century, and then offers a more detailed (though still selective) account of nineteenth- and early twentieth-century thinkers, before focusing more closely still on literary modernism itself. Nineteenth-century sources get heavy coverage – not at the expense of their twentieth-century counterparts (I hope), but because, as I seek to show at points throughout this book, ideas originating in the nineteenth century play a pivotal role in twentieth-century thinking. This is especially the case where music is concerned, music being the topic onto which questions about sound and hearing often devolved.[1] Brad Bucknell has shown the particularly strong appeal that nineteenth-century musical aesthetics held for twentieth-century writers, especially those for whom language, their own chosen medium, was both dynamised and chastened by music's example: as he states, '"music" for many writers [in this period] refers obliquely to an art which transcends referential or lexical meaning, and which has the power of some kind of excessive, yet essential, element to which the literary may point, but which it can never fully encompass.'[2] The transcendence of 'lexical meaning' is indeed one way of thinking about the modernist project across the arts (though certainly not the only one) – such meaning being, for many, a kind of checkmate to the artist, occluding the full richness of experience. In Walter Benjamin's idiosyncratic variation on this theme, as we shall see, we are 'in' meaning, or language, almost precisely insofar as we are far from God.

Sound in Philosophy from Aristotle to Marx

It is to Aristotle that we owe some of the earliest significant reflections on sound and humans' ability to hear it. In *De Anima* (c. 350 BC), hearing is defined as 'of the audible and inaudible', accounting for the fact that we can sense when sound is absent as well as when it is present.[3] Like other senses, hearing is conceived as an arbiter between opposing qualities within the objects it perceives – for instance, sharp or flat (in terms of musical pitch) or rough and smooth (in terms of tone) (p. 184). As they are acted on, the senses are constantly remoulded by their objects, despite remaining untouched by them at a fundamental level; a difficult idea which Aristotle renders by means of an analogy with sealing wax, which similarly takes on the 'forms' of objects pressed upon it without being affected by them in its essential substance (p. 187). However, Aristotle's account in this respect is inconsistent, for he elsewhere claims that sense impressions are produced precisely by a sense organ's being made over, as it were, in the image of whatever object it perceives: before it is affected, it is 'unlike [. . .], but on being affected it becomes like what has acted on it' (p. 170). Perhaps it is a question of whether the sense organ concerned is able to register impressions while still maintaining its physical integrity; hence Aristotle's warning that 'excesses of the sense-objects destroy the sense-organs' (p. 188).

A wider point made by Aristotle is that the senses must be distinguished from the 'intellect' and other mental faculties that may draw upon the senses' data. This, in turn, seems to have potentiated the distinction drawn by early Christian commentators between the physical and 'spiritual' or 'inner' senses. For Origen (c. AD 185–254), there are five such senses, corresponding to the 'grosser' senses of sight, hearing, touch, taste and smell, themselves rooted in the body.[4] In his *Confessions* (397–8), St Augustine builds on this distinction to draw a 'moralised' contrast between the spiritual insights accessible via the inner senses and the corrupting pleasures represented by their physical counterparts; it is only by eschewing the latter, he concludes, in favour of the former, that salvation can be reached.[5] Although such ideas are clearly rooted in distrust for what the senses, on their own account, can offer, there is no reason in principle why this should always be the case. When Virginia Woolf, for instance, invokes the ideas of 'inner voice' and 'inner harmony', as we have seen her do in this book's 'Introduction', it is with a sense that these are complementary, and not opposed, to the 'exterior' acoustic phenomena on which they are modelled.

A final legacy of Aristotle worth noting is his 'ranking' of the senses, according to which sight is privileged as the most estimable (because most ostensibly knowledge-yielding) sense, and taste and touch deprecated as the least.[6] Such hierarchies are a mainstay of much subsequent commentary on the senses, at least until the great systems of Kant and Hegel in the late eighteenth and early nineteenth centuries. In Kant's *Anthropology from the Pragmatic Point of View* (1798), hearing is ranked slightly below vision on the grounds of its allegedly closer relation to touch (though touch itself, surprisingly, despite being criticised for 'clumsi[ness]', is ultimately adjudged 'the most reliably instructive of all the senses').[7] Meanwhile, inner and outer senses are cast in a dialectical relationship, impacting on and changing into one another. The 'outer' senses, touch, sight and hearing,

> lead the subject through reflection to cognition of the object as something outside ourselves. When the sensation, however, becomes so strong that the awareness of the activity of the organ becomes stronger than the awareness of the relation to an external object, then outer perceptions are changed into inner perceptions [. . .] [P]ersons are unable to attain a concept of the object because of the intensity of the sense impression; their attention centers only on the subjective idea, namely, the modification of the organ. (pp. 43–4)

Here, in a passage that compares interestingly with Woolf's account of 'inner voice', the 'inner' idea leads away from trustworthy knowledge of its object, leading to unchecked subjectivity. (There is an echo here of Aristotle's remarks about sensory 'excess', though now it is the subject's absorption rather than the impression provoking it that seems excessive.) Objective knowledge is reduced to, at best, a phenomenology of one's own body. And yet, there are other ways in which inwardness need not be identified with solipsism or a withdrawal from reality. In his remarks on sound itself, Kant suggests a link between the derived or expressed quality of sounds – it is always something 'else' that makes a sound, since sound cannot make itself – and the cognitive procedure that is or that issues in abstraction. Since 'sounds are nothing in themselves or at any rate not objects [. . .] they are the best means of expressing concepts' (p. 42). When such concepts are exchanged or shared in speech, 'people are most easily and completely able to share their thoughts and feelings with others' (p. 42). In speech, then, the mouth of one interlocutor couples with the ear of another: the 'inwardness' of one party in such discussion thus turns to 'outward' stimuli for the other; this then may turn to still further 'inward' thoughts, and so on. Inwardness itself devolves to dialogue and sociability.

With this in mind, it is easy to see how sound might go on to play a key role in certain versions of romanticism, the literary and philosophical movement for which the expression on 'inner feelings' is a paramount imperative. Hegel speaks to this in stating: 'When a body sounds, we feel we are entering a higher sphere; sound affects our innermost feeling. It speaks to the inner soul since it is itself inner and subjective'.[8] It follows that of all the senses, hearing is the most connected with 'the flight from materiality, with the transition to the immaterial and ideal' (p. 139). Though this might appear to lift sound out of everyday reality and into an eternity of frozen, static forms, sound is actually, says Hegel, a correlate of process or becoming, a point confirmed elsewhere in his writings when he states that sound 'is purely evanescent in its perceptible existence', hence its likeness to an 'ever-flowing stream'.[9] As an object of aesthetic contemplation, sound thus has a privileged relationship with time; a relation crystallised by music, which is of course the sonic art par excellence, and which Hegel regards (like others, as we shall see) as predicated on time's passing and unfolding. Is there a connection between sound's close relationship with time and its relation to the 'inner' life or soul? There is, Hegel thinks, and it resides in the fact that the self is *itself* 'in time', and that this timeliness is one of the self's own quintessential attributes. Since time 'provides the essential element in which sound gains existence in respect of its musical value, and since the time of the sound is that of the subject too, sound on this principle penetrates the self' (p. 908). When we are impressed or moved by music, in other words, it is because we recognise in it (consciously or otherwise) an echo of our own subjective life. And it is this, Hegel concludes, that constitutes the source of music's 'elemental might' (p. 908).

It is to Marx, though, Hegel's follower and critic, that we owe an observation that helps root musical reception – and, indeed, the apprehension of all sense impressions – more specifically in certain forms of social and historical reality. Noting that 'music alone awakens in man the sense of music' (because the ear must be trained to recognise and understand it as such), Marx points out that the senses must be educated before making the sort of fine discriminations that Hegel seems to have in mind.[10] Imagining that this educative process adumbrates the entire history of humankind from its earliest stages up to his own present, Marx continues:

> the *senses* of the social man are *other* senses than those of the non-social man. Only through the objectively unfolded richness of man's essential being is the richness of subjective *human* sensibility (a musical ear, an eye for beauty of form – in short, *senses* capable of human gratifications, senses confirming themselves as essential powers of *man*) either cultivated or brought into being. For not only the five senses but also the so-called mental senses – the practical senses (will, love, etc.) – in a word, *human* sense – the humanness of the senses – comes to be by virtue of its object, by virtue of *humanized* nature. The *forming* of the five senses is a labour of the entire history of the world down to the present.[11]

Not only does this anticipate Benjamin's and Adorno's accounts of the senses' historicity, considered in this book's 'Introduction', it also argues that the senses' objects, like the senses themselves, are historical as well. In other words, the 'how' as much as the 'what' of sensing is contingent on specific forms of social life. Moreover, Marx suggests that shifts in one of these two things are profoundly connected to shifts in the other: if the senses change over time, then, this is at least in part because the things they are prevailed on to consider change too, each change representing an aspect of a single process. The 'humanness of the senses' thus denotes an attunement of the senses to a largely human-made environment: a transformation that affects the senses in their 'internal' structure at the same time as corresponding transformations take place in 'external' stimuli as well. With this in mind, we can say that subsequent commentators follow Marx whenever they also depict the senses as either implicitly or explicitly conditioned by their own present; which means, in practice, whenever such commentaries are either framed or inhabited by implicit or explicit theories of modernity.

DARWIN, KANT (AGAIN) AND PHYSIOLOGY

If Hegel provides one rationale for music's 'elemental might', Marx's contemporary, Charles Darwin, provides another. In *The Descent of Man* (1873), Darwin proposes that the origin of music lies in animal courtship, a phase or form of behaviour during which the males of many species make sounds to intimidate their rivals or attract mates. (The privileged example of this is bird song, which Darwin thinks is sexually selected, so that the more 'charming' songs are favoured by females and so passed on via hereditary transmission.[12]) The strong emotions aroused by music amongst humans are thus a form of atavism, transporting people back in time to an era when they, or their ancestors, had sexual interests vested in antecedent soundings. In Darwin's words, such feelings 'appear from their vagueness, yet depth, like mental reversions to the emotions and thoughts of a long-past age'.[13] Though seemingly rather arbitrary (certainly, one cannot imagine how it might be tested), Darwin's hypothesis taps a rich vein of association between music and sexual love familiar in English literature since at least the sixteenth-century.[14] And in doing so, he, like Marx, historicises sensory experience – albeit in a rather different way. For although Marx, as we have seen, argues that sense experiences change over time, he does not necessarily thinks this happens in a way allowing individuals in one historic epoch to 'tap into' those of another, or allow the same individual to compare impressions at different times of life. Darwin, on the other hand, argues that the whole of historic – and at least part of prehistoric – time is condensed whenever musical emotions are aroused, giving listeners a kind of synoptic, if oblique impression of this whole past at one fell swoop.

The prestige of Darwin's evolutionary theory meant that his account of music, however fleetingly developed, became a platform for further enquiries into the ontology of music later in the nineteenth century. Perhaps the most significant of these is Edmund Gurney's *The Power of Sound* (1880), which, perhaps anticipating objections to Darwin's own argument, tries to turn these to its advantage. 'These ideas may seem at first sight somewhat startling', says Gurney, having quoted the text by Darwin I quote above, 'but when we realise the extraordinary depth and indescribability of the emotions of music, the very remoteness and far-reachingness of the explanation is in favour of its validity.'[15] Since music's appeal proves impossible to rationalise on other grounds, in other words, it must relate to areas of life anterior to and even inaccessible by rationality itself. In elaborating these claims, Gurney makes a detailed case for music's relation to the body, which he believes to be more intimate than in the case of any other art form, partly because of perceived parallels between musical and bodily events or states. Thus, rhythm, as 'the perpetual satisfaction of expectation', is 'represented in the nervous organisation by the adjustment of nerve-substance in readiness for a discharge by stimulants at certain instants' (p. 425). Similarly, melody is both continually suggestive of 'physical movement' and, as such, productive of 'a direct impulse to move; which is not only felt but constantly yielded to in varying degrees' (p. 103; emphasis removed). Music is therefore related to the inward life, not as something spiritual and immaterial (as Hegel thought), but rather, as a commentary on the most material aspects of existence. Hearing music is a displaced or mediate experience of our own bodies.

It is at this point that we can note coeval nineteenth-century developments in the scientific study of the body, where researchers were equally concerned with the neural and anatomical structures potentiating all aesthetic judgements. As Jonathan Crary writes, nineteenth-century sense-psychology coheres around 'the notion that our perceptual and sensory experience depends less on the nature of an external stimulus than on the composition and functioning of our sensory apparatus'.[16] Though this was not a new idea in philosophy – it was Kant, in his *Critique of Pure Reason* (1781), who first suggested that our knowledge of the world is formed inward-outwards, by the innate structures of the mind, rather than, as it were, outward-inwards, by external objects impinging on those structures – this was increasingly recast as a conclusion borne out by experimental physiology as the century wore on.[17] For Gustav Fechner, pioneer of so-called 'psycho-physics', 'the body's external world is functionally related to the mind only by the mediation of the body's internal world'; a formula that can be glossed as stating that what we perceive is always, to some extent, an artefact of our sense organs.[18] Immediate reality comes to be seen as a chimera, the vanishing point of all perception. Mediation, in this view, is perception's unsurpassable horizon.

But mediation by *what*, exactly? If the body is one answer, another might be the character or attitude of perceivers – and for Nietzsche, the great con-tumely-monger of the late nineteenth century, both character and attitude are too craven in the vast majority of human beings to make our senses anything other than 'hostile and reluctant', especially in the face of new impressions.[19] 'To hear something new is hard and painful for the ear', he claims, so we men-tally convert it into something we have heard already; thus, 'we fabricate the greater part of the experience and can hardly be compelled *not* to contemplate some event as its "inventor"' (p. 97; emphasis in original). Nietzsche is just one of many thinkers of this period to insist that there is no 'pure' or unprejudiced sensation. In *Time and Free Will* (1889), for instance, Henri Bergson argues: 'every sensation is altered by repetition [. . .] I perceive it through the object which is its cause, through the word which translates it. This influence of lan-guage on sensation is deeper than is usually thought'.[20] In *Laughter* (1900), Bergson adds: 'we do not see the actual things themselves; in most cases we confine ourselves to reading the labels affixed to them [. . .] The word, which only takes note of the most ordinary function and commonplace aspect of the thing, intervenes between it and ourselves.'[21] Language is thus a parasite on the body of sensation, draining the life out of its host, even as it falsely assumes that host's identity. For a potentially limitless array of impressions, it substi-tutes a clutch of pallid clichés.

Nietzsche's and Bergson's criticisms are all the more powerful – and were seen as so being by their followers – because they foreshadow a sort of 'ethic' of sensation that would be capable of meeting them. If Nietzsche's figure of the future is the 'over-man', as is well known, one form this personage might take is a subject capable of registering and cultivating sense impressions in ways that that are not attenuated and standardised like those of ordinary, all-too-human beings. For Bergson, this sort of figure already exists, and is, in fact, the artist. 'Could reality come into direct contact with sense and consciousness', *Laughter* states, 'probably art would be useless' – but since this is held to be impossible, it is all the more important that art should offer its 'more direct vision of reality' by way of compensation.[22] This view was, to say the least, congenial to artists themselves in Bergson's lifetime. As Clement Greenberg writes of the late nineteenth-century avant-garde: 'There is a common effort in each of the arts to expand the expressive resources of the medium, not in order to express ideas and notions, but to express with greater immediacy sensations, the irreducible elements of experience.'[23] If one thing this entailed was a certain violence towards ideas, another was a rhetorical (if not, of course, practical) insistence that these should play no role in the genesis of actual artworks. Thus, Greenberg speaks of Courbet ('the first real avant-garde painter'), as having painted 'only what the eye could see as a machine unaided by the mind' (p. 29). The metaphor is a resonant one in early twentieth-century culture. Another painter, Frank Budgen, called his friend Joyce a 'delicate recording instrument', and went on to praise the dialogue in Joyce's *Ulysses* and *A Portrait of the Artist as a Young Man* (1915) as follows: 'we might think that a recording instrument had been hidden in the room or bar and whisked away when it had served the auditor's purpose'.[24] Authenticity is served by (quasi-) automaticity. This brings us on, then, to the question of sound recording technology, and its place in evolving understandings of the senses in the late nineteenth and early twentieth centuries.

TECHNOLOGY, AND THE DIALECTIC OF SENSORY EXCITEMENT AND EXHAUSTION

As we saw in this book's 'Introduction', the machine intoning 'sllt' in Joyce's *Ulysses* exemplifies the category of 'all sound' that Douglas Kahn has identified with late nineteenth-century technologies such as the gramophone and phonograph, and the changing perceptual habits these machines sponsor. A text that Kahn draws on is Rainer Maria Rilke's 'Primal Sound' (1919), which invokes the phonograph's invention, and offers perhaps the most vivid account available of the shock this device generated when it first appeared. Describing an apparatus built out of cardboard, a clothes brush and other makeshift materials by schoolboys in a science class, Rilke writes: 'When someone spoke or sang into the funnel [. . .] the sound which had been ours came back to us tremblingly, haltingly from the paper funnel, uncertain, infinitely soft and hesitating and fading out altogether in places.'[25] A metaphysically-attuned interpretation follows: 'We were confronting, as it were, a new and infinitely delicate point in the texture of reality'; an 'independent sound, taken from us and preserved outside us'; seemingly 'far greater than ourselves', yet simultaneously 'indescribably immature' (p. 128). As well as indicating just how poor (by our own, twenty-first-century standards) the quality of early sound recordings was, this commentary reveals the existential stakes raised by sound recording – despite, we might say, this poor quality.[26] The mouth/ear partnership, so important in Kant's account of human speech, discussed above, has been disrupted, so that one's own speech is experienced at a temporal remove, unnervingly detached from one's own person. By making this detachment, the phonograph also effectively revises Marx's account of the 'humanization of the senses'. For while it is clearly human (and 'humanized') sound that the phonograph produces, at least in this instance, this does not, in Rilke's view, strike the ear with an effect of pleasing recognition (as Marx's argument would anticipate) but rather as alien and estranged. Human artifice thus marks the presence of inhumanity in human life.

A wider question raised by Rilke's essay is whether technologies like the phonograph simply augment, or qualitatively alter, the senses to which they are coupled. Rilke goes on to say that visual devices like microscopes and telescopes 'increase the range of the senses upwards and downwards': the phonograph, by inference, might thus make us hear more and better (p. 131). (A parallel to this is Freud's argument, in 'Civilization and its Discontents', 1930, that 'With every tool man is perfecting his own organs, whether motor or sensory, or removing the limits to their functioning.' In this respect, he adds, the phonograph represents a materialisation of memory.[27]) But no sooner has Rilke said this than he makes the seemingly opposing claim that such extensions of sensory range 'lie in another sphere' from that of sense perception itself, since the very increase they represent 'cannot be interpenetrated by the senses, cannot be "experienced" in any real sense' (p. 131). What this seems to mean is that microscopy and other such techniques lie aslant from everyday reality, and cannot enter into our apparatus-free relationships with nature and each other. (In this respect, Rilke differs from another classic of early-twentieth-century theory, Benjamin's 'The Work of Art in the Age of Mechanical Reproduction', 1936, which argues that the perceptual enhancements made possible by film, such as slow motion and close up, *do* enter into our habitual modes of perception.[28]) The melancholy view of technology latent here becomes explicit in the work of American historian Henry Adams, for whom twentieth-century reality was, in crucial ways, impenetrable to sensory experience. Recalling the world of 1900 from the vantage point of just a few years later, Adams writes:

> man had translated himself into a new universe which had no common scale of measurement with the old. He had entered a supersensual world, in which he could measure nothing except by chance collisions of movements imperceptible to his senses, perhaps even imperceptible to his instruments.[29]

Everything that is novel and of consequence in this world – Adams singles out X-rays, discovered in 1895, radium, isolated in 1898, and radio, first used to transmit messages in 1895 – contradicts the impression of reality to which our senses have accustomed us. Microscopes may have helped us in the past, but it now seems that sense-experience and reality itself have definitively parted company.

So, the question may be asked, did early-twentieth-century people sense 'more' or 'less' of their reality than their predecessors? Unlike Adams, Jinny, in Woolf's *The Waves* (1931), answers this question with a confident assertion of moderns' pre-eminence: '"our senses have widened"', she affirms; '"Membranes, webs of nerve that lay white and limp, have filled and spread themselves and float round us like filaments, making the air tangible and catching in them far-away sounds unheard before."'[30] Though the last part of this comment, especially, suggests radio, it prompts a follow-on assertion from Jinny's interlocutor, Louis, concerned instead with the surrounding city, London: the city's '"roar"', he responds, '"is round us. Motor-cars, vans, omnibuses pass and repass us continuously. All are merged in one turning wheel of single sound."'[31] Quite apart from the fact that Louis's words suggest an eclipse (rather than increase) of sensory discrimination, however, the very same stimuli, or similar, were adduced by other people as responsible for a lessening or confusion of the senses. Characterising the same metropolis in *The Soul of London* (1905), Ford Madox Ford has his ears 'deafened by the cries of vendors of all things meet for a Saturday night, by the incessant whistle of trams looming at a snail's pace through the massed humanity; by the incessant, as if vindictively anvil-like, peals of notes of barrel organs'.[32] This is Aristotle's argument about 'excesses' of sense-objects 'destroy[ing] the sense-organs' with a vengeance. A no less taxing sonic character was ascribed to another city, New York, when, after a twenty-one year absence, Henry James returned there in 1904. Here, James reports, he was confronted by 'a welter of objects and sounds in which relief, detachment, dignity, meaning, perished utterly and lost all rights'. The result was 'confusion carried to chaos', beyond all prospect of 'any intelligence, any perception'.[33]

The multiplicitous and, as we see, often assaultive character of urban sense impressions is also, of course, famously the occasion of Georg Simmel's 'The Metropolis and Mental Life' (1903). By contrast to the aghast response of James, and the enthused one by Louis, Simmel adds a twist to the effect that long exposure to such stimuli will leave city-dwellers jaded and indifferent. The blasé attitude, Simmel argues, is the dialectical product of the city's stimulatory excess, precipitated out of such anything-but-blasé reactions as Louis's and James's as the latter are exhausted. In this attitude,

> the concentration of men and things stimulate the nervous system of the individual to its highest achievement so that it attains its peak. Through the mere quantitative intensification of the same conditioning factors this achievement is transformed into its opposite and appears in the peculiar adjustment of the blasé attitude.[34]

Like many nineteenth- and early twentieth-century observers, Simmel feels that the highest forms of 'civilization' that metropolitanism represents go hand in hand with a diminished sensory capacity. Charles Baudelaire, for example, speaks to this, when, in 'The Painter of Modern Life' (1863), he contrasts the blunted sensibilities of most of his contemporaries with those of the child, the drunkard, the convalescent – and the artist.[35] A spectre haunts many such accounts: the spectre of primitivism.[36] Darwin, for one, notes 'The inferiority of Europeans, in comparison with savages, in eyesight and in the other senses'; similarly, Proust's narrator, in *Swann's Way* (1913), refers to 'those primitive men whose senses were so much keener than our own'.[37] The remarkable obduracy of this idea, according to which Europeans and their descendents have less discriminating senses than their 'primitive' or 'savage' counterparts, might be reckoned as one of the key catalysts behind modernists' attempts to hone and intensify, while representing, their own senses impressions.[38] It is to these attempts that we now turn.

Sound in Literary Modernism

Having sketched some of the major theories of hearing and the other senses in the run-up to and during the modernist period, it is time for a more detailed look at what sound means within modernism itself. Though instances will doubtless be found that fall outside such categories, a provisional taxonomy for this may be sketched as follows: there is a 'shock' approach to or experience of sound; a 'depth' approach or experience; and what we might call (a little awkwardly) appeals to the musico-immaterial or -ineffable.

A fine example of the first approach appears in Joseph Conrad's memoir, *A Personal Record* (1912):

> How quiet everything was at the end of the quays on the last night on which I went out for a service cruise as a guest of the Marseilles pilots! Not a footstep, except my own, not a sigh, not a whispering echo of the usual revelry going on in the narrow, unspeakable lanes of the Old Town reached my ear – and suddenly, with a terrific jingling rattle of iron and glass, the omnibus of the Jolliette on its last journey swung round the corner of the dead wall which faces across the paved road the characteristic angular mass of the Fort St. Jean. Three horses trotted abreast with the clatter of hoofs on the granite setts, and the yellow, uproarious machine jolted violently behind them, fantastic, lighted up, perfectly empty and with the driver apparently asleep on his swaying perch above the amazing racket. I flattened myself against the wall and gasped. It was a stunning experience.[39]

It makes for stunning reading. Sound emerges against a background of silence, increases suddenly, and then bursts upon the auditor accompanied by its cause, which is itself equally present to vision. (This is what I meant in my 'Introduction' by saying that sound is best conceived as a 'configuration': it is not opposed to, but harnessed with and ratcheted up by other forms of sensation.) We might think of this as an instance of what Jürgen Habermas has called 'the dialectic of shock and revelation', paradigmatically modernist in its attempt to dislodge things from their familiar frames of reference, clear them of what might be disparaged as the stale muck of association, and present them in such a way that they seem lustrous, extraordinary and, above all, *new* (we have now seen how this approach is intimated in Nietzsche and Bergson).[40] As an aesthetic, this goes with an existential ethos that sees the self's legitimacy and continued well-being in terms of its ability to absorb and profit from just this sort of experience: as Dorothy Richardson says paradigmatically of her heroine Miriam in *Pilgrimage*, 'the registration of impressions was a thing that she must either do or lose hold of something essential'.[41] Judith Ryan has called the strain of writing this represents 'empiricist modernism', and traced its roots to late nineteenth-century psychologists such as Ernst Mach (1838–1916), for whom subjectivity is not so much receptive of but constituted by perception.[42] And Conrad himself describes the way such perceptions are, so to speak, passed on from writer-artists to their readers, ideally speaking, when he famously defines his own task, in his 'Preface' to *The Nigger of the 'Narcissus'* (1897) as this: 'by the power of the written word to make you hear, to make you feel – it is, before all, to make you *see*!'[43] Though this 'before all' appears to privilege the visual, we will shortly see how this privileging itself comes under the sign of the acoustic.

Alongside this 'shock' approach, meanwhile, there is what we might call the 'depth' approach to sound, where 'depth' designates a temporality '*beneath*' or extending back from one's own present. As preceding portions of the present chapter allow us to identify, this is 'Darwinian' insofar as it assumes the experience of sound to offer access to the past, and 'Marxist' insofar as it identifies this experience as an index of where one stands on an historical continuum. A key exhibit here is T. S. Eliot's theory of the 'auditory imagination', a faculty he believes to be essential to good poetry, and which he defines as 'the feeling for syllable and rhythm, penetrating far below the conscious levels of thought and feeling, invigorating every word; sinking to the most primitive and forgotten, returning to the origin and bringing something back'.[44] In *The Use of Poetry and the Use of Criticism* (1933), where this account appears, poetry itself is said to originate 'with a savage beating a drum in a jungle' – a formula that makes the link between primitivism and (supposed) aesthetic potency explicit (p. 148). The poet, Eliot suggests, is effectively '*older* than other human beings' – not in terms of actual years, but in some loftier, lifespan-independent sense allowing this poet privileged access to or empathy with prior epochs (p. 148; emphasis in original). In *Fantasia of the Unconscious* (1922), D. H. Lawrence makes the related claim that certain people's voices resound with a quality in which we recognise the 'deeper resonance' of ancient modes of consciousness (the same experience, he adds, may also be found in 'savage music, and in the roll of drums, and in the roaring of lions, and in the howling of cats').[45] W. B. Yeats's late poem 'Hound Voice' (c. 1936–9) revolves around a similar idea: here, those who have 'hound' voices speak to and thereby recognise each other as the bearers of a primordial and (the poem prophesies) ultimately renascent communal legacy.

Finally, for an example of modernism's interest in the musico-immaterial and -ineffable, we may look no further than Proust's famous account of Swann's fascination with a haunting melody in a piano and violin sonata by the fictitious composer, Vinteuil:

At first [Swann] had appreciated only the material quality of the sounds which these instruments secreted [. . .] But then at a certain moment, without being able to distinguish any clear outline, or to give a name to what was pleasing him, suddenly enraptured, he had tried to grasp the phrase or harmony – he did not know which – that had just been played and that opened and expanded his soul, as the fragrance of certain roses, wafted upon the moist air of evening, has the power of dilating one's nostrils. Perhaps it was owing to his ignorance of music that he had received so confused an impression, one of those that are none the less the only purely musical impressions, limited in their extent, entirely original, and irreducible to any other kind. An impression of this order, vanishing in an instant, is, so to speak, *sine materia*. Doubtless the notes which we hear at such moments tend, according to their pitch and volume, to spread out before our eyes over surfaces of varying dimensions, to trace arabesques, to give us sensations of breadth or tenuity, stability or caprice. But the notes themselves have vanished before these sensations have developed sufficiently to escape submersion under those which the succeeding or even simultaneous notes have already begun to awaken in us.[46]

The most important thing to note here is that music is esteemed not despite, but *because*, it eludes complete perceptual capture and cognitive arrest. Though it hints at other sources of aesthetic pleasure – from the scent of flowers to visible designs or ballet postures (both meanings of 'arabesque') – it can never be fully explicated in the latter's terms; not least, as its definitively continual elaboration in and over time means that it outstrips or gives the lie to these very analogic models. Of special interest here is the way the musical amateur or dilettante is privileged as the subject most likely to understand music, or be fully receptive to the aesthetic charge that music represents. Swann does not even know which of two elementary aspects of musical form ('the phrase [i.e. melody] or harmony') is responsible for his excitement – but it is precisely this unwittingness on which the intensity and, so to speak, calibre of his experience is based. The 'confused' impression, Proust insists, is thus the 'only *purely* musical' impression: by implication, those who know music 'too' well may, by very virtue of this fact, find themselves unable to experience the full extent of music's (to recall Hegel's phrase) 'elemental might'. Meanwhile, everything that we have seen Hegel himself consider as a signature of music as an art form – from its transience and self-displacement in time to its apparent immateriality (Proust's '*sine materia*') – is used to explain why music is ultimately trans-discursive or ineffable. The ineffable itself, accordingly, becomes installed as an aesthetic ideal, as well as, here, the 'thing' that music best evokes or represents.

The three approaches to or paradigms of sound sketched here are not of course (and as I have already suggested) best conceived as carving up between them the full range of possibilities that sound in modernism represents. For instance, this schema ignores the more straightforward treatment of sound as a plot-point, narrative device or conceptual issue in its own right (the latter of which Proust again provides a prime example of, via his extended meditation on 'the problem of sound' in *The Guermantes Way*, 1920–1).[47] Furthermore, there may be cases where each of the three approaches appears together, either consecutively or in tandem; another tranche of cases where each appears in modified, as well as, or instead of, in their 'pure' form; and further cases still where all three or any one are modulated by the plot-related, narratological or conceptual interests in sound just identified. For all of these reasons, the remainder of the present section is devoted to an extended analysis of Conrad's *Heart of Darkness* (1899), in which all these 'cases' coincide. To take the 'shock' approach to sound first: the narrative consists in part of an extended series of vivid sensory and affective impressions, much like a cognate of *A Personal Record*'s Marseille episode writ large. The 'depth' approach to sound, meanwhile, is represented by the systematic use of sonic signatures to differentiate between past and present, two temporal fields that are thus equally available to be 'sensed' in close succession if not at the same time. The third approach, meanwhile, that of invoking music's ineffable or trans-discursive character, is represented by the text's insistently voiced sense of itself as an exercise in gesturing at meanings lying beyond the limits of articulation or conceptual determination – exactly the locus of significance that, according to Proust (and others, as we shall see) music occupies. Finally, in a preface written a few years after the text's initial publication, Conrad even represents the text *as* music: the tale's 'sombre theme', he recalls, is such that it 'had to be given a sinister resonance, a tonality of its own, a continued vibration that, I hoped, would hang in the air and dwell on the ear after the last note had been struck'.[48] One reason why this analogy suggests itself so readily, as we shall see, is that the text climaxes with an utterance invoking all that lies beyond the reach of words.

Perhaps it is no accident, then, that there is a theorist of music who – quite inadvertently and *avant la lettre* – provides an almost perfect guide to *Heart of Darkness* at a more basic topical level: Richard Wagner. As we saw in this book's 'Introduction', Wagner evolves the category of 'sound-world' to describe a quasi- or actually autonomous realm to which music gives access or which music might create. In a text written a decade earlier than the essay in which this definition of a sound-world appears, Wagner anticipates this account by sketching the intended effects of what he calls 'endless melody' (unlike conventional melodies, in Wagner's overall aesthetic theory, this is supposedly coterminous with the entire work in which it appears). Such a melody should exert on [the listener] somewhat the effect produced by a noble forest, of a summer evening, on the lonely visitant who has just left the city's din behind; the peculiar stamp of this impression [. . .] is that of a silence growing more and more alive [. . .] [W]hen, overwhelmed by this first general impression, the forest's visitor sits down to ponder; when, the last burden of the city's hubbub cast aside, he girds the forces of his soul to a new power of observing; when, as if hearing with new senses, he listens more and more intently – he perceives with ever greater plainness the infinite diversity of voices waking in the wood.[49]

These are the sound effects – admittedly, with some adjustments – dominating *Heart of Darkness*. In Conrad's novella, the 'wood' is a Congolese jungle, and is listened to, by proxy, by four auditors of a story told by Marlow, a sailor, aboard a ship moored outside London, the 'city' which provides an implicit auditory contrast for the sounds (or lack of them) said to characterise the African environment. For Wagner's 'new power of observing' we may substitute Marlow's acute auditory sensitivity, goaded at points into heightened activity by suspensions or diminutions of the visible: '"I watched the fog for the signs of lifting"', he tells us at one point; '"but for anything else our eyes were of no more use to us than if we had been buried miles deep in a heap of cotton-wool."'[50] Wagner's 'infinite diversity of voices', furthermore, is mirrored by Marlow's tendency to assign vocal status to even the most fugitive or modest sounds. For example, the coast of Africa is imagined as '"mute with an air of whispering"', while '"The voice of the surf"' is likened to '"the speech of a brother"' (pp. 150–1). The voice itself, in part because of this, becomes one of the text's dominant concerns, both as a thematic preoccupation and as the very form of Marlow's narration.

But perhaps the most immediately striking consonance between Wagner's text and Conrad's tale is their shared concern with silence. For Aristotle, we recall, hearing encompasses a sense of sound's absence as well as of its presence, meaning that silence is always, to some extent, the ground against which sound, *qua* figure, must appear. Marlow's imagining of Africa as '*mute* with an air of whispering', moreover, suggests an appetite on the part of avid listeners to hear the sound *in* silence (or vice versa), as if silence were not the opposite of sound but an incipiency or latency in sound itself. Recalling his impression of the jungle as he prepares to venture into it in search of Mr Kurtz, Marlow reflects: '"the silence of the land went home to one's very heart – its mystery, its greatness, the amazing reality of its concealed life"' (p. 170). There is more than a hint here of a further significance that silence acquires in *Heart of Darkness* as a whole: in Marlow's hands, silence becomes the privileged sign of 'African-ness', which he conceives, in high-primitivist fashion, as all that is 'primitive' 'savage' and above all, primordial. Here is Marlow's recollection of the beginning of his voyage up the Congo River:

'Going up that river was like travelling back to the earliest beginnings of the world, when vegetation rioted on the earth and the big trees were kings. An empty stream, a great silence, an impenetrable forest [. . .] There were moments when one's past came back to one [. . .] in the shape of an unrestful and noisy dream, remembered with wonder amongst the overwhelming realities of this strange world of plants, and water, and silence.' (pp. 182–3)

The more silent a landscape is, the more it represents or is a vestige of 'the earliest beginnings of the world'. So powerful is this backwards temporal pull, indeed, that even one's private past may be dragged into it, as if some magnetic force were dragging memory away from sound (despite its 'nois[iness]' in dreams) towards the soundless. This, then, is Conrad's version of the 'depth' approach to sound elaborated elsewhere by Eliot, Lawrence and Yeats; though here, unlike in these other writers, the past is represented not so much by specific sounds as their cessation.[51] Primordiality, we may therefore say, in Marlow's narration, *is* silence; conversely, sound becomes the sign of historicity.

This is not to say, however, that primordial or 'savage' life may not make sounds. Like many in the nineteenth and twentieth centuries, Marlow identifies racial 'savagery' with sonic dissonance and raucousness.[52] Here is his description of black Africans confronting his boat: '"A complaining clamour, modulated in savage discords, filled our ears [. . .] to me it seemed as though the mist itself had screamed"' (p. 192). The way this passage treats human agency as if it were a mere condition of the atmosphere (the 'mist') suggests that Marlow does not exactly think highly of Africans' ability to raise themselves above nature at its 'purest'. That the equation of savagery with silence rather than discord, though, is uppermost in Conrad's mind in the novella as a whole, may be seen by comparing *Heart of Darkness* with *A Mirror of the Sea* (1906), his memoir of his maritime career. In the following passage, Conrad recalls the sonic signature of London – the city, it bears repeating, outside of which Marlow tells his tale of darkest Africa: 'the hum of men's work fills the river with a menacing, muttering note as of a breathless, ever-driving gale'.[53] And here is how those sounds diminish after nightfall in a heavy fog:

After the gradual cessation of all sound and movement on the faithful river, only the ringing of ships' bells is heard, mysterious and muffled in the white vapour from London Bridge right down to the Nore, for miles and miles in a decrescendo tinkling, to where the estuary broadens out into the North sea [. . .]. (pp. 114–15)

The reason why silence evokes primordiality so readily, we may therefore speculate, is that that it represents the suspension of all that sailors identify with 'civilized' endeavour and activity.

However, it does not require much interpretative ingenuity to complicate or undermine this 'civilized'/'savage' opposition. In one of the passages just quoted, the sounds of 'civilization' are associated with weather-effects (a 'gale'), much like the 'scream[ing]' of ('savage') Africans in *Heart of Darkness*. Moreover, further inspection of the London passages in *The Mirror of the Sea* shows this city to be itself likened to a 'jungle' – as if the metropole, too, no less than Africa, were a place of 'savage' energies. Describing a particular stretch of riverside docks, Conrad writes: 'It recalls a jungle by the confused, varied, and impenetrable aspect of the buildings that line the shore, not according to a planned purpose, but as if sprung up by accident from scattered seeds' (p. 107). The interpenetration of 'civilized' and 'savage' staged here recalls the same effect implicit in the famous comment launching Marlow's narrative in *Heart of Darkness*, where he observes that '"this too"' (i.e. the Thames, below London) has been '"one of the dark places of the earth"' (p. 138). Indeed, it may be the putting into question of the 'civilized'/'savage' opposition that Conrad has in mind when speaking of the 'sombre theme' (in his 1902 preface) governing the entire text. What then of Kurtz, the flawed, spoiled, or all too paradigmatic embodiment of western civilisation, whose 'conversion' to savage modes of life articulates this theme at the level of plot, and who therefore does more than anyone else in the novella to demonstrate the sound/silence opposition's contingency, if not invalidity? Remarkably, Kurtz's hold on Marlow's imagination is rendered by another vividly evoked sound effect, complementing the equation of silence with primordiality, the colonialist becoming nothing *but* sound; specifically, a disembodied voice. Here is Marlow's anticipation of their meeting:

> 'I had never imagined him as doing, you know, but as discoursing. I didn't say to myself, "Now I will never see him," [. . .] but, "now I will never hear him." The man presented himself as a voice.' (p. 203)

And here is how Kurtz turns out to be in practice:

> 'He was very little more than a voice. And I heard – him – it – this voice – other voices – all of them were so little more than voices – and the memory of that time itself lingers around me, impalpable, like a dying vibration of one immense jabber, silly, atrocious, sordid, savage, or simply mean, without any kind of sense.' (p. 205)

Something is being said throughout these passages about the sinister, if not demonic, nature sounds acquire when detached from their visible supports. Similarly, something is being said about the character sounds acquire when stripped of linguistic sense.

At this point, it is worth pausing to consider the various historical factors that might explain why a voice may be represented in just this way in literature at this specific juncture. For a start, we may return to a phenomenon that has now been identified as decisively important in raising consciousness of sound earlier in the present book, the invention of the phonograph. According to Ivan Kreilkamp, the way to understand the peculiar emphasis on the voice in *Heart of Darkness* is precisely as a consequence of (and commentary on) this technology.[54] In this reading, not only Kurtz's vocal disembodiment, but also Marlow's entire narration, are seen as analogues for the phonograph and the sundering of voices from bodily origins it instantiates. (At this point, we must note that the disembodiment of Kurtz's voice of which Marlow speaks is reduplicated in the way that Marlow's auditors hear about it: speaking of Marlow as his tale unfolds, the narrator says, 'It had become so pitch dark that we listeners could hardly see one another. For a long time already he, sitting apart, had been no more to us than a voice', p. 173.) One of the sources for Kreilkamp's reading is Friedrich Kittler's influential claim that the phonograph, along with other technologies such as the typewriter and film, helped precipitate a wider decomposition of language across a wide swathe of early twentieth-century culture. This mean that elements of language hitherto considered indissociable – in particular, physical inscription (for example, the grooves or spiral etchings in a phonograph recording), acoustic event (in the same example, the sound these grooves produce when a record is played), and semantic 'sense' (in all instances, the increasingly elusive or unstable-seeming property these other elements leave out) – are broken up and set on separate courses.[55] From this perspective, Kurtz's 'immense jabber' might be said to foreshadow the emphasis on verbal slips in psychoanalysis, the deliberately nonsensical 'sound poetry' of Kurt Schwitters, and any number of other salient artefacts of modernist culture.[56] At a more modest level, I would like to propose a literary coordinate for Conrad's tale: Tolstoy's *The Kreutzer Sonata* (1890), another text in which oral testimony is reported by an auditor-narrator, and where the testimony-giver's voice is isolated from his body (at one point, the narrator of Tolstoy's novella says of its storyteller, 'It was so dark that I could not see his face, only hear his forceful, pleasant voice' – just like Marlow in *Heart of Darkness*).[57] If Conrad's tale is 'phonographic', then, this may be partially explained by the existence of earlier texts that are phonographic too.

But ultimately, I would like to offer a more 'philosophical' and seemingly (though *only*, I think, seemingly) ahistorical reading of Kurtz's voice, drawing on Mladen Dolar's recent study, *A Voice and Nothing More* (2006). For Dolar, the voice is distinguished from all other sounds on the basis of its 'inner relationship with meaning'; thus: 'The voice is something which points toward meaning, it is as if there is an arrow in it which raises the expectation of meaning'; 'it is a sound which appears to be endowed in itself with the will to "say something," with an inner intentionality'.[58] Unlike other sounds, then, the voice carries an implicit promise to make sense: not *this* or *that* sense, but sense as such. We might say that the voice is a promise that meaning *can* be communicated. As we saw earlier, Marlow is fascinated with Kurtz's voice despite, if not because, it represents a 'jabber [. . .] without any kind of sense'.[59] And it is this that makes it exemplary of Dolar's reading of the voice in general. Kurtz's voice, we might say, is a voice 'with an arrow in it' – an arrow pointing towards meanings which the voice itself does not quite meet, but towards which it nonetheless reaches. Marlow is impressed by this because, deprived of its bodily support, Kurtz's voice reveals itself, as it were, as quintessential: not any one voice, but the voice as such.

This brings us on then, finally, to what I referred to earlier as the insistently voiced sense, in Conrad's novella, of the text as an exercise in gesturing at meanings beyond the limits of articulation or conceptual determination. The most spectacular instance of this is Kurtz's notorious death-bed utterance, '"The horror! The horror!"' (p. 239) – about which almost nothing can be said in terms of its substantial content, but which seems to conjure illimitable reservoirs of significance by implication. This is the text's climactic utterance (as I also mentioned earlier), evoking all that lies beyond the reach of words. Here, language itself – and not this time, the language-laden voice – strains towards some point outside itself. (To use Dolar's terms again, we might say that here, it is Kurtz's words that have 'an arrow in them'.) For Proust, as we have seen, music is privileged among the arts for representing the ineffable, an aesthetic pleasure beyond words. Is it possible that Conrad, in assigning such a status to Kurtz's voice (and his final words), has music in mind here as his model? As we have seen, his 1902 preface likens *Heart of Darkness* as a whole to a musical performance; moreover, in the final pages of the tale, another character tells Marlow that '"Kurtz had been essentially a great musician"' (p. 243) – a remark which might otherwise seem throwaway or unaccountable, but which from our present vantage point might even be taken as a key to *Heart of Darkness* as a whole. I leave it to others to decide whether this text is anything 'like' music in any other than this specific, Proust-suggested sense; now, we may move on to the wider question of what music (not just sound) means in literary modernism – and indeed, what music means in modernist constructions of wider constellation of the arts.

MUSIC AMONGST THE OTHER ARTS

It is in fact quite likely that music played some role in Conrad's conception of Kurtz's voice in *Heart of Darkness*, because we know that it played a quite definite role in his conception of artistry as such. As we have seen, his 'Preface' to *The Nigger of the 'Narcissus'* defines the writer's task as 'by the power of the written word to make you hear, to make you feel – it is, before all, to make you *see!*' But we neglected to say earlier that in the same text, he also sets out further prescriptions based on literature's relationship with other art forms. Thus, of fiction, he writes: 'It must strenuously aspire to the plasticity of

sculpture, to the colour of painting, and to the magic suggestiveness of music
– which is the art of arts.'[60] Vision may be privileged as literary source material among the senses ('before all, to make you *see*!'), but an auditory medium,
music, is literature's paragon amongst the arts.

Conrad's source for this idea appears to be Walter Pater.[61] In 'The School of
Giorgione' (1877), Pater makes an oft-cited and enormously influential claim
that

> *All art constantly aspires towards the condition of music.* For while in all
> other kinds of art it is possible to distinguish the matter from the form,
> and the understanding can always make this distinction, yet it is the con-
> stant effort of art to obliterate it.[62]

Any work of art, in any medium, should thus strive towards the unity of form
and content that music, according to Pater, manages effortlessly, simply by
being itself. (It may help here to quote further what Pater says of music: 'In its
consummate moments, the end is not distinct from the means, the form from
the matter, the subject from the expression; they inhere in and completely satu-
rate each other', p. 88). In other words, music's 'subject matter' (insofar as it
has one) *is* its form: it has no other 'content' besides the pitch, time, rhythmic,
tonal, harmonic and other values that are also its formal conditions of possibility. For an artist working in a non-musical medium to take a leaf out of music's
book, then, would mean selecting and rendering his or her subject matter in
such a way that this activity fuses with an investigation and enactment of the
formal possibilities his or her chosen medium offers – the things that make
painting 'painterly' or writing 'writerly', and so on. To draw on Conrad's
example again, we might say that *Heart of Darkness* meets these conditions
insofar as this is a story about storytelling (in addition, of course, to being
many other thing); a story, therefore, in which form and content coincide.

There are perhaps three key principles underlying Pater's argument. The first
stems from a tradition stretching back at least as far as Leonardo Da Vinci
(1452–1519), in which prescriptions for each art form are made on the basis of
what (allegedly) distinguishes each art from every other.[63] The key text here is
Gotthold Ephraim Lessing's *Laocoon* (1766), which Pater cites himself within
'The School of Giorgione', and whose general influence extends deep into the
twentieth century. Lessing's basic claim is that some arts appeal to the ear,
whereas others are directed at the eye; it is folly for members of either camp to
'confuse' or swap their offices. Supplementing this distinction is an existential
or ontological one between time and space, each of which are pegged to one
of Lessing's designated senses (space to vision, time to hearing), and which
are further seen as irreconcilable within any given artwork. Thus, painting,
because consisting of marks or figures juxtaposed in space, 'must relinquish
all representations of time', whilst poetry, being expressive only of '[o]bjects

which succeed each other, or whose parts succeed each other in time', must, conversely, renounce all attempts at representing space.[64] Though not discussed in *Laocoon* – in Lessing's unpublished notes, there are suggestions of how this would have been done in a projected follow-up volume – it is clear that music, as an auditory art, embodies time, according to this schema.[65] It is to Lessing, then, that we may trace Hegel's identification of music with time (as cited earlier in this chapter) – and we may briefly note here some of the many others who have followed since in making this identification. Kierkegaard, for example, equates music with language on the basis of their shared temporal foundation.[66] Similarly, Adrian Leverkühn, the fictional composer in Thomas Mann's *Doctor Faustus* (1947), considers music to be an 'organization of time'.[67]

Lessing's text presents itself as a response to those whose 'false taste' has led them to endorse the cross-contamination of poetry and painting.[68] The same is also true of Irving Babbitt's *The New Laokoon: An Essay on the Confusion of the Arts* (1910), one of several twentieth-century texts to explicitly rally under Lessing's standard. One of Babbitt's targets is Wagner, whose theory of the 'total work of art', considered in this book's 'Introduction', is often railed at in this context (though it is worth remembering that according to that theory, at least its letter, the individual arts are *not* called upon to mimic or leech upon one another, but rather complement each other by precisely doing only what each, uniquely, does best).[69] Babbitt's grievances had at any rate gone some way towards being addressed by the time of Greenberg's 'Towards a Newer Laocoon' (1940) – at least according to this famous essay's argument, which recasts Lessing's prescriptions as descriptions of immanent trends in the history of trans-disciplinary modernism (we have quoted from this text already, in relation to Courbet and the late nineteenth-century avant-garde). Here, the visual arts, especially, are said to have achieved a renewed clarity of purpose at some point in the late nineteenth century by abandoning attempts at emulating musical *effects*, in favour of paralleling music's *form*:

> only when the avant-garde's interest in music led it to consider music as a *method* of art rather than as a kind of effect did the avant-garde find what it was looking for. It was when it was discovered that the advantage of music lay chiefly in the fact that it was an 'abstract' art, an art of 'pure form' [. . .] Only by accepting the example of music and defining each of the other arts solely in terms of the sense or faculty which perceived its effect and by excluding from each art whatever is intelligible in the terms of any other sense or faculty would the non-musical arts attain the 'purity' and self-sufficiency which they desired [. . .]. (pp. 31–2; emphasis in original)

In other words, the non-musical arts achieved their 'modernist' maturity when they cottoned on to music's example in pretty much the way outlined above with respect to Pater, painting becoming 'about' paint, literature 'about' language, and so on. The point of learning from music, in this view, is to renounce it – or at least renounce the temptation to mimic its sensuous effects. From now on, each art, à la Lessing, will address itself only to the sensory and other 'faculties' to which it corresponds. Meanwhile, the wider significance of music appears to reside in what Greenberg calls its 'abstract' or non-mimetic character. To repeat, music, does not set out to represent anything in the external world; in Greenberg's view, it is a circle closed upon itself. The way for other arts to meet their aspiration to the condition of music (as Pater puts it) is accordingly to ditch – or at least downgrade – their commitment to representation.

It is at this point that the first key principle underlying Pater's argument, the enquiry into what differentiates each art from every other, dovetails with the second: the claim that music is intrinsically (or at least is better when it is) non-representational. Though this may seem obvious at first sight – especially to listeners of 'classical' and other instrumental music – it is in fact quite novel, both as a fait accompli and as a creed to be lived up to. As recently as the late eighteenth century, as Bellamy Hosler writes, instrumental music without a determined 'subject' or extra-musical referent was deemed 'boring', or at any rate inferior to music accompanying sung words or that had a definite mimetic purpose.[70] The inversion of this hierarchy was a momentous one, insofar as (the writer this time is John Neubauer) 'for the first time in the history of Western aesthetics, an art that subordinated didactic messages and representations of specific contents to pure forms was acclaimed as profound art'.[71] Central to this inversion was a trans-valuation of music's meaningless-ness – there is no 'meaning', after all, to a melody, say, in any strict semantic sense – from the sub-linguistic to the trans-linguistic, from the embarrassingly inarticulate to what now came to be seen as prestigiously and preciously ineffable. We have seen Proust speak from, as it were, the far side of this trans-valuation, and can now trace its origin to changes in music as actually composed and played; in particular, the development of instrumental genres such as the symphony, by composers such as Haydn, Mozart, and Beethoven, in the late eighteenth and early nineteenth centuries. Here, music was increas-ingly played in contexts where that music's content was freed from any ritual or other definite symbolic function (other than that, perhaps, of symbolising the implicit solidarity of those gathered to listen to it – a possibility I will touch on again in the next chapter). A key text celebrating this development is E. T. A. Hoffmann's review of Beethoven's Fifth Symphony (1810), which credits that composer, in particular, not only with writing better music than his predecessors, but also, in so doing, penetrating deeper into 'the peculiar nature of music' itself.[72] It is this claim that wordless, instrumental music represents the 'truth' of music ('music at its purest') that implicitly grounds both Pater's and Greenberg's treatment of music as a model for the other arts.

If writers such as Hoffman saw music's formal self-reflexivity as a reason for esteeming it as the most venerable art, then this view effectively fuses with the third and final underlying principle of Pater's wider argument: the claim that non-representational art is superior to representational art; that it accesses a 'higher' (or, as comes to the same thing, a 'deeper') truth. Hoffmann is himself an important exponent of this view, but its most influential advocate in the nineteenth century is Arthur Schopenhauer. In *The World as Will and Representation* (also known as *The World as Will and Idea*, 1819), Schopenhauer attempts to answer a question that, as we recall, interested Hegel, and would later exercise both Darwin and Gurney: namely, how does music, which seems so (literally) nonsensical, produce effects in its listeners that so often outstrip those produced by the figurative or sign-based arts?[73] Schopenhauer's answer juxtaposes the terms of his book's titular distinction between the world as will (a primal, omnipresent urge) and as idea or representation (that urge's embodiment in organic and inorganic modes of being). By contrast to the other arts,

> [m]usic is as *immediate* an objectification and copy of the whole *will* as the world itself is, indeed as the Ideas are, the multiplied phenomenon of which constitutes the world of individual things. Therefore music is by no means like the other arts, namely a copy of the Ideas, but a *copy of the will itself*, the objectivity of which are the Ideas. For this reason the effect of music is so very much more powerful and penetrating than is that of the other arts, for these others speak only of the shadow, but music of the essence.[74]

Music here appears as an almost organic force – indeed, *as* an organic force, insofar as it is a primal expression of the world's will. (It will be seen how this anticipates Gurney's view that music mirrors and stimulates the body: in Schopenhauer's view, music *is* a kind of body.) Unlike the derived or mimetic arts, music is 'essential', just like human beings; a view which can, paradoxically, make it sound as though music were outside human agency altogether – something that we encounter, as much as, or instead of, something we create. For Schopenhauer, as Terry Eagleton notes, music is thus a prosecution of the task that philosophy takes up more explicitly; an enquiry into what lies hidden underneath the play of mere appearance.[75] A more emphatic repudiation of the view that music is 'inferior' to the mimetic arts, because non-representational, could hardly be imagined.

Schopenhauer's theory, as is well known, exerted an important influence on many subsequent thinkers and musicians, including Wagner. But while many scholarly accounts of musical aesthetics (or music's place in aesthetics) accordingly quote the passage above or others like it, remarkably few note the tenacity and rigour with which Schopenhauer follows his basic tenet up. The reason why we can be moved by music, he says, is that it is *us*, or at least our mirror image: thus, in '*melody*, [. . .] in the uninterrupted significant connexion of *one* thought from beginning to end [. . .] I recognize the highest grade of the will's objectification, the intellectual life and endeavour of man' (p. 259; emphasis in original). This conceit, according to which the various parts and instrumentation typically found in polyphonic music – melody in the treble register, accompaniment in the bass, and so on – represent different 'grades' of being, then becomes a means for understanding the place of humankind in nature more generally. So, 'for us the ground-bass is in harmony what inorganic nature, the crudest mass on which everything rests and from which everything originates and develops, is in the world' (p. 258). Animals and plants are represented respectively by 'the descending fifth and third' in a diatonic scale (relative to humankind's first or tonic note) (p. 153). And so on. These are not 'mere' analogies for Schopenhauer because, as we have seen, he sees music as having the same ontological primacy as other forms of nature – indeed, as a revelation of that nature, down to its inner structure and deepest expressive inclination. Again, humans *are* the will; and, because music is this too, it reveals this to its listeners while at the same time elucidating their fundamental kinship with all other forms of embodied will.

Music, Language and Meaning

As we have now seen on several occasions, modernist literature invests heavily in the idea of music's close association with the ineffable, defined as something 'beyond' but nonetheless in close proximity to language. For this reason, I close this chapter with a brief closer look the music's relationship with language – the medium, of course, which (more than any one sense faculty) represents the formal base of literature.

It is a relationship that has intrigued, and sometimes baffled, many. Perhaps because of the changes in musical history noted earlier, it especially occupies thinkers of the late eighteenth and early nineteenth centuries, along with writers from later periods for whom the music of the earlier era is particularly important (that era is, we recall, the one in which music lost its hitherto inferior status with respect to the mimetic arts in favour of a newly confident self-image as their superior). Kierkegaard, for one, as mentioned earlier, sees music and language as connected by their shared temporal articulation. However, he defies what was by his time of writing the fashionable preference for ineffable music over definitely meaningful language, considering this to be 'one of those sentimental misconceptions that that sprout only in empty heads'.[76] Such a view can only hold, he adds, if, as its logical correlative, 'it is assumed that saying "Uh" is more valuable than a complete thought'.[77] So much for Proust's privileging of Swann's impression of the Vinteuil sonata.

Some of the issues at stake in these disputes become clearer when we note how closely they were tied to the rival productions and aesthetic programmes of musicians. Beethoven's Ninth Symphony (1824) is many people's cause célèbre in this respect. In its fourth and final movement, the orchestra is joined first by solo, then by choral voices singing Friedrich Schiller's poem 'Ode to Joy' – an eruption of determinate meaning into otherwise 'pure' music that Wagner, for one, interpreted as signalling the 'end' of the symphonic tradition and the beginning of his own, supposedly superior successor (in a then unpublished fragment of c. 1871, the young Nietzsche calls this an 'incredible aesthetic superstition').[78] Wagner's programme for a 'total work of art', as we have noted before, sparked running battles throughout the second half of the nineteenth century and the early decades of the twentieth century. One of Wagner's critics was Eduard Hanslick, whose Vom Musikalisch-Schönen (first edition 1854; there would be nine more by the end of the century) anticipates Pater by privileging music's 'indivisibility of form and content'.[79] Turning his ire especially on those who seek determinate emotional or conceptual content in instrumental music, Hanslick argues that this search rests on a false analogy between music and language, and a corresponding attempt to have each do things that can only be done by the other (it will be seen that there is more than a hint of Lessing in this charge). The likes of Kierkegaard notwithstanding, language and music are in fact quite different, Hanslick writes, as is shown especially starkly when we compare the latter to an act of speech: 'All specifically musical laws radiate from the self-sufficient significance and beauty of sounds in themselves, whereas all the laws governing speech are concerned with the correct use of sounds for the purpose of expression' (p. 31). Language can always, in principle, be split into sound (or whatever other vehicle is used to carry meaning, such as script) and sense; earlier, we considered Kittler's commentary on precisely this. But with music, such a split is impossible.

It is to the twentieth century, though, that we owe perhaps the greatest, and certainly the most strenuous reflection on music's relationship with language – a reflection that is all the more impressive because it refuses any too-complacently discerned identity between the two terms while nonetheless keeping a clear eye on the fact that there must be *some* intense relation between them to which attempts in this direction point. In 'Music, Language, and Composition' (1956), Adorno writes: 'Music is similar to language' without *being* language; thus, 'The person who takes music literally as language will be led astray by it'.[80] The word 'similar' has a lot of work to do in the first of these quotations, and might be best thought of as representing a charged space, holding the two poles, 'music' and 'language', together, without allowing them to either fly apart or collapse into each other. Thus further, music does not separate itself once and for all from signifying language, as if there were different realms. A dialectic reigns here [. . .] Music without any signification, the mere phenomenological coherence of the tones, would resemble an acoustical kaleidoscope. As absolute signification, on the other hand, it would cease to be music and pass, falsely, into language [. . .] Music points to the true language as to a language in which the content itself is revealed, but for this it pays the price of unambiguousness, which has gone over to the signifying languages. And as if to give it, the most eloquent of all languages, comfort for the curse of ambiguity [. . .] intentions stream into it. Time and again it points to the fact that it signifies something, something definite. Only the intention is always veiled. (p. 114)

'Intention,' we should say, had earlier been Hanslick's word for that illicit hinge at work whenever people claim that music 'expresses' this or that linguistic content (in reality, he says, music expresses nothing other than itself – there is no 'hinge') (p. 26). For Adorno to say that intention is 'always veiled', then, is to say that while music is not language, it must nonetheless have language's coherence to be successful, else it will fall into a pile set of sonic fragments, as in 'an acoustical kaleidoscope'. This is why Adorno tacks to and fro from one side to another of a set of interlocked bipolar oppositions – signifying and non-signifying, ambiguous and unambiguous, and, of course, music and language themselves – without ever allowing himself to say something too definitive about how these sets of poles match up: the effect may well be maddening, of course, but is part of a sincere and no doubt self-consciously doomed attempt on Adorno's part to have language – the very language of his essay – echo the definitively 'veiled' nature of musical meaning itself. And what might the 'true language', in which, by contrast to all other languages, 'the content itself' of language is revealed, be? The answer takes us down a path we have not had cause to tread before: theology.

In fact, Adorno's thinking here is strongly influenced by Benjamin's theo-ontological theory of language, according to which naming – a uniquely self-grounding linguistic operation – is identical with God's creation. In the beginning of the world, Benjamin argues, all objects had their proper, non-arbitrary name: it is only with man's Fall that the original identity of word and object is undone, and the reign of 'signifying languages' (to use Adorno's phrase) begun. 'In stepping outside the purer language of name', Benjamin writes, 'man makes language a means' of abstract knowledge, 'and therefore also, in one part at any rate, a *mere* sign' – a formula which sufficiently indicates the lesser status of the sign over the name in Benjamin's eyes.[81] (Signs are not part of the objects they designate; names, in this view, are.) Music, meanwhile, is identified as 'the last remaining universal language since the tower of Babel', and – in what is, in the light of this, a jaw-droppingly assumption-trumping move – as 'the opposite of meaning-laden speech': a conjunction that would seem to make music, paradoxically, a *language without meaning*.[82] And indeed, that is pretty much what a language of pure 'naming' would be, according to another formulation, stating that names represent 'a primordial form of perception, in which words possess their own nobility [. . .] unimpaired by cognitive meaning' (p. 36). Thus Adorno's equally oracular claim, quoted above, that 'Music points to the true language as to a language in which the content itself is revealed'. We might thus paraphrase: 'music is a bit like a language of pure names, from which the "things"' names name are not removed – and certainly, it is the closest that humankind will get to this, after the Fall'. Or, as Adorno says himself elsewhere:

> As language, music tends toward pure naming, the absolute unity of object and sign, which in its immediacy is lost to all human knowledge. In the utopian and at the same time hopeless attempt at naming is located music's relation to philosophy, to which, for this very reason, it is incomparably closer, in its idea, than any other art. But the name appears in music only as pure sound, divorced from its bearer, and hence the opposite of every act of meaning, every intention toward meaning.[83]

Intention, then, again, denotes the meaning-ward or signifying gesture which music must renounce to be itself. And as we have seen Hanslick say as well, 'pure sound' (which music is) is, by definition, senseless.

This, however, is not quite the final word, because, as quoted, Adorno sees intentions as 'stream[ing] into' music, as if it were part of music's vocation to reach towards its own impossibility, to open itself up to the very semantic energy it must definitively exclude. What, then, does music 'say'? 'Among its intentions', Adorno writes, 'one of the most urgent seems to be "That is the way it is" – the judicious, even judging, affirmation of something that is, however, not expressly stated'.[84] Amongst the works that most consummately 'say' this, he continues, is none other than Beethoven's Ninth Symphony – but not the final, vocal final movement seized upon by Wagner; rather, an earlier, instrumental passage – in which 'this intention [. . .] becomes distinctly eloquent'.[85] (Beethoven, in fact, is never far from Adorno's mind when discussing music – neither, for that matter, is Hanslick.) Music is the eloquence of 'saying' without statements. The final word, accordingly, is this: music may strike us as, like language, reaching the highest pitch of aptness and logical coherence, but its aptness has no external measure, its logic no extra-musical correlative.

NOTES

1. As if to set a seal of approval on this fact, perhaps the greatest scientist of sound and hearing in the nineteenth century, Hermann von Helmholtz, writes, in his

epochal *On the Sensations of Tone, As a Physiological Basis for the Theory of Music* (first edn 1862; final edn 1877): 'it is clear that music has a more immediate connection with pure sensation than any other of the fine arts, and, consequently, that a theory of the sensations of hearing is destined to play a much more important part in musical esthetics than, for example, the theory of *chiaroscuro* or of perspective in painting' (Hermann von Helmholtz, *On the Sensations of Tone, As a Physiological Basis for the Theory of Music*, 3rd edn, translated by Alexander J. Ellis, Bristol: Thoemmes, [1870] 1998, p. 4; emphasis in original). Music, on this account, is a theorisation of sound and hearing in itself.

2. Brad Bucknell, *Literary Modernism and Musical Aesthetics: Pater, Pound, Joyce and Stein* (Cambridge: Cambridge University Press, 2002), p. 1.

3. Aristotle, *De Anima (On the Soul)*, translated with an introduction and notes by Hugh Lawson-Tancred (London: Penguin, [c. 350 BC] 1986), p. 180. Subsequent references to this edition are given in the text.

4. See Louise Vinge, *The Five Senses: Studies in a Literary Tradition* (Lund: C. W. K. Gleerup, 1975), p. 27.

5. Elizabeth Sears, 'The Iconography of Auditory Perception in the Early Middle Ages: On Psalm Illustration and Psalm Exegesis', in Charles Burnett, Michael Fend and Penelope Gouk (eds), *The Second Sense: Studies in Hearing and Musical Judgement from Antiquity to the Seventeenth Century* (London: Warburg Institute, 1991), pp. 19–42; p. 28 cited.

6. Anthony Synnott, 'Puzzling over the Senses: From Plato to Marx', in David Howes (ed.), *The Varieties of Sensory Experience: A Sourcebook in the Anthropology of the Senses* (Toronto: University of Toronto Press, 1991), pp. 61–76; pp. 63–4 cited.

7. Immanuel Kant, *Anthropology from a Pragmatic Point of View*, revised and edited by Hans H. Rudnick, translated by Victor Lyle Dowdell (Carbondale and Edwardsville: Southern Illinois University Press, [1798] 1996), pp. 42, 41. Subsequent references to this edition are given in the text.

8. G. W. F. Hegel, *Hegel's Philosophy of Nature: Being Part Two of the Encyclopaedia of the Philosophical Sciences, 1830. Translated from Nicolin and Poggeler's Edition, 1959, and from the Zusatz in Michelet's Text, 1847*, translated by A. V. Miller (Oxford: Clarendon Press, 1970), p. 138. Subsequent references to this edition are given in the text.

9. G. W. F. Hegel, *Aesthetics: Lectures on Fine Art*, 2 vols, translated by T. M. Knox (Oxford: Clarendon Press, [1835] 1975), vol. 2, p. 906. Subsequent references to this edition are given in the text.

10. The other clear influence on Marx here is Friedrich Schiller's *On the Aesthetic Education of Mankind* (1795).

11. Karl Marx, *Economic and Philosophic Manuscripts of 1844*, translated by Martin Milligan, in Robert C. Tucker (ed.), *The Marx–Engels Reader*, 2nd edn (New York: Norton: 1978), pp. 88–9. Emphases in original.

12. Peter Kivy, 'Charles Darwin on Music', *Journal of the American Musicological Society* 12:1 (Spring 1959), pp. 42–8.

13. Charles Darwin, *The Descent of Man, and Selection in Relation to Sex*, with an introduction by James Moore and Adrian Desmond (Harmondsworth: Penguin, [1873] 2004), p. 638.

14. See John Hollander, *The Untuning of the Sky: Ideas of Music in English Poetry, 1500–1700* (Princeton: Princeton University Press, 1961), pp. 199–201.

15. Edmund Gurney, *The Power of Sound*, with an introductory essay by Edward T. Cone (New York: Basic Books, [1880] 1966), p. 119. Subsequent references to this edition are given in the text.

16. Jonathan Crary, *Suspensions of Perception: Attention, Spectacle, and Modern Culture* (Cambridge, MA: MIT Press, 2001), p. 12.
17. See Louis Menand, *The Metaphysical Club* (London: Flamingo for HarperCollins, 2002), pp. 268–70.
18. Gustav Fechner, *Elements of Psychophysics*, vol. 1, edited by David H. Howes and Edwin G. Boring, translated by Helmut E. Adler (New York: Holt, Rinehart and Winston, [1860] 1966), p. 9.
19. Friedrich Nietzsche, *Beyond Good and Evil: Prelude to a Philosophy of the Future*, translated with an introduction and commentary by R. J. Hollingdale (Harmondsworth: Penguin, [1886] 1972), p. 97.
20. Henri Bergson, *Time and Free Will: An Essay on the Immediate Data of Consciousness*, translated by F. L. Pogson (Mineola: Dover Publications, [1889; 1913] 2001), p. 131.
21. Henri Bergson, *Laughter: An Essay on the Meaning of the Comic*, translated by Cloudesley Brereton and Fred Rothwell (London: Macmillan, [1900] 1911), p. 153.
22. Bergson, *Laughter*, pp. 150, 157.
23. Clement Greenberg, 'Towards a Newer Laocoon' (1940), in John O'Brian (ed.), *The Collected Essays and Criticism, Volume 1: Perceptions and Judgements, 1939–1944* (Chicago: University of Chicago Press, 1986), pp. 23–38; p. 30 cited. Subsequent references to this edition are given in the text.
24. Frank Budgen, *James Joyce and the Making of Ulysses* (London: Grayson and Grayson, 1934), pp. 72, 92.
25. Rainer Maria Rilke, 'Primal Sound' (1919), in *Rodin and Other Prose Pieces*, translated by G. Craig Houston, with an introduction by William Tucker (London: Quartet Encounters, 1986), pp. 127–32; p. 127 cited. Subsequent references to this edition are given in the text.
26. Even commercially built devices of the early phonograph era made comparably 'alien' and fragile sounds: see, for example, the fictionalised account in Dorothy Richardson's *Pilgrimage*, 4 vols (London: Virago, [1915–67] 2002), vol. 3, pp. 96–7.
27. Sigmund Freud, 'Civilization and its Discontents' (1930), in *The Standard Edition of the Complete Psychological Works of Sigmund Freud*, 24 vols, translated and edited James Strachey, in collaboration with Anna Freud, assisted by Alix Strachey and Alan Tyson (London: Hogarth Press, 1948–74), vol. 21, p. 90. See also Tim Armstrong's commentary on this passage in *Modernism, Technology and the Body: A Cultural Study* (Cambridge: Cambridge University Press, 1998), pp. 77–8.
28. Walter Benjamin, 'The Work of Art in the Age of Mechanical Reproduction' (1936), in *Illuminations*, edited with an introduction by Hannah Arendt, translated by Harry Zohn (London: Fontana Press for HarperCollins, 1992), pp. 211–44; pp. 228–30 cited.
29. Henry Adams, *The Education of Henry Adams*, with an introduction by D. W. Brogan (Boston: Riverside Press, [1907] 1961), pp. 381–2.
30. Virginia Woolf, *The Waves* (Harmondsworth: Penguin, [1931] 1964), p. 115.
31. Woolf, *The Waves*, p. 115.
32. Ford Madox Ford, *The Soul of London*, edited by Alan G. Hill (London: J. M. Dent, [1905] 1995), p. 16.
33. Henry James, *The American Scene*, edited with an introduction by John F. Sears (Harmondsworth: Penguin, [1907] 1994), p. 65.
34. Georg Simmel, 'The Metropolis and Mental Life' (1903), in *The Sociology of Georg Simmel*, edited, translated and with an introduction by Kurt H. Wolff (New York: Free Press, 1964), pp. 409–24; p. 415 cited.

35. Charles Baudelaire, 'The Painter of Modern Life' (1863), in *Selected Writings on Art and Literature*, translated with an introduction by P. E. Charvet (Harmondsworth: Penguin, 1992), pp. 390–435; pp. 397–8 cited.

36. My argument here is loosely based on Michael Taussig, *Mimesis and Alterity: A Particular History of the Senses* (New York: Routledge, 1993). See especially pp. 200–1.

37. Darwin, *The Descent of Man*, p. 51; Marcel Proust, *In Search of Lost Time*, 6 vols, translated by C. K. Scott Moncrieff and Terence Kilmartin, revised by D. J. Enright (London: Vintage, [1913–27] 1996), vol. 1, p. 33.

38. I do not know where this idea comes from, but one source of its popularity must be the 'Leatherstocking' novels of James Fenimore Cooper (1789–1851), where the sensory acuity of Native Americans is routinely contrasted with the relative dullness of sense in (most) Anglo-Americans. For more on the conjunction of primitivism and modernism, see Elazar Barkan and Ronald Bush (eds), *Prehistories of the Future: The Primitivist Project and the Culture of Modernism* (Stanford: Stanford University Press, 1995).

39. Joseph Conrad, *The Mirror of the Sea: Memories and Impressions* (1906), published together with *A Personal Record: Some Reminiscences* (1912) (London: J. M. Dent, 1923), p. 128.

40. Jürgen Habermas, 'Modernity: An Unfinished Project' (1981), in Maurizio Passerin D'Entrèves and Seyla Benhabib (eds), *Habermas and the Unfinished Project of Modernity* (Cambridge: Polity, 1996), pp. 38–55; p. 48 cited. On 'shock' as an experiential and aesthetic category, see Tim Armstrong, 'Two Types of Shock in Modernity', *Critical Quarterly* 42:1 (2000), pp. 60–73.

41. Richardson, *Pilgrimage*, vol. 1, p. 431.

42. Judith Ryan, *The Vanishing Subject: Early Psychology and Literary Modernism* (Chicago: University of Chicago Press, 1991).

43. Joseph Conrad, 'Preface', in *The Nigger of the 'Narcissus'*, edited with an introduction by Jacques Berthoud (Oxford: Oxford University Press, [1897] 1984), p. xlii; emphasis in original.

44. T. S. Eliot, *The Use of Poetry and the Use of Criticism: Studies in the Relation of Criticism to Poetry in England* (Cambridge, MA: Harvard University Press, 1933), p. 111. Subsequent references to this edition are given in the text.

45. D. H. Lawrence, *Fantasia of the Unconscious* (1922), published together with *Psychoanalysis and the Unconscious* (1921) (Harmondsworth: Penguin, 1971), p. 67.

46. Proust, *In Search of Lost Time*, vol. 1, pp. 250–1; emphasis in original.

47. Proust, *In Search of Lost Time*, vol. 3, pp. 77–82.

48. Joseph Conrad, 'Preface' to *Youth: A Narrative, and Two Other Stories* (1902), in *Conrad's Prefaces to His Works*, with an introductory essay by Edward Garnett, and a biographical note by David Garnett (London: J. M. Dent, 1937), pp. 71–4; p. 73 cited.

49. Richard Wagner, 'Zukunftsmusik' ['Music of the Future'] (1860), in *Richard Wagner's Prose Works*, 8 vols, translated by William Ashton Ellis (London: Kegan Paul, Trench, Trübner, 1892–99), vol. 3, pp. 293–345; p. 339 cited.

50. Joseph Conrad, *Heart of Darkness, and Other Tales*, edited and with an introduction by Cedric Watts (Oxford: Oxford University Press, 1990), p. 197. Subsequent references to this edition are given in the text.

51. In fact, there are reasons to suspect that Eliot's elaboration of the 'depth' model is influenced by the portrayal of sound in *Heart of Darkness*. References to the latter text play an important role in Eliot's 'The Hollow Men' (1925).

52. Gurney, to offer one point of comparison, refers to 'the harsh and noisy music of savages' (*The Power of Sound*, p. 9).

53. Conrad, *The Mirror of the* Sea, *A Personal Record*, p. 106. Subsequent references to this edition are given in the text.

54. Ivan Kreilkamp, *Voice and the Victorian Storyteller* (Cambridge: Cambridge University Press, 2005), ch. 7.

55. Friedrich Kittler, *Discourse Networks, 1800/1900*, translated by Michael Metteer with Chris Cullens, with a foreword by David E. Wellbery (Stanford: Stanford University Press, 1990). See also Kittler's *Gramophone, Film, Typewriter*, translated with an introduction by Geoffrey Winthrop-Young and Michael Wutz (Stanford: Stanford University Press, 1999).

56. On Schwitters, see Rex W. Last, *German Dadaist Literature: Kurt Schwitters, Hugo Ball, Hans Arp* (New York: Twayne, 1973), pp. 57–60. The *locus classicus* for psychoanalysis's interest in verbal slips is of course Freud's *The Psychopathology of Everyday Life* (1901).

57. Leo Tolstoy, *The Kreutzer Sonata and Other Stories*, translated with an introduction by David McDuff (Harmondsworth: Penguin, 2004), p. 38.

58. Mladen Dolar, *A Voice and Nothing More* (Cambridge, MA: MIT Press, 2006), p. 14.

59. As a final cross-reference to Conrad's autobiographical writings, we might note here his observation in *A Personal Record*, with reference to political persuasion: 'The power of sound has always been greater than the power of sense' (p. xiii).

60. Conrad, 'Preface', in *The Nigger of the 'Narcissus'*, p. xli.

61. See Ian Watt, *Conrad in the Nineteenth Century* (London: Chatto and Windus, 1980), p. 86.

62. Walter Pater, 'The School of Giorgione' (1871), in *The Renaissance*, edited with an introduction and notes by Adam Phillips (Oxford: Oxford University Press, [1873] 1998), p. 86; emphasis in original. Subsequent references to this edition are given in the text.

63. Vinge, *The Five Senses*, p. 73.

64. Gotthold Ephraim Lessing, *Laocoon: An Essay upon the Limits of Painting and Poetry*, translated by Ellen Frothingham (Mineola: Dover Publications, [1766] 2005), pp. 90, 91.

65. See Simon Richter, 'Intimate Relations: Music in and Around Lessing's "Laokoon"', *Poetics Today* 20:2 (1999), pp. 155–73.

66. Søren Kierkegaard, *Either/Or*, part 1, edited and translated, with an introduction and notes by Howard V. Hong and Edna H. Hong (Princeton: Princeton University Press, [1843] 1987), p. 68.

67. Thomas Mann, *Doctor Faustus*, translated by H. T. Lowe-Porter (Harmondsworth: Penguin, [1947] 1968), p. 310.

68. Lessing, *Laocoon*, p. x.

69. Irving Babbitt, *The New Laokoon: An Essay on the Confusion of the Arts* (London: Constable, 1910), pp. 106–8.

70. Bellamy Hosler, *Changing Aesthetic Views of Instrumental Music in Eighteenth-Century Germany* (Ann Arbor: UMI Research Press, 1981), p. 212.

71. John Neubauer, *The Emancipation of Music from Language: Departure from Mimesis in Eighteenth-Century Aesthetics* (New Haven: Yale University Press, 1986), p. 2. See also Carl Dahlhaus, *The Idea of Absolute Music*, translated by Roger Lustig (Chicago: University of Chicago Press, 1989).

72. E. T. A. Hoffmann, 'Review of Beethoven's Fifth Symphony' (1810), in *E.T.A. Hoffmann's Musical Writings: 'Kreisleriana', 'The Poet and the Composer', Music Criticism*, edited, annotated and introduced by David Charlton, translated

by Martyn Clarke (Cambridge: Cambridge University Press, 1989), pp. 234–51; p. 237 cited.

73. It should be said though that Hegel did not think music superior to other art forms for this reason, but on the contrary continued to rank other art forms higher. See Bucknell, *Literary Modernism and Musical Aesthetics*, pp. 21, 47.

74. Arthur Schopenhauer, *The World as Will and as Representation*, vol. 1, translated by E. F. J. Payne (New York: Dover, [1819] 1969), p. 257; emphases in original. Subsequent references to this edition are given in the text.

75. Terry Eagleton, *The Ideology of the Aesthetic* (Oxford: Blackwell, 1990), p. 167.

76. Kierkegaard, *Either/Or*, p. 69.

77. Kierkegaard, *Either/Or*, p. 69.

78. Friedrich Nietzsche, 'On Music and Words' (c. 1871), translated by Walter Kaufmann; reprinted as an appendix to Carl Dahlhaus, *Between Romanticism and Modernism*, translated by Mary Whittall (Berkeley: University of California Press, 1980), pp. 103–19; p. 113 cited.

79. Eduard Hanslick, *Vom Musikalisch-Schönen* (1854) [excerpts], translated by Martin Cooper, in Bojan Bujić (ed.), *Music in European Thought, 1851–1912* (Cambridge: Cambridge University Press, 1988), p. 36. Subsequent references to this edition are given in the text.

80. Theodor W. Adorno, 'Music, Language, and Composition' (1956), translated by Susan H. Gillespie, in *Essays on Music*, selected with an introduction, commentary and notes by Richard Leppert (Berkeley: University of California Press, 2002), pp. 113–26; p. 113 cited. Subsequent references to this edition are given in the text.

81. Walter Benjamin, 'On Language as Such and on the Language of Man' 1916), in *One Way Street, and Other Writings*, translated by Edmund Jephcott and Kingsley Shorter, with an introduction by Susan Sontag (London: Verso, 1997), pp. 107–23; p. 120 cited; emphasis in original.

82. Walter Benjamin, *The Origin of German Tragic Drama* (1924–5), translated by John Osborne, with an introduction by George Steiner (London: Verso, 1998), pp. 214, 211. Subsequent references to this edition are given in the text.

83. Theodor W. Adorno, 'On the Contemporary Relationship of Philosophy and Music' (1953), translated by Susan H. Gillespie, in *Essays on Music*, pp. 135–61; p. 140 cited.

84. Adorno, 'Music, Language, and Composition', p. 115.

85. Adorno, 'Music, Language, and Composition', p. 115.

Chapter 2

SOUND AND SOCIAL LIFE

'Sllt' says the machine in a print shop in Joyce's *Ulysses*, prompting Bloom's reflection, 'Everything speaks in its own way'. This takes place in the 'Aeolus' section of Joyce's novel, but receives full-scale elaboration hundreds of pages later in 'Circe', a hallucinatory section largely set in a Dublin brothel. Here, everything indeed does speak in its own way, including a gas jet ('Pooah! Pfuiiiiii !', 'Pwfungg !'), a timepiece ('Cuckoo. / Cuckoo. / Cuckoo'.), a nanny goat ('Megegaggegg ! Nannannanny !'), trees, a waterfall, a door handle, and a gong – and this is far from an exhaustive list.[1] 'Walls have hears', Bloom says at one point, punningly summing up the conceit of the whole section: that inanimate objects, no less than animate ones, are both sensible and cognisant of sound; as such, they not only listen to one another, but also make various critical, satirical, assenting, dissenting or at any rate responsive sounds in turn (p. 421). In the present book's 'Introduction', we saw how such sounds exemplify Douglas Kahn's category 'all sound', and how acknowledging this takes us some way towards understanding the 'modernity' of modern sound – but here, my interest in them concerns the way that all these sounds, in Joyce's imagining, are thoroughly and irrepressibly *social*. As 'Circe' unfolds, all sorts of human and inhuman 'speakers' are variously laughed at, heckled, cheered, questioned or impugned. Almost nobody, and no thing, speaks without some form of answer. This is a sound-world (to re-invoke Wagner's category, also cited in our 'Introduction') as it might be imagined by Mikhail Bakhtin: a world of carnival, in which everyone and everything is up for criticism, and nobody is beyond the range of laughter, be it bawdy, mocking or obscene.[2] Bloom's reflection, 'Everything speaks', is therefore shadowed by an implied counterpart, to the effect that all speaking is dialogic. Speaking to another and hearing that other speaking in return are complementary gestures – as indeed, we saw Kant suggest in the last chapter. Or, in the words of Bakhtin's colleague (and maybe nom de plume) V. N. Vološinov: '*Any utterance*, no matter how weighty and complete in and of itself, *is only a moment in the continuous process of verbal communication.*'[3]

Contributing to the Bakhtinian resonance of 'Circe' is Joyce's writing of the whole section as if it were a stage play, complete with stage directions and other para-dialogic apparatus whose cumulative effect is to underscore the ensemble and by turns fractious and friendly character of what is being said. On one occasion, for example, Bloom comments '*Bitterly*', Zoe responds in '*sudden Sulks*', prompting Bloom to speak '*Repentantly*', and so on (p. 471; emphases in original). The to and fro of sociability is here embodied in the very accents – a key Vološinov term – and emphases that speakers give to language.[4] So it is that 'Circe' functions as an introduction to the topic of this chapter: how sound articulates the social, in all its myriad forms, facilitating and expressing concrete forms of social interaction. Sound is not, I think, intrinsically any more or less social than any other object of sensation, but that it *is* social is attested both by its mediation and potentiation of peoples' interactions with each other, and by its giving these interactions sensuous, objective forms.

In pursuing this theme, this chapter will address a number of more specific topics, some of them also referenced in 'Circe'. First, and in some ways foremost, there is music, which Joyce invokes throughout this portion of *Ulysses*, as in others, via numerous allusions to and quotations from popular songs.[5] More specifically, there is music's reproduction by technologies such as the gramophone, which here, causes listeners to '*squawk*' when a disc '*rasps gratingly against the needle*' (p. 478; emphases in original). Another new technology, radio, is imagined by Joyce as enabling not only '*intercontinental*' but also '*interplanetary*' communications – though we will later see it associated, more prosaically, with new varieties of (terrestrial) crowd formation (p. 456; emphases in original). Meanwhile, this chapter also addresses non-Joycean themes, such as the literary representation of London and New York, and the association of such cities with 'foreign' accents.

But I begin with an extended discussion of Dorothy Richardson, and her interest in 'sound-space': the production by specific spaces of distinctive sonic signatures; or, conversely, the inscription of information about such spaces' size, configuration, inhabitants and so on, by the sounds produced within them.[6] Previous commentators have drawn attention to the significance of sonic (as well as visual) elements in Richardson's work, and to her sensitivity to built environments, and in what follows, I try to build on this work by showing how both concerns coincide with an interest in different forms of interactions with, and consciousness of, others.[7] A contrast with vision may be salutary here. For unlike vision, we might say, the priority and privilege afforded sound in *Pilgrimage* resides in the fact that it may occupy both sides of a shut door.

Dorothy Richardson and Sound-Space

At a point in *Dawn's Left Hand* (1931), *Pilgrimage*'s protagonist, Miriam, sits at her window listening to

> street-sounds. The pealing voice of the newspaper boy would still come up from far enough below to describe to her mind's eye the height of the confronting rows of quiet grey balconied houses and, with the brief-ness of its stay, accompanied by the painty crackling open of large front doors, low-toned words clearly audible, calling up a picture of boy and buyer pleasantly in league, and the quiet satisfied wooden flump of each leisurely closed door, to tell of its perfect length between tree-filled square and tree-filled square.[8]

The 'pictures' called up here, in one respect, are all about social interaction and togetherness. But in another, equally important, sense, they are about discretion and distanciation: not so much the meeting between 'boy and buyer' as that meeting's brevity and circumscription. Encounter and withdrawal, or sociabil-ity and its cessation, should not be thought of as opposed here; rather, they help form a single affective and behavioural complex that, in turn, helps define the urban square as a distinctive social space. Here, people live together, but in what one might call a 'side-to-side', rather than amongst-each-other way, and in ways that do not preclude privacy or even exclusivity. The 'satisf[action]' indicated by the 'flump' of these closed doors is thus one of knowing both that sociability is close to hand and that it may easily be regulated and contained.

In addition to this passage, *Pilgrimage* is, it seems safe to say, unique amongst major modernist artworks in featuring not one but two more exten-sive meditations on the sounds made by different doors. This alerts us to the way doors function in *Pilgrimage* as both a barrier to sociability and a frame *around* that sociability, furthering certain types of intimacy or togetherness while foreclosing others. Here is one of those 'sustained meditations', this one retrospective, as Miriam remembers sounds on the inside of a boarding house where she has lived:

> the sound of each of the Tansley Street doors came back at once, and some stood out clearly from the others. The dining-room door, quiet, slowly-moving because of its size and weight, closing solidly with a deep wooden sound, slamming, very rarely, with a detonation that went up

through the house. The state bedroom behind it, whose door moved discreetly on its hinges over a fairly thickish carpet and shut with a light, wooden sound [. . .] The upstairs drawing-room's softly, silkily closing door, a well-mannered, muffled sound, as if it were intent on doing its duty in such a way as not to interrupt the social life going on within. (vol. 4, p. 195)[9]

Again, the keynotes of this passage are 'discre[tion]' and the maintenance of boundaries. Just as front doors divide houses from all that lies outside them, in a square, so different doors inside a house act as thresholds and divides between the shared space of the dining room and drawing room, the private space of bedrooms, and so on. Each of the sounds from each of the doors is associated with a particular form of sociability – or sociability's suspension. But as this passage again reminds us, these two alternatives are not as straightforwardly opposed as they may first appear: being alone and yet being proximate to others who are not alone, on the contrary, are part and parcel of the same experience.

It is this coincidence of sociability with its (seeming) opposite that provides the key to the significance of 'sound-space' in *Pilgrimage*, and the particular attitude towards the social with which it is associated. To further specify the latter, we may proceed via a distinction drawn by Richardson's contemporary, Martin Heidegger, between 'Being-with' and 'Being-among-one-another'.[10] If the former is, for Heidegger, an essential, inalienable and entirely 'authentic' aspect of human existence – our being as the entities we are being inextricable from, and indeed partly predicated on, our sharing of the world with others like us – the latter is a degraded and inauthentic manner of experiencing this existence, in which authentic selfhood is lost or obscured by absorption into that of other people. In Richardson, a less systematically drawn but corresponding set of distinctions is sonically configured. Compare the following two descriptions: one of what might be called 'bad' sociability, the other of 'good' social *awareness*, as Miriam listens to her pupils from her bedroom:

The dining-room was full of sound [. . .] a fabric of sound unbroken at any point in the rows of tables set against the walls, and all, even the one she had selected, fully occupied. All the heads were averted, intent towards centres. (vol. 3, pp. 470–1)

quick little steps sounded on the stairs and the children shouted from their rooms. A door was opened and shut and for five minutes there was a babel of voices. Then the steps came out again and went away down the passage leading off the landing to the bathroom and a little spare room at the further end. They passed the bathroom, and the door of the little room was opened and shut and locked. (vol. 1, p. 375)

In the first instance, the inclination of the speakers' heads away from Miriam denotes their insensitivity towards her, as well as the willed abandon of their own selves into a kind of communal morass. By contrast, Miriam's auditory impressions of children – by measuring the distance between her and these children, as well as their proximity – denote the self-sufficiency and (in a positive sense) self-centredness of the perceiver. Again, a door (several, in fact: one locked) suggests that social exclusion and inclusion may be two sides of a single coin. This, then, is Richardson's affirmation of what Heidegger calls 'Being-*with*' and its superiority to the more obvious 'sociability' of 'Being-among-one another'.

Given this privileging of 'Being-with' – or what we earlier called 'side-to-side'-ness – it seems no accident that most of *Pilgrimage* takes place in settings that materialise, as it were, these concepts as a set of physical and insti-tutional structures: boarding schools (*Pointed Roofs*, 1915, *Backwater*, 1916); boarding houses (*The Tunnel*, 1919, and other volumes); houses converted into dental surgeries and other medical businesses (also *The Tunnel*, *Interim*, 1919); and hotels (*Overland*, 1927).[11] As a touchstone or counterpoint for all of these, parts of the novels are set within houses occupied by one family, usually involving Miriam's married sisters, which collectively serve to highlight, by way of contrast, the way Miriam's milieus typically sort people into discrete spaces, closely proximate to one another, but with only limited communica-tion. Despite what this contrast might suggest, however, there *is* a space in Richardson's imaginary and value-scheme for face-to-face inter-subjectivity – and this, too, is both sonically and spatially configured. Consider the following episode, where Miriam and her room-mate Selina Holland are talking together in their room:

> Clearly, almost audibly, the silence was knitting up the broken fabric of their intercourse [. . .] To [Selina] it was not a strange, strange adventure that their two voices should be sounding together in the night, a double thread of sound in a private darkness, making a pattern with all the other sounds in the world. (vol. 3, pp. 430, 436)

As in the dining-room passage cited earlier, dialogue here becomes a 'fabric' – a metaphor extended first as spoken sound becomes a 'thread' and then as it helps constitute a 'pattern'. But unlike the *'unbroken'* or oppressively thick 'fabric' made by dining guests in the earlier cited passage, 'intercourse' in the present instance is closer to the essence of fabric, we might say, as it should be: an organisation, or alternation, of presence and absence, something and nothing. Though it is significant that Miriam's and Selina's friendship (and living arrangement) ultimately founders on the disjuncture of their sensibili-ties, even this is, as it were, prefigured by the latter's failure to perceive the 'strange[ness]' of their conversation. For Selina, it turns out, is tin-eared (later,

Miriam will marvel at the moral–intellectual, as much as sensory, obliviousness that allows Selina to sleep through the 'night-sounds' of their neighbourhood; vol. 3, p. 499), and no one like that, in this text, can be a worthy candidate for lasting friendship.

The 'knitting up' of sound by silence in this instance also opens up one of *Pilgrimage*'s wider oppositions, between 'Unifying sound' and 'unifying silence' as 'the medium of [. . .] social life' (vol. 4, p. 273).[12] In the specific context that these words appear in, they serve to differentiate Quakers (for reasons we shall come to) from all those who are not Quakers, but in the wider economy of Richardson's ideas, they are more broadly *gendered*. Miriam's conviction that 'between men and women there can be no direct communication' helps explain not only the relative failure of her romantic-sexual relationships with men, but also the relative success of her strong friendships with women such as Amabel and Jean (vol. 4, p. 223). For similar reasons, silence is identified as the only proper medium for communion between lovers (vol. 4, pp. 645–6). Language itself is criticised throughout the novel sequence as an artefact and prop of patriarchy, locating Richardson in the vanguard of Virginia Woolf, Hélène Cixous and any number of others who have made such arguments. And then there is Quakerism, which fascinates Miriam not least for the way in which periods of collective silence, famously, often feature in its prayer meetings. Here is how she weaves her appreciation for this practice into a critique of spoken language:

> Words are separators, acknowledgment of separateness. The strength drawn when several people talk together in a room comes from one person, is paid out by him from some definite level of advantage, and disappears at the moment of separation. Spirits meet and converse and understand each other only in silence. Hence the strength available in a vitally silent Friends' [i.e. Quaker] Meeting. In Meeting, people live together, grow aware of each other's uniqueness. And consequence. Each silent figure is miraculous [. . .] Certainties state themselves, with or without words, within the mind of everyone in the gathering. (vol. 4, pp. 620–1)

Quakerism, then, is a collective version of that 'good' social awareness showcased when Miriam listens to her pupils from her bedroom. By keeping silent, Quakers maintain their 'uniqueness' as individuals while at the same time ensuring that the group of which those individuals are part is strengthened *as* a group. This is to say that in *Pilgrimage* as a whole, Quakerism stands for a synthesis of 'Being-with' and 'Being-among-one-another' – a form of solidarity that does not negate or ride roughshod over individuality, but rather nurtures it. So it is that though sound is cherished, as we have seen, throughout this text, for the evidence it bears of other peoples' lives, it is silence that bears the weight of Richardson's investment in communion and fellow feeling.

Music as Paradigm of Sociality

Ultimately, however, this privileging of Quakerism turns out to be qualified. Backing off from full endorsement at the last, Miriam states that for all its virtues, the Quaker worldview's (alleged) neglect of aesthetic pleasure 'makes the idea of a Quakerized world intolerable' (vol. 4, p. 603). Translating this criticism into the sphere of interpersonal relations, Miriam ends the novel sequence as an outsider. In a familiar – if not banal – gesture, *Pilgrimage* ends up affirming that the individual, to be healthy, must preserve a space outside any determinate social group.

In a synoptic commentary on her work, Richardson indeed explicitly says as much, using a metaphor that is itself significantly chosen. In her own relations with the various political, religious and intellectual groups that Miriam has dealings with throughout the novel sequence, the author recalls finding herself in a position 'where alone I could be everywhere at once, hearing all the voices in chorus'.[13] The term 'chorus', then, designates a form of collectivity *outside* specific forms of belonging or identification. Unison and/or harmony – the simple facts that in a chorus, more than one singer is present, and that, typically, different groups of (or single) singers sing distinct parts – become metaphors not so much of determinate forms of *sociability* as what we might call underlying or transcendent *sociality*.[14] The use of such terms to articulate such concepts lead us on to our next topic.

There is, in fact, a long tradition for which the use of musical terms to articulate ideas of sociality is not 'mere' metaphor, because music is considered as itself innately social. Here is an argument to this effect by Kant, based on music's phenomenal properties:

> Music is a communication of feelings in the distance to all present within the surrounding space, and it is a *social* pleasure which is not diminished by the fact that many people participate in it.[15]

And here is an argument by Rousseau, in his *Essay on the Origin of Languages* (c.1762), based on music's ontological and genealogical properties (Rousseau's overarching claim is that music is the earliest form and origin of language):

> [Music] always gives us some idea of our fellows.[...] [O]ne cannot hear either a song or an instrumental piece without immediately saying to oneself: another sensitive being is present.[16]

Here, meanwhile, is a claim by Adorno and Eisler resonant with Richardson's interest in the sociality of 'sound-space':

> This direct relationship to a collectivity, intrinsic in the phenomenon [i.e. music] itself, is probably connected with the sensations of spatial depth,

inclusiveness, and absorption of individuality, which are common to all music.[17]

And here, finally, is Nietzsche in *The Birth of Tragedy* (1872), commenting on Beethoven's Ninth symphony – a piece of music we have already heard Adorno speak of, in Chapter 1:

> Now, with the gospel of world harmony, each man feels himself not only united, reconciled, and at one with his neighbour, but *one* with him, as if the veil of Maya had been rent and now hung in rags before the mysterious primal Oneness.[18]

As the 'Dionysiac' art par excellence (as is well known, Nietzsche sees the 'Dionysiac' as one of two motive principles behind all art, the other being the 'Apolline' principle of individuation), music provides listeners with as direct an intuition as is possible of their fundamental kinship with each other. Drawing on Schopenhauer's idea of music as philosophically disclosive – 'veil of Maya' is Schopenhauer's term for the illusory world of mere appearances – Nietzsche thus sees 'unit[y],' in social terms, as humankind's otherwise occluded existential core.[19]

It is against this background that we should return to the work of Proust. Here, music is inextricable from social relations – for the very simple reason that it is always other people than the narrator whose music the narrator hears performed and who perform it. (We often forget this now, but before the widespread diffusion of sound reproduction technologies, listening to music was synonymous with social gathering: the only way to hear it otherwise than in such gathering was by playing on an instrument oneself.) However, music also marks that point within the social when the narrator feels his incommunicable individuality. Hearing music,

> the sounds seem to follow the very movement of our being, to reproduce that extreme inner point in our sensations which is the part that gives us that peculiar exhilaration which we experience from time to time and which, when we say 'What a fine day!' 'What glorious sunshine!' we do not in the least communicate to others, in whom the same sun and the same weather evoke quite different vibrations.[20]

Just as there will always be a multiplicity of different responses to the 'same' weather – the 'vibrations' it evokes being incommensurable with the labels with which we ostensibly share them – so for every one piece of music there will be as many responses as there are listeners. Music discloses the irreducibly multiple within the singular.

The narrative possibilities of this idea are explored in the significant number of modernist short stories based around concerts. In Woolf's 'The String Quartet' (1921), the 'outward' verbal exchanges of concertgoers are juxtaposed with paragraphs of visionary prose designed to replicate the 'inward' character of musical reception, the implicit point being that there is no mediation between the two. In Herman Grab's 'The Moonlit Night' (published 1957, but written before Grab's death in 1949), characters gather at a concert before departing to their private hopes and sorrows: though the music they hear represents a pinnacle of shared experience, the story shows their responses as ultimately atomised and idiosyncratic. And in Katherine Mansfield's 'Miss Brill' (1922), the protagonist's pleasure in an ersatz intimacy with her fellow concert-goers is shattered when she inadvertently discovers herself to be the object of derisive scrutiny by a couple hitherto imagined only as objects of her own judgement, not as judges. In each case, the individualising (and indeed isolating) effects of musical performances are contrasted with the supposed social, and socialising, ontology of music itself.

Of course, it is possible, given such evidence, to say that such claims for music's ontology are themselves faulty, and conclude instead that music and the social simply have different principles of consonance and dissonance, or unity and differentiation. Wallace Stevens's 'The Man with the Blue Guitar' (1937) entertains at least three distinct variations on this theme: the first, positing that individual listeners can be identified with music, if not musicians or each other ('The blue guitar / And I are one', the poet states at one point); the second, positing that insofar as individual members of a given audience can indeed be identified with each another, then this collective identity may be both realised within and transcended by a piece of music ('play', an audience asks the guitarist, 'A tune beyond us, yet ourselves'); and the third, suggesting that notwithstanding this last thesis, it may be foolish to expect music to abolish or make irrelevant manifest differences within an entire population (importantly, the poet asks sceptically if all the guitarist's audience can be accommodated on 'one string? [. . .] And all their manner, right and wrong, / And all their manner, weak and strong?').[21] Social multiplicity, it seems, is recalcitrant to musical synopsis. And finally, it may be that even if an equation between musical and social 'harmony' is given, one decides that one would simply rather have nothing to do with either. This is the position set out in two utterances by the same party in a two-way conversation (I here omit the pair's intervening exchanges) in D. H. Lawrence's *Aaron's Rod* (1922):

> 'What I can't stand is chords, you know: harmonies. A number of sounds all sounding together. It just makes me feel ill. [. . .]'
> [. . .]'But perhaps the flute is different. I have a feeling that it is. I can think of one single pipe-note – yes, I can think of it quite, quite calmly.'[22]

The speaker's interlocutor is, needless to say, a flautist. So it is that music, as well as sponsoring dreams of social unity, may also be enlisted in support of radical individualism.

PARTIES, CITY STREETS AND FOREIGN ACCENTS

As our last chapter showed, the 'depth' approach to sound in modernism identifies particular sounds as depositories of an ancestral, if not pre-human past. As a further example of this, take Richardson's description, not of a concert, but of the sound made by a concert-going crowd: 'Though composed of a multitude of voices, it was a single, rhythmic, continuous sound: beastlike' (vol. 4, p. 295). In Aldous Huxley's *Point Counter Point* (1928), a similarly primitivist image grabs Walter Bidlake's imagination as he enters a party, to hear a 'jungle of noise', in which people are as if the 'roots' of trees and 'their voices [. . .] the stems and waving branches'.[23] In F. Scott Fitzgerald's *The Great Gatsby* (1925), a similarly profuse (if not, on this occasion, primitivist) image fuses party guests with the pleasures they are gathered for: 'cocktails permeate the garden outside, until the air is alive with chatter and laughter [. . .] Laughter is easier minute by minute, spilled with prodigality, tipped out at a cheerful word.'[24] Each of these examples makes a naturalising gesture, rendering collective sound as either animal ('primitive beast'), vegetable (a 'jungle') or liquid.

Such ascription of ahistorical or primordial qualities to modern or contemporary sound is not an aberrant, but a regular feature in conceptions of modern sound – as indeed, we have already indicated in this book's 'Introduction'. Nowhere is this more evident, in fact, than in descriptions of what might at first glance seem the most distinctly 'modern' environment of all: the metropolitan, technology-pervaded city. Twice in close succession in *Pilgrimage*, London's sound is likened to the sea, a likeness also ascribed to a London train station in Woolf's *The Waves* (meanwhile, the same city emits a dog-like 'growl' in Woolf's *Flush* (1933) – a novel, it should be noted, that is actually about a dog).[25] The horses whose hoofs clatter through the streets of John Dos Passos's New York (*Manhattan Transfer*, 1925) indicate one important reason for such likenesses: though we now tend to think of the city almost exclusively in terms of humans and human-made things, its great exemplars in the early twentieth century were full of animals, and could scarcely have functioned at all without horses, at least until the whole-scale triumph of the motor car and its derivatives.[26] Michael Gold's *Jews Without Money* (1930) indicates another – this time thoroughly unwanted – animal sound typical of certain districts of New York: 'At night [cats] alarmed the tenement with their weird cries like a congress of crazy witches [. . .] We tortured them, they tortured us.'[27]

New York itself, of course, was regarded by many in our period as the quintessential modern city, and was thus to many observers, also, clearly the loudest.[28] Henry Roth, a fellow denizen of Gold's Jewish Lower East Side, records further reasons for this in *Call it Sleep* (1934):

Here in 9th Street it wasn't the sun that swamped one as one left the doorway, it was sound – an avalanche of sound. There were countless children, there were countless baby carriages, there were countless mothers. And to the screams, rebukes and bickerings of these, a seemingly endless file of hucksters joined their bawling cries. On Avenue D horse-carts clattered and banged. Avenue D was thronged with beer wagons, garbage carts and coal trucks. There were many automobiles, some blunt and rangy, some with high straw poops, honking. Beyond Avenue D [. . .] was the East River on which many boat horns sounded. On 10th Street, the 8th Street Crosstown car ground its way towards the switch.[29]

The social, *pace* Richardson, is here is not a 'fabric' – broken or unbroken – but an 'avalanche', hurling sound without remission, and in doing so threatening to paralyse its auditors. Everyone, and nearly every thing (the boat horns may be an exception) make sounds that speak of some emergency. However, a later passage indicates the protagonist David's growing ability to winnow out from this sound mass items to linger over and savour – much as Miriam, in *Pilgrimage*, does with doors:

He knew his world now. With a kind of meditative assurance, he singled out the elements of the ever-present din – the far voices, the near, the bells of a junk wagon, the sing-song cry of the I-Cash-clothes-man, waving his truncheon-newspaper, the sloshing jangle of the keys on the huge ring on the back of the tinker. (p. 171)

In contrast to the 'avalanche' on 9th Street, these sounds encode the social as a treasure trove of characters, rituals and institutions.

In doing so, the last example also illustrates one of the most abiding literary techniques for rendering the multistranded character of urban sound: writing multi-item lists. Hence is Djuna Barnes in New York's Greenwich Village, hearing

[a] rattle of music through an open window, the weeping of a baby in a tenement, the click of a typewriter in a basement [...].[30]

And here is London's Kentish Town in Compton Mackenzie's *Sinister Street* (1913):

A train roared over the bridge; a piano organ gargled its tune; a wagon-load of iron girders drew near in a clanging tintamar of slow progress.[31]

Finally, here is T. S. Eliot describing London's Bloomsbury to his brother Henry in a letter from 1914:

> The noise hereabouts is like hell turned upside down. Hot weather, all windows open, many babies, pianos, street piano accordions, singers, hummers, whistlers.[32]

In each of these instances, the arrangement of each item paratactically, without hierarchical differentiation, identifies these items as equally characteristic of a given locale. Thus we understand that while these sounds may have no fixed causal or temporal relation to each other, they nonetheless constitute a 'set', and that their locale itself may best be characterised by the co-presence or coincidence of just these things.

A similar idea animates the proposal by the more recent urban theorist Henri Lefebrve of analysing the manifold activities of city life into interpenetrant, competing, and overlapping 'rhythms' (anticipating this idea, the Vienna of Robert Musil's *The Man Without Qualities*, 1930–42, moves to 'one great rhythmic beat as well as the chronic discord and mutual displacement of all its contending rhythms').[33] Meanwhile, back in the early twentieth century, others see sounds that have occurred over time in close proximity becoming 'fixed,' and also mingling and coalescing, as if by some quasi-geological process of sedimentation. Here is Barnes again, describing a tout at New York's pleasure park, Coney Island:

> A thin little girl like an old woman steps up onto the sidewalk [. . .] She begins to cackle, copying the crowd; [. . .] she seems to be an outcome of past cries, curses, shouts, laughter, music, dancing, hubbub, and merry insolence. She is a little girl who has collected herself from the gutter and molded herself into this saucy, angular body from the refuse of great noises [. . .].[34]

The girl is thus an auditory collage or concretion. Putting Barnes's idea of 'trapped' or non-departing, and Lefebrve's idea of overlapping, sounds together, one arrives at a fabulous conceit whereby privileged locations in a city act as a kind of sonic 'mirror' or gallery of its inhabitants. Here is British writer Stephen Graham walking with a friend through London's Greenwich foot-tunnel at 3 a.m.:

> It was an eerie place [. . .] We stopped short, sure that we were being followed; and as we listened there outbroke on our ears the sharp noise of steps on the iron stairway. Was it a watchman? Or a police-man? We waited, standing stock-still, and as we did so we heard our own footsteps coming stealthily toward us and then again the clatter of steps of people coming down the iron stairway. Then we understood that they were echoes. The long, snake-like way was possessed by all manner of wandering sounds which could not escape into outer air and get lost. There were sounds there of people who had gone through it hours before.[35]

Here, then, in a manner that may recall the 'clattering' of planks in Faulkner's *As I Lay Dying* (as discussed above in this book's 'Introduction') the tunnel functions 'phonographically', preserving sound and re-releasing it, long after its efficient cause has gone. And though this conceit is scarcely plausible as 'fact' – for surely, one cannot help wondering, the walkers are more likely here to have heard their *own* footsteps as echoes, and misrecognised these sounds as those produced by other people? – one cannot help envying the walkers the moment at which this conceit must have struck them as 'true'. For what an experience to have! For the two walkers, it is as if the tunnel allows them to step back in time while somehow retaining their place in their own present, and thus appear to themselves as both within and outside an acoustic crowd. Hearing one's footsteps alongside departed others', then, on this account, one hears oneself as 'in' oneself, as opposed to others, and also, simultaneously, 'beside' oneself, among them.

Graham is in fact, besides this episode, an especially vivid chronicler of urban sound throughout his two 'Nights' books, *London Nights* (1925) and *New York Nights* (1927), each of which details nocturnal walks in the cities they respectively designate. Here is a description from the New York book of a rooming house (a very different establishment, one notes, seemingly, from the boarding houses in Richardson):

> Doors on various floors stand half-open all the evening and most of the night. You hear a medley of guitar-playing, songs, *bla-bla* of announcers on loud-speakers, noisy discussions over cards [. . .] The second-floor front is a large room where companions from Babel gather about a billiard-table every evening [. . .] In the third-floor front two men in the B.V.D.'s ['Bradley, Voorhees and Day's', a brand of underwear] dance to a gramophone. And ever and anon the telephone rings insistently, till some one is moved to lift the receiver and yell a name up and down the stairs.[36]

Despite the impression of unbridled sociability this gives, however, Graham goes on to note that day by day, the men inhabiting this house are too discrete to speak to or even acknowledge one another. Once more, in this hybrid, public–private space, 'Being-among-one-another' is subordinate to 'Being-with'.

Why does Graham designate some of these men 'companions of Babel'? Because at least some of their languages, to him, are unintelligible – Babel of course being the biblical city whose inhabitants God punished for building a tower towards heaven by ensuring that they henceforth spoke mutually unintelligible languages. To many observers, New York was a modern Babel, being the place in the English-speaking world where one was most likely to have the privilege of one's own language queried by the presence of 'foreign' counterparts (the reason being, of course, New York's status as the entry point for great numbers of immigrants coming to the USA throughout the late nineteenth and early twentieth-centuries).[37] In the fiction of Abraham Cahan, a Lithuanian-born émigré Jew, this process is explored, as it were, from the reverse side, via the effect of English on the speech of those whose first language is Yiddish. In *Yekl* (1896), almost every sentence characters speak (in Yiddish, though written as English) is studded with italicised, phonetically-spelled words to indicate English words these characters have incorporated into their vocabularies, and the accents in which they speak them (for example, '"settled"' becomes '"*tzettled*"').[38] In *The Rise of David Levinsky* (1917), we hear how the 'singsong' of the narrator's childhood Talmud reading survives in the English-language, business-centred discourse of his adulthood.[39] And in Roth's *Call it Sleep*, an episode of misunderstanding surrounds different pronunciations of a street name ('"Boddeh Stritt,"' '"Poddeh Street"' and '"Barhdee Street"') (pp. 96, 99). For Henry James, it was just this sort of thing that had disastrous effects upon native English speakers, never mind immigrants, and even upon the English language itself. In a harrowed report from the Lower East Side, he describes its cafes as 'torture-rooms of the living idiom' and predicts a future in which spoken English is unrecognisable as such 'in any sense for which there is an existing literary measure'.[40] Others, thankfully, put a more positive spin on this sort of thing, but there is no doubt that James, like Cahan, was right in noticing how the languages they spoke were rendered non-identical with themselves as they and their respective speech communities came into contact (this was true for Yiddish, of course, as much as English, or any other language). What the history of English in New York and places like it shows is thus the ability of languages to be internally divided, so that each language appears as 'other' whenever spoken by those who share a different history and manner of usage from oneself. As that part of speech whose acoustic perception may outpace linguistic comprehension, the 'other's' accent is perhaps the most obvious sign of this phenomenon. What Cahan, Roth and James all document, then, in different ways, is that process whereby language may cease to be experienced simply as 'sense', and start appearing also or instead as sheer, sense-affecting sound.

TELEPHONES, RADIO AND GRAMOPHONES

The rooming house described by Graham in the passage quoted above is also distinguished by another feature we have not yet noted: the presence of technologies such as the gramophone and telephone, which serve to open up the space they are used in to sounds and agencies coming from outside. (I suspend here consideration of the passage's eroticism, as manifested by the two men dancing, though I shall avert to it below.) This prompts the question of what sort of social relations such technologies enable. For surely these facilitated new forms of 'Being-among-one-another' and 'Being-with'? We shall attempt to explore this issue via three of the most significant technologies: the telephone, the radio, and the gramophone and phonograph.

An initial answer, linking the telephone to still other technologies, comes from Louis in Woolf's *The Waves*:

> 'I am half in love with the typewriter and the telephone. With letters and cables and brief but courteous commands on the telephone to Paris, Berlin, New York, I have fused my many lives into one; [. . .] I love the telephone with its lips stretched to my whisper, and the date on the wall; and the engagement book. Mr Prentice at four; Mr Eyres sharp at four-thirty.'[41]

The key thing to note here is the reversibility, so to speak, of the passage's key line: instead of 'I have fused my many lives into one' we might just as easily read, 'I, who am one person, have a multitude of lives'. That each multiple represents engagement with *another* person is furthermore indicated by the telephone's implied relation to the engagement book, suggesting that Mr Prentice's meeting has been arranged by a call to his telephone, Mr Eyres's by a call to his, and so on. Meanwhile, the weird eroticism of those inorganic 'lips' is picked up in an episode in Dos Passos's *Manhattan Transfer* where Ellen takes calls from different suitors in quick succession, and offers different levels of encouragement to each of them as they pursue their suits.[42] Here, then, the telephone represents the promise of romantic, possibly sexual, encounter.

The dramatic possibilities of this 'switching' effect, meanwhile, whereby the telephone is used to rapidly open, close and alternate discussions with a multitude of different interlocutors, are systematically exploited in Ben Hecht and Charles MacArthur's stage play *The Front Page* (1928; cinematised as *His Girl Friday* by Howard Hawks in 1940). Here, the stage is set around seven telephones, each communicating with a newspaper office, in the pressroom of a criminal court. Throughout the play, the leading characters, all newspaper reporters, combine face-to-face dialogue with each other, with numerous telephone conversations with other people, either phoning into or being phoned from inside the pressroom. At one point, questions posed by one reporter to an interviewee on the telephone are accompanied by sardonic commentary from his colleagues on stage, making the reporter pivot between two distinct (but for him, overlapping) sonic worlds: one at his end of the telephone, that his colleagues too are part of, the other, at the other end of the telephone, which only he can hear.[43] On another occasion, one reporter finishes a conversation with his girlfriend on one phone and then commences an entirely different conversation with another person on another, this having been answered by a colleague moments earlier (p. 64). The play's climax sees several reporters phone their respective offices simultaneously, all reporting versions of the same, just-breaking story (p. 75). The 'fusion' and self-splitting identified in Woolf's novel are rewritten as grand farce.

Just because it *can* be used this way, however, the telephone does not of course automatically entail more sociability, more often, for every user. It can also be used to cool or even terminate relationships; the conversations during which Nina and Adam first break their engagement, and then all contact with each other, in Evelyn Waugh's *Vile Bodies* (1930) are salutary in this respect.[44] Still other feelings towards interlocutors are shown by protagonists in Faulkner's *Pylon* (1935) and Patrick Hamilton's *Hangover Square* (1941) – in both cases, coincidentally or not, while using public telephones. In the first instance, the 'sweatclutched' handpiece and breath-cupping mouthpiece of the apparatus present an image of self-cornered vulnerability; in the second, George Harvey Bone enters a phone box to become 'a different sort of person in a different sort of world – a muffled, urgent, anxious, private, ghostly world, composed not of human beings but of voices, disembodied communications'.[45] Here, the telephone is as much what divides the persons using it from other people as what connects them.

Bone's experience, it might be thought, borders on the hallucinatory – and this is no coincidence: he suffers from psychotic episodes, which will eventually lead to him killing the woman with whom he is infatuated (in Chapter 5, we will see how his illness is conceptualised in terms of another technology, cinema). But in certain of its features, according to Hamilton's description, it also resembles the mundane and, for most people, surely *non*-pathological experience of radio, another communications – and, from the 1920s onwards, mass-broadcast – medium, inaugurating what its early theorist Rudolf Arnheim calls 'a world of sound differentiated from reality by its own formal laws'.[46] Two other early radio theorists, Hadley Cantril and Gordon W. Allport, focus their investigation on the types of social bond the new medium constructs. Arguing that radio 'plays havoc with the traditional theories of crowd formation', they attempt to characterise what we would now call the 'virtual' crowd of radio listeners, formed by individuals lacking any necessary spatial proximity to, communication with, or even knowledge of, each other.[47] The two diagrams reproduced in Figure 2.1 summarise their findings: in contrast to what the first caption calls 'congregate assemblies', the audiences formed by radio are atomised and consist of individuals who (with some exceptions) lack the ability to influence either each other or whatever broadcasters or performers they are listening to. One may object that the concert-goers portrayed in, say, Herman Grab's 'The Moonlit Night' (see above) behave more like the crowd in the second diagram here than the 'congregate assembly' this analysis predicts they 'should', but the basic distinction Cantril and Allport draw here is surely uncontroversial. Though nothing in its technical capability necessitates it (the facts, indeed, are to the contrary) radio did in fact, early in its history,

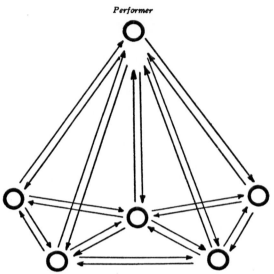

Fig. I.—The social formation of the *congregate assembly*, showing circular relationship between performer and auditors, as well as the influence of one auditor upon another.

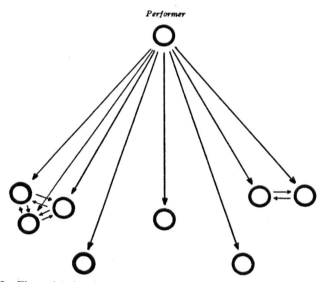

Fig. II.—The social situation in *radio*, showing the linear relationship between the speaker and his auditors, and, excepting where listeners are grouped in their own homes, a complete absence of social facilitation in the audience.

Figure 2.1 Diagram from Hadley Cantril and Gordon W. Allport, *The Psychology of Radio* (New York: Harper and Brothers, 1935)

become a predominately 'one-way' rather than two-way medium.[48] Thus radio testifies to and depends on what we have called sociality without necessarily enhancing sociability.

Having arrived at this conclusion, Cantril and Allport proceed to further observations about the psychology of radio listeners vis-à-vis each other, some of which are fascinatingly self-contradictory. Thus on one hand, they claim (identifying themselves with such listeners), 'We do not feel the compulsion to conform or to express the feelings that others are expressing. We are less emotional and more critical, less crowdish and more individualistic'; on the other, however, they state, 'it seems to be the nature of radio to encourage people to think and feel alike' (pp. 13, 20). Similarly, at one point they identify radio as 'Inherently' a 'foe of Fascism and of cultural nationalism'; at another, though, they cite as evidence of its political effectiveness its use by Goebbels to spread the creed of National Socialism in Germany (pp. 22, 60). None of these points are necessarily unmerited in isolation, but together, scarcely add up to a coherent theory of what social, much less political, arrangements radio does and does not sponsor. Decades before Marshall McLuhan famously declared 'The medium is the message', Cantril and Allport have not quite clarified the distinction (or, conversely, the relation) between radio's form and content.

In one respect at least, however, their study seems to have been prescient. In 1938, thousands if not millions of American listeners panicked while listening to Orson Welles's adaptation of H. G. Wells's *The War of the Worlds* (1938), apparently convinced that the Martian invasion depicted therein was 'real'. Responding to this incident, Cantril wrote a dedicated study, *The Invasion from Mars: A Study in the Psychology of Panic* (1940), attempting to explain what had happened. Some of his suggestions interestingly complicate what he and Allport had argued just a few years earlier. For instance, the distinction between 'congregate assemblies' and radio audiences is blurred here by the fact that people frightened by the broadcast 'often hastened to telephone friends or relatives', thus passing on their fear to others.[49] Those who happened to hear (or hear about) the broadcast while outside their homes became 'more confused and more terror-stricken because they were away from home, worried about their families, and surrounded by so many other people who were frightened' (p. 146). The latter point suggests that fear is contagious (Cantril uses the term himself), and that as such, it and maybe other emotions can either sidestep or subvert whatever barriers technology puts in their place (remember, Cantril and Allport originally saw radio listeners as characterised by mutual isolation). Other contributory causes of the panic Cantril considers are ignorance and inequality amongst audience members, the contemporaneous threat of war in Europe, and radio's established use as a medium for public announcements – but we should also note one that he neglects: the sheer brilliance of Welles's production and the script of Welles's staff-writer, Howard

Koch.[50] Showing a formal self-reflexivity more commonly associated with 'high' modernist masterpieces, these simulate both the deliberate and accidental signatures of 'live' broadcasting in order to suggest that Welles's production too is a news-based, rather than rehearsed and scripted broadcast. For example, the play begins with apparently routine programming, and then has a presenter break in to bring unscheduled, supposedly live reports broadcast from outside (p. 11). Subsequent reports are punctuated by breathless, hesitant or frightened pauses, while at the play's climax, an outside line falls ominously silent, inviting the audience to infer that actual reporters are now amongst the Martians' victims (p. 31). Evidently, then, Welles's production frightened so many, at least in part, because it so successfully simulated the vicissitudes of live broadcasting *in and as a broadcast*.

'Liveness' is, of course, intrinsic to both radio and telephony, insofar as listeners to either expect the sounds to which they listen to coincide, in origin, with the time of their own listening.[51] But this is definitely not the case with the phonograph and gramophone – whose very *raison d'être*, we might say (in common with other forms of recording) is to allow the time of a communicative or performative act to become uncoupled from that of its reception. As Rilke's 'Primal Sound', discussed in Chapter 1, helps show, one effect of this is to allow one's own voice to be experienced in unaccustomed otherness, as if the self could enter into 'social' relations with its temporally distributed parts. Other, more clearly interpersonally social possibilities are explored in Mark Twain's and William Dean Howells's *Colonel Sellers as a Scientist* (1883), one of several stage plays written in the wake of the phonograph's invention to explore the new technology's effects.[52] In one scene, two lovers are reunited after one of them, who has believed the other dead, hears the latter's recorded voice in a house he is visiting; in another, somewhat laboured comedy is derived from the prospect of a ship's mate recording profanities in order that these may be played back to exhort crew members in his absence.[53] Though both these episodes may seem far-fetched, they lay their finger on a point of real-world consequence: that by separating playback from recording, gramophones and phonographs give people influence over others in situations from which they are removed in time as well as space.

Given this, it is perhaps no surprise that these technologies were associated with the condition in which temporal and spatial absence are ineluctable and absolute, namely death.[54] In the words of Thomas Edison, the phonograph's inventor, one use the device immediately suggested itself for was recording 'the last words of dying persons'.[55] Bloom parodically re-imagines the same idea in *Ulysses* (p. 109). But the disjuncture between addressor and addressed such scenarios emphasise was not always (or even often) upmost in users' minds: just as often, if not more so, the gramophone or phonograph were prized by listeners for facilitating close physical proximity with one another. Graham, again, provides a helpful sign of this, with his vaguely eroticised image of two guests dancing to a gramophone in a New York boarding house. Similarly, phonographs provide music for the crowded, hedonistic parties of Carl Van Vechten's *Nigger Heaven* (1926), while in *Manhattan Transfer*, an unattended record, still spinning after its music has come to an end, stands in coyly for more overt representation of a couple having sex.[56] But the most elaborate account of the phonograph's place in romantic, if not sexual, liaisons is surely the scene in Fitzgerald's *Tender is the Night* (1934) where Nicole brings her machine and record collection to play to Dick under the Swiss night sky:

> They went to the cache where she had left the phonograph, turned a corner by the workshop, climbed a rock, and set down behind a low wall, facing miles and miles of rolling night.
>
> They were in America now [. . .] They were so sorry, dear; they went down to meet each other in a taxi, honey; they had preferences in smiles and had met in Hindustan, and shortly afterward they must have quarrelled, for no-body knew and nobody seemed to care – yet finally one of them had gone and left the other crying, only to feel blue, to feel sad.
>
> The thin tunes, holding lost times and future hopes in liaison, twisted upon the Swiss night. In the lulls of the phonograph a cricket held the scene together with a single note. By and by Nicole stopped playing the machine and sang [. . .].[57]

Even before Nicole starts singing, we understand the central role recorded music is taking on here in the construction of the couple's romance. For in that middle paragraph above, Fitzgerald's prose suddenly takes on a ventriloquising function, paraphrasing and combining fragments from the lyrics of the songs whose recordings Nicole plays ('they went down to meet each other in a taxi, honey' echoes 'The Darktown Strutter's Ball', a 1917 song by Shelton Brooks; 'Hindustan' is a 1918 song by Oliver G. Wallace and Harold Weeks, and so on).[58] Just as Fitzgerald mimics the lyrics of these songs, then, so Nicole and Dick's feelings are shaped by the sentimental content of the songs themselves – to the extent that the couple are figuratively transported to 'America', the country or continent from which these recordings originate. Here, it is not so much Nicole who is playing records for herself and her future husband; rather, it is these records that are 'playing' Fitzgerald's characters.[59]

And in this respect, Nicole and Dick's experience is emblematic. For if a generalisation may be risked, we may say that here, Fitzgerald sketches nothing less than an entire expressive culture, in which people have learned to articulate their feelings not by playing music (as nineteenth-century people would have assumed) but by consuming it. As late as the early 1890s, Edison and other pioneers of sound recording believed that the future of their industry lay in business's use of their machines for recording-keeping and dictation purposes: by 1899, however, their strategic focus had decisively shifted forwards the marketing of pre-recorded sound, increasingly involving not the spoken word but music.[60] Ever since then, people like Nicole and Dick have been able to mix and match recordings, play them as often or as rarely as they like, and take them more or less anywhere they go (as in Nicole's taking of her phonograph outside), thus weaving the emotional avowals and associations of the music they consume into the affective fabric of their own lives. Sound recording may not have created this culture out of nothing – clearly, the emotional appeal of music is both chronologically and ontologically prior to its recording – but it has undoubtedly given this culture greater breadth and depth: after all, how else can most people, especially those who do not compose, or play an instrument, make music a regular, if not constant prompt and regulator of their moods? So it is that an invention that Edison saw mainly as a medium of inventories and memoranda became the engine of music's apotheosis as a cultural reserve of shared referents and as a caster of romantic spells. Hitherto confined to a relatively small number of people and situations, music became a royal road that almost anyone could travel to aspiration, memory and desire.

LOVE AND THE PIANO

Nonetheless, it bears repeating that recording is not, or at least not primarily, responsible for whatever emotional appeal and significance music has. As long as music has existed, its capacity to arouse extreme emotional responses has been noted; Plato, for instance, notoriously excludes many forms of it from his ideal republic on just this basis.[61] We must be clear, then, that whatever the effects on music of recording may be – and as we shall see in Chapter 4, these have been considerable – recording hardly created an appetite or social space for music where none hitherto existed. Rather, gramophone and phonograph recordings found niches in contexts and environments largely shaped by anterior modes of musical production and reception.

To see this, it is worth considering the musical landscape of *Tender is the Night* as a whole. Like other novels by Fitzgerald, this has an extensive 'literary soundtrack' – a term T. Austin Graham uses to designate 'a series of written references to specific pieces of music that [. . .] heighten, color, or otherwise comment upon the text that contains them'.[62] (In this respect, we can now see, Fitzgerald's writing absorbs and recapitulates the listening habits of his leading characters.) Waiting for a train, for instance, Rosemary hears an orchestra play 'the "Nice Carnival Song" and last year's American tune', thus locating her own journey in relation to the rhythms of international tourism (p. 23). Elsewhere, the lyrics to 'Thank Your Father', a 1930 jazz number, comment uncomfortably on Nicole's history of child-abuse (p. 311). And in an erotically charged telephone conversation between Dick and Rosemary – notice here how the association between telephony and sexual intrigue, noted earlier, is inscribed again – Dick overhears the 1925 jazz duet 'Tea for Two' coming from an unnamed source in or near Rosemary's hotel room (p. 107). Recalling this a few weeks later, Dick acts as follows:

> He went into the house, forgetting something he wanted to do there, and then remembering it was the piano. He sat down whistling and played by ear:
>
> 'Just picture you upon my knee
> With tea for two and two for tea
> And me for you and you for me – '
>
> Through the melody flowed a sudden realization that Nicole, hearing it, would guess quickly at a nostalgia for the past fortnight. He broke off with a casual chord and left the piano. (p. 187)

Again, what music provides a character here is a vocabulary out of which to construct his own sentimental narrative.

The 'consumption' of music, then, as identified above, should not be seen as necessarily passive, but rather as a sometimes active element in an ongoing process that may also include music's interpretation (Dick's 'whistling' and accompaniment 'by ear'), adaptation, and even (though this is not represented here) composition. Similarly, use of one musical technology, like the phonograph, at certain times, does not preclude use of other productive or reproductive instruments, like the piano, at others – just as one may provide a 'live' supplement to a recording by singing along, perform music 'live' that one only then hears recordings of subsequently, and so on. Music's commentary and citational capacity – what we have called its function as a 'sound-track' – thus builds not only on the inherent translatability of music between different media (the fact that, say, the 'same' music can be played by a full jazz orchestra and by an amateur playing alone on the piano) but also on an equally inherent tendency for musical production, consumption and reproduction to overlap. To these tendencies within music we may add another, already implicit in our earlier discussion of Nicole's and Dick's phonograph listening: its oft-avowed capacity to arouse feelings both 'directly,' as if in an unmediated encounter with each individual listener or player, and also transferentially, between them.[63] All these things contribute to the associations we have already traced between music and the social. But there is one musical instrument whose literary representation, at least, tends to bind them up especially tightly: the one Dick is playing in the last-cited passage, the piano.

There are several historical reasons for this. For a start, the piano's rise coincided in the early nineteenth century with that of musical romanticism – a movement which, like its literary and philosophical equivalents (as we saw in Chapter 1) privileges the expression of 'inner feelings'.[64] Secondly, it became an important item of furniture and a status symbol within the nineteenth-century (and later) bourgeois household, thus becoming more or less strongly linked in turn with what we tend to think of as typically 'bourgeois' affective dispositions: interiority (implicit in the instrument's resemblance to that other meditative site, the desk); intimacy (made manifest in musical terms by the duet, whether played by two people at the piano or one pianist and another person with another instrument, or singing); and, in a more diffuse way, the emotional convulsions and self-consciousness of adolescence and early adult-hood (the piano became central to musical education at a time when the latter was especially esteemed as a means to personal attainment and formation, meaning that many middle-class children acquired familiarity with the instru-ment in their teenage years).[65] Related to its educational use is a third reason: the fact pupil–tutor relations in piano instruction were often, if not always, strongly gendered, with pupils disproportionately tending to be female and tutors male.[66] This, and such well-known instances as the romance and sub-sequent marriage between pianist-composers Clara Wieck (1819–1896) and Robert Schumann (1810–1856) helped give the piano a discrete but definite aura of romantic sexuality. And finally, while generally at the forefront of attempts to privilege music's 'pure', non-representational nature (again, see Chapter 1), the dedicated repertoire written for solo piano by composers such as Frédéric Chopin (1810–1849) tended, at least in its popular recep-tion, to create an association between piano music and specific emotional states. Chopin himself, for instance, is famous for (amongst other things) his twenty-one Nocturnes – pieces intended to be played at night, or evoke 'nocturnal' moods. The same composer, similarly, wrote several equally cel-ebrated pieces entitled 'Impromptu', a term denoting expressive freedom and spontaneity.

Given all this, it is no surprise that Kate Chopin (no relation) makes piano music central to the burgeoning eroticism of Edna Pontellier in *The Awakening* (1899). While visiting her friend Mademoiselle Reisz, an accomplished pianist, Edna discovers that the latter has received a letter from Robert le Brun, with whom Edna is in love. Giving Edna the letter to read, Mademoiselle Reisz goes to the piano and 'without further comment' plays music that includes none other than one of those Impromptus by Frédéric Chopin. This is how Edna responds:

> Edna did not know when the Impromptu began or ended. She sat in the sofa corner reading Robert's letter by the fading light. [. . .]
>
> The shadows deepened in the little room. The music grew strange and fantastic – turbulent, insistent, plaintive and soft with entreaty. [. . .]
>
> Edna was sobbing [. . .].[67]

The social relations of this episode are complex. At the most obvious level, Mademoiselle Reisz is using music to convey her implicit understanding of Edna's passion – her playing constituting a social bond between two women, listener and performer. But at another level, the pianist seems to be 'playing' Edna's feelings for an absent, third person. The all-female dyad of the first relation thus acts as a proxy or mediator for a second, female–male, relation, between Edna and Robert. Moreover, a further female–male relation prevails between the letter's original recipient (Mademoiselle Reisz) and its writer (Robert) – a fact which, further, helps account for the choice of Chopin's music as the letter's 'sound-track' when Mademoiselle Reisz hands it on to Edna (within the letter, Robert explicitly asks that this music should be played if Edna comes to visit; p. 70). The piano thus creates a musical and sentimental space in which three distinct two-way relationships can operate upon one another or converge.

To some extent, of course, this 'erotic' view of music comes as no surprise. As we saw in Chapter 1, thinkers in the evolutionary tradition from Darwin onwards identified a sexual ontology and genealogy for all music, of whatever genre or instrumentation. Moreover, certain texts coincident or overlapping with this tradition go even further than *The Awakening* in associating music (as Chopin hints at here) with quasi-telepathic emotional transactions: Tolstoy's 'The Kreutzer Sonata,' for instance – a text averted to above, in Chapter 1 – has a plot that turns on an alleged adulterous liaison between a violinist and a protagonist's piano-playing wife; the same text also underscores an association between musical duets and sexual intimacy.[68] But there is a further musical referent helping to explain the association of music with specifically erotic emotional convulsions in Chopin's text: Wagner's *Tristan and Isolde* (1856), portions of which are also amongst the music Mademoiselle Reisz plays to Edna on the occasion when the latter reads Robert's letter, as an excursus within her recital of Chopin's 'Impromptu' (p. 71). With this part of her performance, the indeterminate emotional freight of 'pure' music and the determinate emotional referents of music when accompanied by words coincide – for *Tristan* is notoriously, in its dramatic content, perhaps the most centred on eroticism in the entire canon of western music to its date. A mythic tale of passionate, transgressive love, the work concludes with the titular protagonists' deaths, in terms famously conflating death itself with sexual fulfilment (the famous Wagnerian term is *Liebestod*, or 'love-death'). And while originally, the piece is written for many voices and a large orchestra, it is via its piano transcriptions, redactions and performance that it functions as a metonym for perilous or morbid passions in a significant number of early twentieth-century texts.

One instance of this is Woolf's first novel, *The Voyage Out* (1915). Spotting Rachel Vinrace's piano score of *Tristan*, Clarissa Dalloway casts her eye over an especially '"thrilling"' passage of duet between Wagner's protagonists, and then recalls an earlier experience at a performance of the composer's *Parsifal* (1882) where she has ended up sobbing on a male stranger's shoulder.[69] In *Swann's Way*, Proust's Madame Verdurin objects on similar grounds to her guests playing Wagner on the piano, 'not because the music [i]s displeasing to her, but, on the contrary, because it ma[kes] too violent an impression'.[70] In Thomas Mann's *Buddenbrooks* (1902), the male dueting partner of Gerda Buddenbrook charges *Tristan* with 'blasphemy, insanity' and 'madness!'[71] But the text in which the opera plays the most decisive role is surely the one Mann named after it, 'Tristan' (1903), in which one male and one female sanatorium patients find themselves together in a room with Wagner's score and a piano.[72] Here is how the male party breaks the news of his discovery of the music to his female counterpart – who, it may be noted, has immediately prior to this been playing one of Chopin's Nocturnes:

> "It's not possible! . . . It can't be true! . . . And yet there is no doubt of it! . . . Do you know what this is? . . . Do you realize what has been lying here – what I have in my hands? . . ."
> "What is it?" she asked.
> Speechlessly he pointed to the title page. He had turned quite pale; he lowered the volume and looked at her with trembling lips.[73]

And here is Mann's commentary on the music the pianist goes on to play:

> It told of two forces, two enraptured lovers reaching out towards each other in suffering and ecstasy and embracing in a convulsive mad desire for eternity, for the absolute . . . (p. 117)

Between the auditor's near-frenzied anticipation and Mann's account of how this expectancy is met, the lineaments of *Tristan*'s peculiar status as a hallowed, if not fetish- object, clearly emerge: it either is, or is believed to be, an intoxicant – perhaps specifically, a love potion (not coincidentally, since just such a thing features prominently in *Tristan*'s plot), and source of ready-made romantic role models which its listeners – especially if predisposed by events in their own emotional lives – may more or less readily identify with.

None of this is to say that Mann is wholly approving of *Tristan*'s (alleged) effects. At the end of 'Tristan', the pianist's already fragile heath deteriorates – apparently, as a direct result of the music she has played (or, given Mann's account, we might now say, that has played her).[74] Moreover, it is notable that in least two other of the cases noted above, the opera's death-centredness is used by writers to hint darkly at how a novel's action will pan out: in both Chopin's case, with Edna, and Woolf's, with Rachel, heroines leave their narratives dead or on death's path. For Nietzsche, this link to death, far from being a mere narrative conceit, was an inherent and indeed materially risky feature of the music – especially in *Tristan*'s third act, where, he wrote,

Wagner's work reaches such peaks of intensity that susceptible persons listening to it without accompanying acting and scenography might actually perish of the experience.[75] It is difficult, of course, to know quite how seriously to take this suggestion: though Nietzsche made it during his period of genuine admiration for the composer, he is after all never less than an extravagant and, at times, perhaps such as this, deliberately hyperbolic writer. More generally, it is significant that Nietzsche's *oeuvre* as a whole encompasses perhaps the full range of possible responses to Wagner's work, from near worshipful enthusiasm in his early work to disillusion and outright scorn in his later (though this periodisation is complicated: for instance, Nietzsche's rebuke for Wagner's 'incredible aesthetic superstition' regarding Beethoven's Ninth Symphony, quoted in Chapter 1, predates the text cited above, *The Birth of Tragedy*, the most 'Wagnerian' of all his works). This, then, is the place to turn to more of Wagner's works, the controversy surrounding them, and the social relations they were explicitly designed to cultivate.

Wagner at Bayreuth

Towards the end of *Pilgrimage*, in anticipation of a performance they are attending together, Hypo tells Miriam:

> 'There is no possible representation that can compete with the vast scenes [Wagner's] music brings to your mind. I shall see, with the lit stage behind me instead of the [. . .] orchestra in front, much bigger scenes than the stage could hold. No one can see and hear to perfection at the same moment. And the wonder of Wagner is that through your ears he makes you see so hugely. All humanity pouring itself into space. A huge, exciting world-party [. . .] Beethoven and Bach are experiences and adventures of the solitary human soul. In all its moods. Wagner is everybody speaking at once.' (vol. 4, p. 170)

If all music is 'social,' then – as we have seen Kant, Rousseau, Adorno and Eisler, and Nietzsche all assert earlier in the present chapter – then Wagner's music, on this account, is somehow more so than that of others.

Certainly, this is what Wagner thought himself. Throughout his early theoretical writings, he stresses the collective nature of the spectatorship envisioned for the ideal 'musical dramas' his own works aspired to be. In our 'Introduction', we have considered this conception, and its companion term, *Gesamtkunstwerk* ('Total Work of Art'), as well as how such works were intended to join together both the arts and their associated senses; more obliquely, we also touched on Wagner's view that through such effects, these works would also serve as remedies for social divisions he saw as endemic to modernity. Now, we can emphasise just how earnest this last, 'social' aspect of his programme really was. As Juliet Koss writes, 'Wagner's descriptions of the interrelation of the individual forms of art and the work of art they would together produce also applied to the spectators for such a work of art, as well to their experiences, individual and communal, within and beyond the auditorium.'[76] In other words, Wagner wished his works to not just depict or prescribe social cohesion, but actually create it, in his audience. Bound up with this desire is a further turn in his theorisation of the *Gesamtkunstwerk*, as somehow incomplete until an audience was assembled and in the process of reception.[77] Clearly, then, he viewed individual spectators as not merely 'Being-with' each other but as mutually benevolent and fellow minded.

It was with all this in mind that decades after formulating this theory, Wagner finally got the chance to put it into practice. Having at last secured the necessary funding and permissions, he built a theatre in the hitherto unheralded town of Bayreuth (chosen for its centrality in Germany, and the lack of competing attractions) to house a festival of his own works that has since become an annual event.[78] To celebrate the laying of the theatre's foundation stone, he conducted a performance of Beethoven's Ninth Symphony – the very work we have noted above as occasioning Nietzsche's remark about individuals' collective absorption in 'primal Oneness' as well as (in the previous chapter) Wagner's own declaration of the 'end' of the symphonic tradition and the anticipation of his own. Later that year, 1876, the festival itself saw the first complete performances of *The Ring of the Nibelung*, the massive tetralogy Wagner had composed for just this purpose (the complete cycle took five days to perform: one night for each individual drama, with one rest day).[79] Like *Tristan*, this is a mythic work – replete with giants, Gods and dragons – designed to have an overwhelming overall effect. And like Wagner's other works, accordingly, it is one in which words, singing, orchestral music, acting, costume, scenography and stage effects all work together in what is meant to be a single, seamless whole.

Was this, however, what the first Bayreuth festival's audience experienced? Contemporary testimony is plentiful, and not all of it favourable. One English reporter, for instance, likened certain stage effects to the 'useless lumber of some forgotten Christmas pantomime'.[80] Many commentators were struck by the festival's status as as much a demographic and logistical as an artistic spectacle, dilating especially on the town's inadequate provision of hotels and restaurants (Tchaikovsky, who sent reports back to a Russian newspaper, quipped that only having sought food and drink at Bayreuth had he understood the meaning of the Darwinian slogan, 'struggle for existence').[81] Eduard Hanslick, whose counter-Wagnerian views we considered in Chapter 1, reported after witnessing one drama that the 'majority of listeners were already more or less exhausted after the second Act', and asked rhetorically, 'Who could endure four consecutive evenings of this exaltation?'[82] But in his comments on the substantial content of the performances, Hanslick indicates why, individual differences of taste notwithstanding, Wagner's project has deep significance not only for nineteenth-century culture but also for cultural developments extending well into the twentieth century and beyond. Marvelling at the various contraptions used to create the production's many stage effects – evidently some of these, at least, impressed him more than the previously quoted English correspondent – he wrote:

> Wagner has utilised all the modern advances of applied science. We have seen in astonishment the colossal machinery, the gas apparatus, the steam machines above and below the stage [. . .] Wagner could have as little composed the *Ring* before the invention of the electric light as without the harp and bass tuba [both instruments significantly modified in the nineteenth century, and in the latter's case invented as recently as 1835]. Thus it is that the element of colour in the broadest sense [. . .] usurps for itself an unheard-of self-sufficiency. It is through its sensually fascinating magic that this music, as a direct nervous stimulant, works so powerfully on the audience and on the female audience particularly.[83]

This is a vision of the artist, and the artwork, as essentially bound up with the most cutting-edge technological developments, from 'gas', 'steam' and electricity to more musically and even work-specific innovations in musical instrumentation (in addition to the two musical instruments named above, these include so-called 'Wagner tubas' specifically created for the *Ring*). The work's effects upon spectators, commensurately, are seen as no less bound up with advanced technique (here pharmacological: 'nervous stimulant'), as if the mind, no less than light or 'colour', were subject to precision engineering.

The anticipatory character of these remarks is striking. For just under two decades after Hanslick made them, an equally, if not even more technology-defined artistic medium emerged; according to its detractors, just as likely to induce narcotic or otherwise disempowering effects on its audience, especially women: cinema. The resemblance, it has been said, is no coincidence. For Adorno, a great scourge of both, it is precisely in Wagner's musical dramas that 'we witness the birth of film out of the spirit of music' (he is of course aping here Nietzsche's full title, *The Birth of Tragedy out of the Spirit of Music*). Thus, he added, does high art transform itself into 'mass culture'.[84] For Siegfried Kracauer, a some-time associate of Adorno, Wagner's conception of the multimedia character of his artworks was relevant to the way early commercial use of film imbricated cinema with other forms of spectacle and live performance. Here is Kracauer's account of how an 'American style of a self-contained show' (basically, a variety show or revue), as seen in a Berlin cinema in 1926, subjects its audience to a *total artwork [Gesamtkunstwerk] of effects.*

This total artwork of effects assaults all the senses using every possible means. Spotlights shower their beams into the auditorium, sprinkling across festive drapes or rippling through colorful, organic-looking glass fixtures. The orchestra asserts itself as an independent power, its acoustic production buttressed by the responsory of the lighting. Every emotion is accorded its own acoustic expression and its color value in the spectrum – a visual and acoustic kaleidoscope that provides the setting for the physical activity on stage: pantomime and ballet. Until finally the white surface descends and the events of the three-dimensional stage blend imperceptibly into two-dimensional illusions.[85]

Again, Wagner's idea of a *Gesamtkunstwerk* is used to explain developments in 'mass' culture decades after his death (1883). And with the benefit of hindsight, we can use Kracauer's account of technical conditions in 1926 as a gloss on much in the history of cinema that, so to speak, came next – for the very next year, important parts of what appears extrinsic to film here started to appear inside the cinematic work itself, most notably, sound (pioneered, as we remember from our 'Introduction', by *The Jazz Singer*); and subsequently, in the various versions of, and fashions for, to date, 3D.

Over and above such phenomenological considerations – although of course, profoundly linked to them – we may note two further features of the specially designed theatre at Bayreuth as pointing towards cinema spectatorship. First, there is the recessed pit for orchestra built between the audience and stage, rendering musicians invisible to spectators. Secondly, there is the near total darkness achievable inside the auditorium (the link here is that in traditional theatres, where the orchestra is not removed from view, there must be enough light within the space musicians share with spectators for the former to read their music).[86] Both these effects anticipate the now familiar experience of sitting in a cinema – though in the latter's case, of course, the 'invisibility' of music is no longer (typically) ensured by a recessed orchestra but by the playing of recordings through loudspeakers. Both techniques, it will be seen, make music 'acousmatic', thus meeting one of the criteria for 'modern' sound mooted in this book's 'Introduction'. This should come as no surprise: Wagner specifically indicated that his orchestra should be made invisible in order to prevent spectators being distracted by the music's mere 'mechanical source', anticipating Pierre Schaeffer's view that listeners freed from a concern with sound's production and dissemination would become more attentive to the sounds themselves.[87] More obliquely, there may even be a sense in which Wagner's project as a whole reprises Pythagoras's putative teaching methods (the original source, we may remember, for 'acousmatic' as a concept), though the latter are, of course, if anything more transparent in their demagogy and cultishness.

We are led back, then, with this last remark, to the vexed question of Wagner's effects upon his audience, and their political or social correlatives. This question is important, beyond what it might be in relation to other artists, because of the alleged connection between Wagner's work and German National Socialism. Adorno is, again, the chief prosecutor for this case, declaring in an essay written towards the end of the Second World War that 'Nobody can escape the awareness of the deep interconnection between Richard Wagner and German supra-nationalism in its most destructive form' and that 'His music itself speaks the language of Fascism'.[88] In this view, not just the bombast of Wagner's fictional world, or the occasional megalomania of his theoretical writings – and no one who has followed my account so far can, I hope, be entirely unaware of these – but also the actual substance of his scores has fascist or proto-fascist content. (In *In Search of Wagner*, 1952, Adorno expands but also modulates this view, associating Wagner's music more with the underlying processes of capitalism, of which he considers German fascism a specific variant.) Moreover, the staging of Wagner's works, at Bayreuth and elsewhere, was, Adorno thought (despite whatever Wagner thought himself), geared towards the creation of a 'mass', submissive audience. There is historical, if circumstantial, evidence to back this view: before and after taking power, Hitler courted and received the society of members of Wagner's surviving family, and received enthusiastic support from at least some of the latter in return. And finally, there is Wagner's own explicit anti-Semitism, as showcased in writings such as 'Judaism in Music' (1850), which dilates upon the Jewish voice in ways interestingly, if obnoxiously, proximate to some of the commentary on Jewish speech considered in our section on New York, above.[89]

Nothing I could say here would either seek to or be capable of completely countering the indictment all this adds up to (though it is perhaps worth remembering, along with Juliet Koss, that at least in some respects, Wagner and his dream of socially rejuvenating art are products of the 1848 democratic revolutionary movements in Germany rather than any of the more 'nationalist' and bellicose trends emerging later).[90] But rather than ending this discussion on an admonitory note, it seems preferable to conclude by returning to the specific sensory effects attributed to Wagner's works, as these do not seem reducible (at least in and of themselves) to any one political ideology. Earlier, we saw Hypo claim that Wagner 'makes you see' through hearing, and Hanslick say – to no less seemingly paradoxical effect – that Wagner gives 'colour' an 'unheard-of self-sufficiency' through music. To these contentions we may now add Nietzsche (again in his 'pro-'-Wagner phase) claiming:

> we feel certain that in Wagner all that is visible in the world wants to become more profound and more intense by becoming audible, that it seeks here its lost soul; and that all that is audible in the world likewise

wants to emerge into the light and also become a phenomenon for the eye
[. . .] [Thus the composer] is continually compelled – and the beholder is
compelled with him – to translate visible movement back into soul and primordial life, and conversely to see the most deeply concealed inner activity
as visible phenomenon and to clothe it with the appearance of a body.[91]

Together, these remarks offer a more circumscribed impression of the
Gesamtkunstwerk than any we have considered hitherto, specifying two senses
in particular as complements and close collaborators. In Wagner's works,
then, vision and hearing, more than any other senses, are seen as capable of
changing places, and of rendering each other – without surrendering their own
distinctive forms.

Over and above the obvious reasons why these two senses should be singled
out above others – neither smell, taste, or even touch have ever featured
quite so much in aesthetic discourse, as canonically defined – we can perhaps
distinguish three reasons why this is the case. The first is that in Nietzsche's
text, especially, the vision-hearing dialectic seems to open up a path between
an 'objective' sense and an 'inner' or 'subjective' one. With our discussion of
such distinctions from Chapter 1, above, in mind, we are now in a position
to see how this distinction draws on that hierarchy of sensation traced from
Aristotle through to Kant and Hegel, and thus see why Wagner's work might
be privileged for traversing, at least to some extent, these very hierarchies. In
Nietzsche's account then, the special merit of Wagner's work appears as that
of spanning the 'inner'/'outer' gulf, translating subjective feelings into forms
that have substantial, quasi-embodied shapes, and vice versa.[92] Clearly, given
the terms that govern this account, this is something no single-sense or single-
media artwork could ever do.

The second answer takes us via another of Hypo's contentions, also quoted
above, that 'No one can see and hear to perfection at the same moment'. This
is perhaps a reference to Ernst Mach's *Contributions to the Analysis of the
Sensations* (1885), which argues influentially that 'the attention cannot be
fixed upon two different senses-organs at once'.[93] Insofar as Wagner's work
seems to resist if not suspend this condition – by making you 'see' *through*
hearing, rather than (seemingly) see *and* hear at the same time – then Hypo
would appear to value it for circumventing or compensating for deficiencies
in the organism that otherwise prevent the senses being fully adequate to their
objects. As we now know, this is a physiologically informed view of art, and
one prominent in the modernist and anterior periods: advocates of it we have
considered elsewhere in Chapter 1 include Nietzsche (again) and Bergson. We
may now say that this view does not seem uncongenial to Richardson herself,
especially as she puts it here in the mouth of one of her own characters.

Finally, we can simply note that for a variety of reasons, to which we turn in the next chapter, a conviction grew throughout the nineteenth and early twentieth centuries that sound was either innately or by contrivance visualisable: that one could literally 'see sound'. As we noted in this book's 'Introduction', Chladni's experiments of the early nineteenth century, in which sounds were found to trace clear patterns when passed through sand, were important for subsequent sound recording and reproduction. We can now add that they also helped create a new sense of sound's 'translatability', especially into visible forms – and will see in the next chapter just how significant such translation was within acoustic science. But scientists were not, of course, the only ones to be excited by such possibilities. Earlier in this chapter, I quoted Nietzsche's claim that in beholding Beethoven's Ninth Symphony, 'each man feels himself not only united, reconciled, and at one with his neighbour, but *one* with him' – but neglected to mention, at that time, that while claiming this, Nietzsche is specifically asking his readers to imagine this music as a painting. What does it mean to imagine music, or any other sound, *as a painting*? If either could be painted, what would they look like?

NOTES

1. James Joyce, *Ulysses: The 1922 Text*, edited with an introduction by Jeri Johnson (Oxford: Oxford University Press, 1993), pp. 480, 542, 444, 513. Subsequent references to this edition are given in the text.
2. Mikhail Bakhtin, *Rabelais and his World*, translated by Hélène Iswolsky, foreword by Krystyna Pomorska, prologue by Michael Holquist (Bloomington: Indiana University Press, 1984).
3. V. N. Vološinov, *Marxism and the Philosophy of Language*, translated by Ladislav Matejka and I. R. Titunik (Cambridge, MA: Harvard University Press, 1986), p. 95; emphases in original.
4. See Vološinov, *Marxism and the Philosophy of Language*, pp. 22–3.
5. On these allusions and quotations, see Zack Bowen, *Musical Allusions in the Work of James Joyce: Early Poetry through 'Ulysses'* (Albany: State University of New York Press, 1974), pp. 253–303.
6. For more on this, see Barry Blesser and Linda-Ruth Salter, *Spaces Speak, Are You Listening? Experiencing Aural Architecture* (Cambridge, MA: MIT Press, 2007), and my 'Weather, Sound Technology, and Space in Wallace Stevens', *Wallace Stevens Journal* 33:1 (2009), pp. 83–96.
7. On sound in Richardson, see David Stamm, *A Pathway to Reality: Visual and Aural Concepts in Dorothy Richardson's 'Pilgrimage'* (Tübingen: Francke Verlag, 2000); on built environments, see Elisabeth Bronfen, *Dorothy Richardson's Art of Memory: Space, Identity, Text*, translated by Victoria Appelbe (Manchester: Manchester University Press, 1999).
8. Dorothy Richardson, *Pilgrimage*, 4 vols (London: Virago [1915–67] 2002), vol. 4, pp. 204. Subsequent references to this edition are given in the text.
9. The second meditation on the sounds of doors appears in *Pilgrimage*, vol. 4, p. 628. Here, however, sounds are not savoured for any particular social association.
10. Martin Heidegger, *Being and Time*, translated by John Macquarrie and Edward Robinson (Oxford: Blackwell, [1927] 1962), pp. 149–68. 'Being-with' is discussed throughout this section, 'Being-among-one-another' more locally on p. 166.

11. See, again, Bronfen, *Dorothy Richardson's Art of Memory*, for excellent commentary on this and related issues.
12. For further commentary, see Bronfen, *Dorothy Richardson's Art of Memory*, p. 180.
13. Dorothy Richardson, 'Data for Spanish Publisher' (1943), *London Magazine* 6 (June 1959), pp. 14–19; p. 18 cited.
14. Sociality may be distinguished from sociability on the grounds that whereas the latter may or may not be present in different individuals, groups and situations (and is in any case a matter of degree, of 'character' and 'mood'), the former is an ontological and – it seems safe to say – inalienable attribute of human beings. Thus sociality has primacy over sociability, being the ground upon which all more local and determinate forms of social interaction may or may not appear.
15. Immanuel Kant, *Anthropology from a Pragmatic Point of View*, revised and edited by Hans H. Rudnick, translated by Victor Lyle Dowdell (Carbondale and Edwardsville: Southern Illinois University Press, [1798] 1996), pp. 423; emphasis added.
16. Jean-Jacques Rousseau, *Essay on the Origin of Languages, and Writings Related to Music*, edited and translated by John T. Scott (Hanover, NH: University Press of New England, 1998), p. 326.
17. Theodor Adorno and Hanns Eisler, *Composing for the Films*, with an introduction by Graham McCann (London: Athlone Press, [1947] 1994), p. 21.
18. Friedrich Nietzsche, *The Birth of Tragedy, Out of the Spirit of Music*, edited with an introduction by Michael Tanner, translated by Shaun Whiteside (Harmondsworth: Penguin, [1872] 1993), p. 17; emphasis in original.
19. There is one other influence on Nietzsche we should mention at this point: Wagner. I take up some of Nietzsche's more explicit commentary on Wagner later.
20. Marcel Proust, *In Search of Lost Time*, 6 vols, translated by C. K. Scott Moncrieff and Terence Kilmartin, revised by D. J. Enright (London: Vintage, [1913–27] 1996), vol. 5, p. 427.
21. Wallace Stevens, *Collected Poetry and Prose*, edited by Frank Kermode and Joan Richardson (New York: Library of America, 1997), pp. 140, 135, 136. I owe the last of these three points to Alan Filreis, 'Stevens in the 1930s', in John Serio (ed.), *The Cambridge Companion to Wallace Stevens* (Cambridge: Cambridge University Press, 2007) pp. 37–47.
22. D. H. Lawrence, *Aaron's Rod* (Harmondsworth: Penguin, [1922] 1950), p. 269.
23. Aldous Huxley, *Point Counter Point*, with an introduction by David Bradshaw (London: Vintage Books, [1928] 2004), p. 65.
24. F. Scott Fitzgerald, *The Great Gatsby*, edited with an introduction and notes by Ruth Prigozy (Oxford: Oxford University Press, [1925] 1998), p. 34.
25. Richardson, *Pilgrimage*, vol. 1, pp. 413, 421; Virginia Woolf, *The Waves* (Harmondsworth: Penguin, [1931] 1964), p. 61; Virginia Woolf, *Flush*, edited with an introduction and notes by Kate Flint (Oxford: Oxford University Press, [1933] 1998), p. 91.
26. John Dos Passos, *Manhattan Transfer* (Boston: Houghton Mifflin, [1925] 1953), p. 19. On early twentieth-century urban horses, see Clay McShane and Joel A. Tarr, *The Horse in the City: Living Machines in the Nineteenth Century* (Baltimore: Johns Hopkins University Press, 2007), pp. 174–6.
27. Michael Gold, *Jews Without Money*, with woodcuts by Howard Simon (London: Noel Douglas, 1930), pp. 65–6.
28. Emily Thompson, *The Soundscape of Modernity: Architectural Acoustics and the Culture of Listening, 1900–1933* (Cambridge, MA: MIT Press, 2002), p. 115.

29. Henry Roth, *Call it Sleep* (Harmondsworth: Penguin, [1934] 1977), p. 141. Subsequent references to this edition are given in the text.
30. Djuna Barnes, 'Becoming Intimate with the Bohemians' (1916), in *New York*, edited with a commentary by Alyce Barry (Los Angeles: Sun and Moon Press, 1989), p. 244.
31. Compton Mackenzie, *Sinister Street*, 2 vols (London: Martin Secker, 1913), vol. 2, p. 855.
32. T. S. Eliot, letter of 8 September 1914, in *The Letters of T. S. Eliot, Volume 1: 1898–1922*, edited by Valerie Eliot (London: Faber and Faber, 1988), p. 55.
33. Henri Lefebrve, *Rhythmanalysis: Space, Time and Everyday Life*, translated by Stuart Elden and Gerald Moore, with an introduction by Stuart Elden (London: Continuum, 2004), ch. 3; Robert Musil, *The Man Without Qualities*, translated by Sophie Wilkins and Burton Pike (London: Picador, [1930–42] 1997), p. 4.
34. Djuna Barnes, 'Surcease in Hurry and Whirl – On the Restless Surf at Coney' (1917), in *New York*, p. 280.
35. Stephen Graham, *London Nights* (London: Hurst and Blackett, 1925), p. 73.
36. Stephen Graham, *New York Nights*, illustrated by Kurt Wiese (New York: George H. Doran, 1927), p. 136.
37. Gavin Jones, *Strange Talk: The Politics of Dialect Literature in Gilded Age America* (Berkeley: University of California Press, 1999), p. 135.
38. Abraham Cahan, *Yekl, and The Imported Bridegroom, and Other Stories of the New York Ghetto*, with an introduction by Bernard G. Richards (New York: Dover Books, 1970), p. 2; emphasis in original.
39. Abraham Cahan, *The Rise of David Levinsky*, with an introduction by John Higham (New York: Harper Torchbook, [1917] 1960), p. 28.
40. Henry James, *The American Scene*, edited with an introduction by John F. Sears (Harmondsworth: Penguin, [1907] 1994), p. 106. In *The Question of Our Speech* (1905), the text of which James gave as a lecture during the tour in which he gained these impressions, he complains similarly that immigrants 'play, to their heart's [*sic*] content, with the English language', and 'dump their mountain of promiscuous material into the foundations of the American' (Henry James, *The Question of Our Speech, The Lesson of Balzac: Two Lectures*, Boston: Houghton Mifflin, 1905, pp. 42–3.)
41. Woolf, *The Waves*, p. 143.
42. Dos Passos, *Manhattan Transfer*, p. 259.
43. Ben Hecht and Charles MacArthur, *The Front Page* (New York: Covici Friede, 1928), pp. 4–5. Subsequent references to this edition are given in the text.
44. Evelyn Waugh, *Vile Bodies* (Harmondsworth: Penguin, [1930] 1938), pp. 183–4.
45. William Faulkner, *Pylon: The Corrected Text* (New York: Vintage, [1935] 1987), p. 63; Patrick Hamilton, *Hangover Square*, with an introduction by J. B. Priestley (Harmondsworth: Penguin, [1941] 2001), p. 60.
46. Rudolf Arnheim, *Radio*, translated by Margaret Ludwig and Herbert Read (London: Faber and Faber, 1936), p. 141.
47. Hadley Cantril and Gordon W. Allport, *The Psychology of Radio* (New York: Harper and Brothers, 1935), p. 4. Subsequent references to this edition are given in the text.
48. For more on this distinction between radio's technical potential and the actual history of its use, see Hans Magnus Enzensberger, 'Constituents of a Theory of the Media', translated by Stuart Hood, in *Dreamers of the Absolute: Essays on Ecology, Media and Power* (London: Radius, 1988), pp. 20–53.
49. Hadley Cantril with the assistance of Hazel Gaudet and Herta Herzog, *The

Invasion from Mars: A Study in the Psychology of Panic (Princeton: Princeton University Press, [1940] 1982), p. 83. Subsequent references to this edition are given in the text.

50. The script is reproduced in Cantril's book.

51. This picture is complicated, of course, by the use of recordings as the actual content of many broadcasts. But though the latter has come to be an important feature of broadcasting – especially where music is concerned – it does not change the basic fact that 'live' presentation is the default mode of commercial radio. At least until the recent adoption by radio stations of the internet as a storage and retrieval facility for programmes, it was at a certain time that a radio listener would have to tune in a given piece of programming – whether the latter was a 'live' event or not.

52. Other examples include another play by Howells, *The Unexpected Guests* (1893), and George W. Hill's *The Phonograph Witness* (1883).

53. W. D. Howells and S. L. Clemens [Mark Twain], *Colonel Sellers as a Scientist* (1883), in *The Complete Plays of W. D. Howells*, edited by Walter J. Meserve (New York: New York University Press, 1960), pp. 224, 240–1.

54. See Sebastian Knowles, 'Death by Gramophone', *Journal of Modern Literature* 27:1 (2003), pp. 1–13.

55. See, for example, Michael Chanan, *Repeated Takes: A Short History of Recording and its Effects on Music* (London: Verso, 1995), p. 3.

56. Carl Van Vechten, *Nigger Heaven* (New York: Alfred A. Knopf, 1926), p. 38; Dos Passos, *Manhattan Transfer*, p. 216.

57. F. Scott Fitzgerald, *Tender is the Night*, edited by Arnold Goldman, with an introduction and notes by Richard Godden (Harmondsworth: Penguin, [1934] 1998), p. 151. Subsequent references to this edition are given in the text.

58. Matthew J. Bruccoli with Judith S. Baughman, *Reader's Companion to F. Scott Fitzgerald's 'Tender is the Night'* (Columbia: University of South Carolina Press, 1997), p. 109.

59. I am thinking here of Niklas Luhmann, *Love as Passion: The Codification of Intimacy*, translated by Jeremy Gaines and Doris L. Jones (Stanford: Stanford University Press, 1998).

60. Andre Millard, *America on Record: A History of Recorded Sound* (Cambridge: Cambridge University Press, 1995), p. 49.

61. See Book III of the *Republic* (c. 380 BC).

62. T. Austin Graham, 'The Literary Soundtrack: Or, F. Scott Fitzgerald's Heard and Unheard Melodies', *American Literary History* 21:3 (2009), pp. 518–49; p. 519 cited.

63. See, for example, the account of C. P. E. Bach's *Versuch über die wahre Art das Clavier zu spielen* (1753) given in Edward Lippman's *A History of Western Musical Aesthetics* (Lincoln, NE: University of Nebraska Press, 1992), p. 79.

64. There is more to the piano's early history, of course. For further details see, for example, Michael Chanan, *Musica Practica: The Social Practice of Western Music from Gregorian Chant to Postmodernism* (London: Verso, 1994), ch. 8.

65. On the piano as 'middle-class', see Max Weber, *The Rational and Social Foundations of Music*, edited and translated by Don Martindale, Johannes Riedel and Gertrude Neuwirth (Carbondale: Southern Illinois University Press, [1921] 1958), pp. 120–4.

66. Arthur Loesser, *Men, Women and Pianos: A Social History* (London: Victor Gollancz, 1955).

67. Kate Chopin, *The Awakening, and Other Stories*, edited with an introduction

and notes by Pamela Knights (Oxford: Oxford University Press, 2000), p. 71. Subsequent references to this edition are given in the text.

68. Leo Tolstoy, *The Kreutzer Sonata and Other Stories*, translated with an introduction by David McDuff (Harmondsworth: Penguin, 2004), pp. 96, 88.

69. Virginia Woolf, *The Voyage Out*, edited with an introduction and notes by Lorna Sage (Oxford: Oxford University Press, [1915] 2001), p. 47.

70. Proust, *In Search of Lost Time*, vol. 1, p. 226.

71. Thomas Mann, *Buddenbrooks*, translated by H. T. Lowe-Porter (London: Vintage, [1902] 1999), p. 407.

72. For related commentary to that which follows, see Walter Frisch, *German Modernism: Music and the Arts* (Berkeley: University of California Press, 2005), pp. 195–200; James Kennaway, 'Singing the Body Electric: Nervous Music and Sexuality in *Fin-de-Siècle* Literature', in Anne Stiles (ed.), *Neurology and Literature, 1860–1920* (Houndmills: Palgrave, 2007), pp. 141–62.

73. Thomas Mann, 'Tristan' (1903), in *Death in Venice, and Other Stories*, translated with an introduction by David Luke (London: Vintage, 1998), pp. 116–17. Subsequent references to this edition are given in the text.

74. Cf. Kennaway, 'Singing the Body Electric', pp. 147–8.

75. Nietzsche, *The Birth of Tragedy*, p. 101.

76. Juliet Koss, *Modernism After Wagner* (Minneapolis: University of Minnesota Press, 2010), p. 14.

77. Koss, *Modernism After Wagner*, p. 13.

78. See Robert Hartford (ed.), *Bayreuth: The Early Years; An Account of the Early Decades of the Wagner Festival as seen by the Celebrated Visitors and Participants* (London: Victor Gollancz, 1980); Frederic Spotts, *Bayreuth: A History of the Wagner Festival* (New Haven: Yale University Press, 1994).

79. Koss, *Modernism After Wagner*, p. 48.

80. J. W. Davison, untitled excerpt in Hartford (ed.), *Bayreuth*, p. 103.

81. Peter Ilyich Tchaikovsky, untitled excerpt in Hartford (ed.), *Bayreuth*, p. 53.

82. Eduard Hanslick, untitled excerpt in Hartford (ed.), *Bayreuth*, p. 83.

83. Eduard Hanslick, untitled excerpt in Hartford (ed.), *Bayreuth*, p. 84.

84. Theodor Adorno, *In Search of Wagner*, translated by Rodney Livingstone, with a new preface by Slavoj Žižek (London: Verso, [1952] 2005), p. 96.

85. Siegfried Kracauer, 'Cult of Distraction' (1926), in *The Mass Ornament: Weimar Essays*, edited, translated and with an introduction by Thomas Y. Levin (Cambridge, MA: Harvard University Press, 1995), pp. 323–8; p. 324 cited; emphasis in original.

86. Spotts, *Bayreuth*, p. 2.

87. Richard Wagner, 'The Festival-Playhouse at Bayreuth, with an Account of the Laying of its Foundation Stone' (1873), in *Richard Wagner's Prose Works*, 8 vols, translated by William Ashton Ellis (London: Kegan Paul, Trench, Trübner, 1892–99), vol. 5, pp. 320–40; p. 333 cited.

88. Theodor W. Adorno, 'What National Socialism Has Done to the Arts' (1945), in *Essays on Music*, selected with an introduction, commentary and notes by Richard Leppert (Berkeley: University of California Press, 2002) pp. 373–90; pp. 374, 375 cited.

89. For instance, when 'we' non-Jews hear Jews talk, Wagner alleges, 'our attention dwells involuntarily on [this talk's] repulsive *how*, rather than on any meaning of its intrinsic *what*' (Richard Wagner, 'Judaism in Music' (1850), in *Richard Wagner's Prose Works*, vol. 3, pp. 75–122; p. 88 cited; emphases in original).

90. Koss, *Modernism After Wagner*.

91. Friedrich Nietzsche, 'Richard Wagner in Bayreuth' (1876), in *Untimely Meditations*,

translated by R. J. Hollingdale, with an introduction by J. P. Stern (Cambridge: Cambridge University Press, 1983), pp. 195–254; p. 223 cited.

92. It should also be said that Wagner himself distinguishes the 'outer' sense of vision from the 'inner' sense of hearing in 'The Art-Work of the Future' (in *Richard Wagner's Prose Works*, vol. 1, pp. 67–213; p. 91 cited).

93. Ernst Mach, *Contributions to the Analysis of the Sensations* (1885), translated by C. M. Williams (Bristol: Thoemmes, [1896] 1998), p. 112.

Chapter 3

SEEING SOUND

In 1860, Wagner conducted selections of his work at three performances in Paris. One of those attending was Charles Baudelaire, and what he wrote about it helped determine literary history. Here is Baudelaire's response to the overture to *Lohengrin* (1850):

> involuntarily, I evoked the delectable state of a man possessed by a profound reverie in total solitude, but a solitude with *vast horizons* and *bathed in a diffused light*; immensity without other decor than itself. Soon I became aware of a heightened *brightness*, of a *light growing in intensity* so quickly that all the shades of meaning provided by a dictionary would not suffice to express this *constant increase of burning whiteness*. Then I achieved a full apprehension of a soul floating in light, of an ecstasy *compounded of joy and insight*, hovering above and far removed from the natural world.[1]

Immediately obvious here are the themes of light and visual expansiveness, as emphasised by Baudelaire's own italics – which have been added, as Baudelaire subsequently indicates, to highlight parallels between his own response and those of two other writers he later quotes: the composer, Wagner, and Wagner's close associate and collaborator (and future father-in-law), Franz Liszt. Like Baudelaire himself, then – though without the latter's prior knowledge, as Baudelaire is at pains to stress – Wagner too has described this music in terms of solitude and massive spaces, whilst Liszt, also, has found himself

thinking of light effects (an *iridescent haze*') and colours ('*gold*' and '*blue*')
(p. 329; emphases in original). A common locus of ideas is found to gravitate
around a single piece of music. Thus Baudelaire aims to substantiate his major
thesis in this essay, that 'true music suggests similar ideas in different minds'
(p. 330).

Further to the substantive drift of these ideas, Baudelaire suggests: 'the
only really surprising thing would be that sound could not suggest colour,
[. . .] since all things always have been expressed by reciprocal analogies, ever
since the day when God created the world as a complex indivisible totality'
(pp. 330–1). The likening of one thing to another is thus grounded in these
things' ontology. But beyond this claim, a more specific 'logic' is at work here:
one identifying sound and sight; or more specifically still, identifying sonic
phenomena as correlates or surrogates for visual ones. If both Baudelaire and
Liszt, especially, are put in mind of colours by Wagner's music, and Baudelaire
has been more particularly put in mind of light effects ('*diffused light*,' yielding
to '*burning whiteness*'), there must, on this account, be something vision-like
in sound, even when that sound is unaccompanied by vision (to underscore
the latter part of this claim, Baudelaire further reports that he has listened to
Lohengrin's overture with his eyes closed). We should remember here that
Baudelaire is not responding to a full staging of Wagner's work, as in the
Bayreuth festival described in the previous chapter, still many years hence,
and bear in mind too that the *Lohengrin* overture is in any case designed to be
played without staged accompaniment, as indeed it was on this occasion. The
relationship of sight and sound asserted in Baudelaire's text, then, is not the
same as the one in Wagner's own conception of the *Gesamtkunstwerk*, where
staging, scenery, music and so on do indeed (ideally) work in tandem: here,
this relation is not simply one of complementarity, but of what we might call
equivalence or *correspondence*.

I use the latter term, of course, advisedly. Baudelaire's poem 'Correspondances'
('Correspondences') (1857) is amongst the most influential documents of incip-
ient or early modernism; later texts indebted to it include Arthur Rimbaud's
'Voyelles' (1872), in which equivalence is posited not merely between broad
fields of sense-phenomena but between individual colours and specific vowel
sounds.[2] But of arguably still greater influence was Baudelaire's 'Wagner'
essay, which, in the work of Symbolist writers of the later nineteenth century,
precipitated a more thorough-going reconceptualisation of the status and
capacities of poetry, of far-reaching import in the subsequent history of modernism.[3] For Symbolists such as Stéphane Mallarmé (1842–1898), music is not
so much an object to be described as something to be realised *as* poetry: something a poem may 'be', rather than merely be about. And it is in this spirit that
many other figures, too, set about exploring other ways in which sight- and
sound-based media might be related. In this chapter, I therefore tack to and fro

between perceived equivalence or correspondence between sensory domains, and equivalence or correspondence between art forms the former sponsor. Literature aside, this will entail looking at such things as 'silent' cinema and painting, the psychiatric analysis of synaesthesia, and 'neurogrammatological' conceptions of the mind.

SUBSTITUTION AND THE WORD

We may begin with Mina Loy's 'Brancusi's Golden Bird' (1922), a poem whose subject, a sculpture by Constantin Brancusi, is, significantly, another artwork in a different medium, for which the poem stands as a tribute or, more ambitiously, a substitute:

> This gong
> of polished hyperaesthesia
> shrills with brass
> as the aggressive light
> strikes
> its significance
>
> The immaculate
> conception
> of the inaudible birth
> occurs
> in gorgeous reticence . . .[4]

At least four distinct ideas are at work here. For a start, there is the sculpture's characterisation as a 'gong', a musical instrument; that is, something that *sounds*. Thus is sound located in an object that in fact, we may not hear but only look at (as anyone who has ever visited an art museum knows, there is no striking sculptures as if they were gongs: normally, we may not even touch them).[5] Secondly, this trans-sensory substitution is both recapitulated by and made dependent on another, between different art forms – the relation between one medium, music (as represented by the gong), and another, sculpture, thus being mediated by a third term, poetry, as instantiated by Loy's text itself. Without this mediation, we may speculate, the sculpture cannot 'be' a gong at all. Thirdly, the golden bird being described is either precipitated out of, or something that induces, heightened sensation ('hyperaesthesia'), an echo of the Bergsonian or Greenbergian idea of art as an intensification and de-familiarisation of sensation, as discussed in Chapter 1. Finally, despite all of the above, there is a weird air of self-cancellation about the whole enterprise. The sound made, embodied or represented by the sculpture is, after all, 'inaudible': notional, we might say; not quite (or not quite yet?) itself.

In a manifesto on 'modern poetry' in general published three year later, Loy recasts some of these ideas as part of a programme for her art. Poetry itself, she says, is 'music made of visual thoughts, the sound of an idea', a 'sound' she further specifies as 'silent'.[6] Again, one art form is called upon to 'be' another ('music' once more, though here this is asserted more explicitly) while the trans-sensory switch that this depends on is simultaneously affirmed and placed in doubt. Beyond Loy's own work, other poets too show interest in the 'light' so crucial to the 'birth' of (soundless) sound conceived by 'Brancusi's Golden Bird'. In Hart Crane's 'Chaplinesque' (1921), for instance, we are told that 'we have seen / The moon in lonely alleys make / A grail of laughter on an empty ash can' – a formulation that makes the play of light on metal a stand-in for, or promise of sonority.[7] Meanwhile, the first line (in translation) of an undated Fernando Pessoa (1888–1935) poem both displaces this idea from moon to sun and inverts Loy's and Crane's sense of the 'sounding-ness' of light-reflective surfaces: 'In broad daylight even the sounds shine.'[8]

It is the novels of Virginia Woolf, though, that best show how these ideas coincide with broader areas of cultural activity. In *Mrs Dalloway* (1925), the shell-shocked Septimus Warren Smith see 'shocks of sound' arise before him in 'smooth columns', seemingly confirming a widespread (as we shall see, though by no means uncontested) association between sensory substitution and psychopathology (in parentheses, Woolf adds 'that music should be visible was a discovery', further linking Smith's percept to the contemporaneous fad for another topic addressed below, 'colour music').[9] In *To the Lighthouse* (1927), Lily Briscoe wonders what two distant characters are saying and then looks over at them, 'as if by looking she could hear them' – as if, in fact, she were practised in the art of lip-reading, the then still relatively new technique for 'hearing' practised by the deaf (in one lip-reading manual from the period, readers are similarly said to '*hear* with their eyes').[10] Finally, in the same novel, two instances feature where Mrs Ramsey imagines the words she is speaking to her daughter Cam acquiring visual forms:

> The words seemed to be dropped into a well, where, if the waters were clear, they were also so extraordinarily distorting that, even as they descended, one saw them twisting about to make Heaven knows what pattern on the floor of the child's mind. (p. 61)

> She could see the words echoing as she spoke them rhythmically in Cam's mind. (p. 124)

On both occasions, words are visualised so that they can be imagined as persisting after their cessation, having a kind of permanence that speech *qua* sound must lack. Since ancient times, a technology has existed whose office is to ensure precisely this: writing.[11]

Writing is, of course, hardly specific to the modern period. But in the genealogy of literary modern*ism*, exceptional significance has sometimes been attached to experiments with writing's 'written-ness' that focus on what normally represents the unexamined ground of printed text, typography. Mallarmé's 'Un Coup de Dés Jamais N'Abolira Le Hasard' ('A Throw of the Dice Will Never Abolish Chance') (1897) is the earliest distinct example. Here, different font sizes and styles (especially, italics and capitalisation) combine with a decomposition of traditional line and verse forms and consequent redistribution of verbal material across the surface of the page (Figure 3.1). As Johanna Drucker writes, 'The shaped forms of the lines stand out against the conspicuously marked white space of the page, activating spatial and temporal relations outside the normal linear sequence of poetic lines.'[12] This creates the possibility of, say, reading all or parts of the poem right to left, or bottom to top, or several such ways at once. Those 'white spaces', meanwhile, no longer appear as a neutral ground against which the poem just happens to be set, but rather as a meaning-charged component of the poetry itself. Interestingly, given the visuality of all this, Mallarmé's preface states the rationale for his technique less in terms of visuality itself than of sound effects:

> from this stripped-down mode of thought, with its retreats, prolonga-
> tions, flights, or from its very design, there results, for whoever would
> read it aloud, a musical score. The differences in the type faces, between
> the dominant motif, a secondary, and adjacent ones, dictates their impor-
> tance for oral expression, and the range or disposition of the characters,
> in the middle, at the top, or at the bottom of the page, marks the rising
> and falling of the intonation.[13]

This, then, is a poem to be read aloud (note the contrast here with Loy on poetry as 'silent sound'). The use of unconventional typography is thus aimed not so much at representing sounds visually as at precipitating sounds in and as themselves. Paradoxically, however, this makes music's utility as a model here turn not on its sonority but its visuality, its written-ness: hence the layout's likeness to a 'musical score'. (Ironically, given Mallarmé's emphasis on 'oral expression', in an actual musical score the notation itself has no expressionistic content, this being left to purely verbal terms, such as *forte* ['loud'], *cantabile* ['singingly'], and so on.) Mallarmé's poem is like music, then, not so much because we 'hear' it visually as because we *see* how it should sound.

Mallarmé's experiment is *sui generis*: in Drucker's words, 'without precedent within literature'.[14] But it was followed, albeit at some interval, by a veritable explosion of typographic and, more broadly, visual-textual experimenta-tion, by Italian and Russian futurists, the French poet and critic Guillaume Apollinaire, the London-based 'Vorticists', and others. A single example will here suffice: Apollinaire's 'Lettre-Océan' ('Ocean Letter', 1914) (Figure 3.2). Here, 'the typographical disposition of elements [. . .] depicts a world mapped

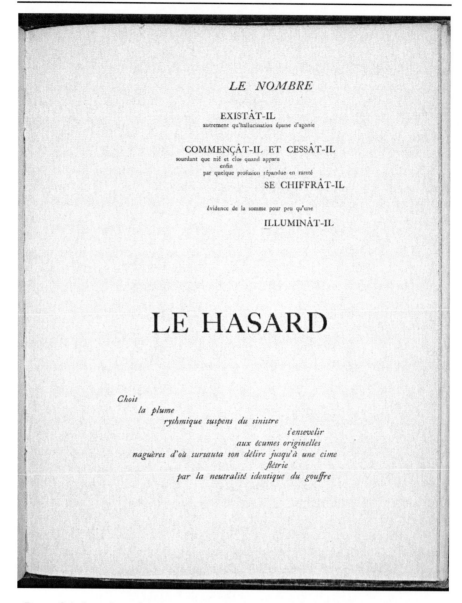

Figure 3.1 Page from Stéphane Mallarmé, 'Un Coup de Dés Jamais N'Abolira Le Hasard' (1897), *Un Coup de dés jamais n'abolira le hasard: Poème* (Paris: Gallimard, 1914), © The British Library Board

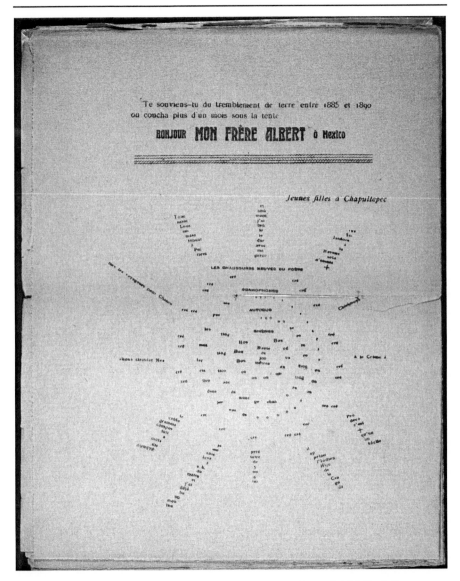

Figure 3.2 Pages from Guillaume Apollinaire, 'Lettre-Océan' (1914), *Calligrammes: Poèmes de la paix et de la guerre (1913–1916)* (Paris: Mercure de France, 1918), © The British Library Board

out in acoustical space. Fragmentary phrases float in the air in precise relation to a central consciousness'.[15] In contrast to Mallarmé's poem, then, what counts here is not whether we can make the sounds configured by the text, as whether these are fully legible as data for the eye alone, as part of a process of reception that is self-sufficient and requires no subsequent enunciation.[16] Thematically, the poem concerns itself with, amongst other things, one of the present book's own recurrent topics: new sound technologies; in particular, the gramophone and radio, which it depicts both verbally and – by the same stroke – quasi-pictorially. To take the gramophone first: this appears as a capitalised word towards the top of the circle formed by this and other words, along with phonemic fragments such as 'ou', and also via the concentric rings that spread out from this circle's centre, which together represent a gramophone disc. Moreover, the various words and phonemes that make up these rings represent the sounds made *by* the gramophone, and the verbal fragments' patterning, these sounds' passage through space. Turning to radio: this is represented by the 'spokes' which surround the outer gramophonic circle, each of which evokes radio transmissions from the Eiffel Tower (we know it is this tower because its height, 300 metres, is stated at the centre of the inner gramophonic circle: its geographical location is also stated elsewhere in the poem). With respect to both technologies, then, the poem thus manages, simultaneously, denotation, physical depiction, and phenomenological evocation of its objects.

For reasons that are partly inherent in the medium itself – the normative, though by no means universal desire for narrative (or other logical) momentum, from which visual effects may form a distraction – such typographic experimentation is less a prominent feature of modernist prose than it is of poetry.[17] But there are exceptions to this rule, perhaps none more salutary, for our purposes, than Faulkner's *As I Lay Dying*. As we have seen already in the present book's 'Introduction', this novel both evokes the phonograph's effects on sound and features the device (or its equivalent, the graphophone) explicitly. We may now add that in addition, it also evokes and even approximates the phonograph scripturally, by means of abnormally extended spacing placed between three iterations of the same onomatopoeic word. Here is Darl's narration of his brother Cash's shaping wood to make a coffin:

I go on to the house, followed by the

                              Chuck.   Chuck.   Chuck.

of the adze.[18]

Each 'chuck' made by the adze (a small hand tool) represents a discrete sonic event, and is presented as such upon the page. But beyond the simple registration of these sounds, the extended spacing surrounding each 'chuck' establishes as well the time *between* these chucks, and in doing so, the silence each sound interrupts.[19] Just as white spaces on the page establish contrastive temporal and acoustic values in Mallarmé, then, spacing here establishes the rhythmicality and deliberation of Cash's labours; the intermittence that is essential to their sonic signature. Thus does typography perform the 'phonographic' work of capturing the 'passing-ness' of sounds and reproducing them in that very passing-ness; more fundamentally, it also shows all sounds as phenomena of time.

A further question raised by Apollinaire, meanwhile, is whether a poem such as 'Lettre-Océan' is best considered as a poem at all, and not, say, a picture or instance of some other kind of visual art. Such distinctions are put under extreme pressure throughout the early twentieth century, with artists on both sides of this 'visual'/'literary' divide, as it were, drawing on each others' example and incorporating thematic foci from each other into their own work.[20] 'Lettre-Océan' itself, for instance, is at least as interested in painterly models as in musical ones – Apollinaire, it is worth noting, wrote the first important critical work on Cubism – and is 'even-handed in its presentation of the visual and auditory, of spatial and temporal'.[21] It is worth asking, then, if correlates of techniques used for 'seeing' sound in literature might not also be found in visual art of the period. Unsurprisingly, given the above, we find they can.

A good way to start examining this is via the series of iconic works by Edvard Munch collectively known as *The Scream* (1893–1910). In the first and probably best-known painting of the series, the sound of the central figure's scream is depicted in at least three ways: by the painting's title; by the figure's open mouth; and by a set of coloured swirls, beginning with the blue one enveloping the figure's head. Nothing connects these swirls to the figure's voice in purely figurative terms – in fact, the blue swirl fairly clearly suggests instead an expanse of water; the red and yellow ones above, a sunset – but viewers rarely doubt that the former represents the latter: that they *translate* the scream out of the acoustic realm and into that of vision. What these swirls convey, in other words, especially given the dominance of straight lines elsewhere on the canvas, is the power of the scream to induce peculiar, areal effects in a sensory arena different to its own. (As Steven Connor comments: 'the power of utterance is [here] represented by its very capacity to bend and buckle visual and spatial forms.'[22]). Insofar as the scream is depicted as an exceptional and indeed horrible event, then, that very exceptionality is represented by audibility's unnerving and unwanted visibility.

A different approach is represented by Gino Severini's *Cannoni in Azione* (1915) (Figure 3.3), one of several paintings of this period directly indebted to the typographic experiments of Mallarmé, Apollinaire and Severini's futurist colleagues such as F. T. Marinetti. Here, a more or less realistic depiction of soldiers grouped around a cannon is overlaid by fragments of text (in French), painted at a variety of angles and in many different sizes, styles and colours. The overall effect is to suggest the ubiquity and magnitude of sound

Figure 3.3 Gino Severini, *Cannoni in Azione* (1915), reproduced in black and white, © Archivio Fotografico Mart, il Museo di Arte Moderna e Contemporanea di Trento e Roverto / © ADAGP, Paris and DACS, London 2012

upon the battlefield – this is a completely 'filled' and saturated image, without any of the gaps evoking silence in Mallarmé or Faulkner – while the effect of individual words and phrases is to suggest the phenomenology of each sound more specifically. The diminishing size of each successive letter in the elongated 'BBBOUMM' athwart the cannon's barrel, for instance, depicts the decay of sound following an explosion; the smaller clumps of regularly sized 's's' and 'z's' elsewhere depict the quieter but more insistent burr of artillery-induced vibrations. In this painting, then, sound does not so much distort the visual field as label that field and encode it.

Viewed another way, however, we could see both Munch's swirls and Severini's quasi-typographic flourishes as cognate answers to the same technical problem: that of representing sound within a medium (painting) that can never, in principle, offer direct access to it. Perhaps surprisingly, this 'problem' seems to have acted more as a spur than a deterrent to an entire painterly tradition, extending back at least as far as the seventeenth century, representing one field of sonic activity especially: music. As Richard Leppert notes in his study of this tradition, artists seeking to depict music pictorially must perform the complex trick of conveying information about the type and quality of music being played 'inside' the painting to those who stand outside it: 'Music's effects and meanings, which in performance are produced both aurally *and* visually, in painting must be rendered visually only. The way of seeing hence incorporates the way of hearing.'[23] An example that falls outside Leppert's frame of reference, but squarely within the modernist period, Nadezhda Udaltsova's *At the Piano* (1914–15) exemplifies the second of these formulae especially. Here, the figure of a woman playing a piano is progressively decomposed, cubist-fashion, along radiating geometric planes, suggesting both the movements of her body and the 'movements' of the music being played (this is by Bach, as is specified by a patch of text near the top-right corner of the canvas). The latter movement thus enters into the image as a correlate of the strictly visual drift from figuration to abstraction. Meanwhile, both modalities of 'movement' derive impetus from sheets of the actual music being played, sketched opposite the player's face.

And how might this relate to cinema, an art form one early commentator located halfway *between* painting and writing, and which others in the period (as we shall see), perhaps more surprisingly, likened to music?[24] As we have seen in this book's 'Introduction', cinema was 'silent', at least in principle, until the advent of synchronised sound-tracking in 1927 (and indeed after this development, in many instances, while the technical regimes concerned overlapped). However, this hardly precluded the treatment of music as subject matter, any more so than it had for centuries in painting. We have already seen (again in this book's 'Introduction') how *L'Inhumaine* addresses jazz alongside its heroine's more formal repertoire, and may now consider the treatment of music in films of the 'silent' era generally. In *The House of Darkness* (dir. W. D. Griffith, 1913), for example, action turns on the discovery that an otherwise violent patient at a lunatic asylum can be calmed by music played on the piano. We know the character and effects this music has by means of the way these are 'performed' by actors' bodily movements and expressions. A similar association of music with transports of emotion features in Erich von Stroheim's *The Merry Widow* (1925), where, in one scene, blindfolded musicians are deployed by the hero in his boudoir to play alluringly while he attempts to woo the heroine; in another scene, the camera lingers on the title page of a musical score to establish the identity of a piece of music being played while the couple dances. The orchestra accompanying the dancers on this occasion represent an institution often featured in early cinema: in *The Play House* (dir. Buster Keaton and Edward F. Cline, 1921), multiple exposures allow Buster Keaton to play every member of an orchestra at once. And in Dziga Vertov's *Man with a Movie Camera* (1929), an orchestra accompanies cinema itself, as part of the

Figure 3.4 Image from *Man with a Movie Camera* (dir. Dziga Vertov, 1929, USSR)

film's self-reflexive portrayal of the conditions under which it or any other film might have been viewed by contemporary audiences. As part of a sequence that enacts the film's own screening, musicians are seen taking up positions inside an auditorium as the audience files in; they then perform with gusto once the film's projection starts.

All these examples depend upon the physical proximity of performers and listeners, under conditions (broadly speaking) of 'live' performance. But this is not the case in my final example, also from *Man with a Movie Camera*, which relates instead to Pierre Schaeffer's category of the acousmatic – as glossed in this book's 'Introduction'. On this occasion, patrons of a social club listen to radio, as depicted by a loudspeaker on which appear superimposed, successively, an accordion, an ear, a piano, and a singing mouth (part of this sequence is reproduced as Figure 3.4). The musical instruments (and mouth) clearly represent the sources of the music being listened to; the ear, listening itself. Their coincidence on the same visual plane thus represents a conflation of hearing with its objects, the loudspeaker standing both for sound's dissemination and its reception. Thus does Vertov attempt to show not only sound but also hearing, and give the latter, too, a visual correlative.

Put another way, we could say that this sequence comments more specifically on 'acousmatic' sounds, which are defined, as we remember, by the invisibility of sound sources to those that hear them. And by the same token, the sequence may also be taken as an apt comment on the whole issue of representing sound in 'silent' film. For by making the accordion, piano and other sound sources visible – importing them, that is, into the visual field from which radio, as acousmatic, normally excludes them – Vertov effectively dramatises the conditions of his own medium, in which sounds normally may not be heard but only 'seen'.[25] The acousmatic and the sight of sound in 'silent' cinema, in other words, are mirror images of one another. (We may think here again of the blindfolded musicians in *The Merry Widow*, who like Vertov's radio, in their sightlessness echo and invert the film's ability to see without hearing them.) Thus is trans-sensory substitution founded – sometimes – on the senses' mutual exclusion.

INTER-ART TRANSLATION OR EQUIVALENCE

We may now switch our attention to the theorisation of cinema *as* music (or at least, as music-like), invoked above as a possibly surprising feature of this period. A key exhibit here is Hugo Münsterberg's *The Photoplay: A Psychological Study* (1916), whose very title illustrates the tendency in early cinematic discourse to understand the new medium in terms of categories derived from earlier ones ('photoplay' was a short-lived designation: subsequent reprints of Münsterberg's work replace it with simply *Film*). On the intercutting of material shot in different locations to indicate simultaneity of events, Münsterberg writes: 'It is as if we saw one through another, as if three tones blended into one chord'.[26] Thinking of a different musical phenomenon (the effect made by the editing together of frames out of their original sequence), he comments: 'A certain vibration goes through the world like the tremolo of the orchestra' (p. 55). To suggest the range and promptness of emotional responses cinema may prompt, he refers to the 'keyboard of [our] imagination' (p. 52). And then, as if to systematise all these remarks, he says:

> we falsify the meaning of the photoplay if we simply subordinate it to the esthetic [sic] conditions of drama [. . .] But we come nearer to the understanding of its true position in the esthetic world, if we think at the same time of [. . .] the art of musical tones. They have overcome the outer world and the social world entirely, they unfold our inner life, our mental play, with its feelings and emotions, its memories and fancies, in a material which seems exempt from the laws of the world of substance and material, tones which are fluttering and fleeting like our own mental states. (pp. 72–3)

Unlike drama, then, the other candidate here as analogue for the newer art (as the term 'play' in 'Photoplay' suggests), music is autonomous, self-referential. Drawing together strands of thought that we have seen exemplified in Chapter 1 by Greenberg, Hegel and Proust, Münsterberg identifies cinema with music on the basis of the latter's supposed status as three things: non-representational; of time and subjectivity; and seemingly immaterial.

As readers of that earlier chapter will recall, the view of music as non-representational, especially, is connected to the demand that each art 'be itself' – a demand voiced often, in fact, in cinema's early decades (as we shall see indeed in Chapter 5, via the claim that the displacement of 'silent' film by sound threatened to betray this principle). For the moment, though, we may attend directly to the underlying wager on which Münsterberg's comparison of music and cinema is staked, which is simply that there exists between these (and maybe other) art forms the possibility of *translation*, rooted in common principles or structures transcending any one of them. A de facto, if oblique, statement of this principle appears via a discussion of language in Wittgenstein's *Tractatus* (1921):

> In the fact that there is a general rule by which the musician is able to read the symphony out of the score, and that there is a rule by which one could reconstruct the symphony from the line on a gramophone record and from this again – by means of the first rule – construct the score, herein lies the internal similarity between these things which at first sight seem to be entirely different. And the rule is the law of projection which projects the symphony into the language of the musical score. It is the rule of translation of this language into the language of the phonograph record.[27]

In other words, the 'rule of translation' states that information stored in one medium – a gramophone disc, musical notation – may always, in principle, be converted into the 'language' of another. Or, to put the same point in terms of art rather than media or information theory (though the effect of Wittgenstein's examples is to provocatively align these very things), we might say that one medium's materials and techniques often, if not always, have cognates in others, and that practitioners working in different fields may thus ultimately be able to 'say' the same things.

It must be emphasised that Wittgenstein's point specifically concerns *language*, and should not be confused with, say, Baudelaire's sense of the universal 'correspondence' between things, outlined above. But to see how this point might nonetheless be related to post-Baudelairian poetics, we may consider Hart Crane's *The Bridge* (1930), in which music functions again as a master-trope of inter-mediality. The poem's final section begins with an epigraph from Plato, '*Music is then the knowledge of that which relates to love in harmony and system*', and proceeds to describe Brooklyn Bridge in New York City as both a musical instrument (with sounding 'strings') and as musical notation (with 'staves').[28] But beyond this making and inscription of music, part of Crane's wider thinking about the bridge is that this massive edifice itself is 'music', in visible, substantial form, simply by virtue of the way it occupies and organises space. Here are the poem's final lines:

So to thine Everpresence, beyond time,
Like spears ensanguined of one tolling star
That bleeds infinity – the orphic strings,
Sidereal phalanxes, leap and converge:
 – One song, one Bridge of Fire! Is it Cathay,
Now pity steeps with grass and rainbows ring
The serpent with the eagle in the leaves . . .?
Whispers antiphonal in azure swing. (pp. 107–8)

The bridge, 'One song', is made of 'Fire' – is essentially a *vision*, into which enter complex and multiply determined images of audiovisual crossover: the bleeding star that 'toll[s]' like a bell (recalling both a 'Swift peal of secular light' seen-heard slightly earlier in the poem, p. 107, and the 'grail of laughter' made by moonlight in another Crane poem, considered earlier in this chapter); the 'leap[ing]' and 'converge[nce]' of musical 'strings' with star formations ('orphic' as in Orpheus, the great musician of ancient Greek mythology; 'sidereal' as in stellar); and the 'whisper[ing]' of the poem's many voices as encompassed by the 'azure swing' of sky. Earlier in the poem, moreover, the bridge has been imagined as a kind of amplifying chamber into which the 'labyrinthine mouths of history' pour testimony (p. 105), again emphasising the bridge's physicality – the very physicality, paradoxically, that allows it to function *meta*-physically, as a depository for otherwise fugitive or latent traces of disparate times (mythical and secular) and spaces (in the final lines, America, along with the Cathay for which Columbus mistook it). The bridge, then, *is* sound, in the same sense that its design or engineering is harmonious: it materialises principles that, in Plato's terms, may properly be assigned to music.

A key term in the quotation Crane takes from Plato is 'harmony', whose use to characterise phenomena outside the musical *per se* we have touched on before, in Chapter 2 (specifically, to designate social solidarity). Several other terms operate similarly within the period – their membership of several 'languages' at once, we might say (recalling Wittgenstein), thus facilitating 'translation'. In *Ulysses*, Bloom reflects while listening to music, 'Numbers it is. All music when you come to think': a reference to Pythagoras, for whom 'number' is the principle of both music and all other things.[29] Almost the next thing Bloom thinks of is another term, 'vibration', which in Isaac Newton's *Opticks* (1704) denotes a common ground of auditory and optical phenomena, and in the physiology of David Hartley (1705–1757) denotes the physical substratum beneath all types of sensation.[30] At least since the ancient Greek philosopher Chryssipus, people have linked 'waves' of sound to those observable in water: in nineteenth-century physics, this idea of 'waves' is extended more broadly to all forms of energy, from sound to heat and light.[31] Gillian Beer has linked the later development to the work of modernist writers such as Woolf; we might also link it to artefacts of visual culture, such as the Munch painting discussed earlier in this chapter.[32]

With all this in mind, we gain a clear view of nineteenth-century acoustic science, perhaps the single field tributary to modernism in which the translation of the auditory into vision was most insistently effected. As we have seen in this book's 'Introduction', Chladni stands near the head of this tradition, with his 'sound figures' traced in sand; an arguably even more important figure in this tradition, Hermann von Helmholtz, continues in this vein (while recalling Newton or Hartley, as just evoked) in his use of a special microscope to observe the vibratory patterns made by violin strings in his *On the Sensations of Tone* (1862–77). As the nineteenth century wore on, such devices migrated from the laboratory to the lecture circuit, 'with popular demonstrations that featured a whole panoply of devices for showing off acoustic principles'.[33] Amongst the most renowned performers in an Anglophone context was John Tyndall, whose *Sound* (1867) not only documents his demonstrations but was also one of the most widely read works of science of its period in its own right. The following description of a 'vowel flame' reacting to a music box (one of many such flames Tyndall produced, in different shapes and sizes) gives a flavour of what his audiences were treated to: 'The flame behaves like a sentient creature; bowing slightly to some tones, but courtesying deeply to others.'[34]

Subsequent developments in acoustic science made prominent use of new sound (and imaging) technologies, of the kind considered throughout this book. Shortly after the phonograph's invention, recordings made by it were placed under a microscope by the American investigator Persifor Frazer Jr. to see what shapes were imprinted on the recording's surface by different vowel sounds (Figure 3.5).[35] Later phonological research similarly linked acoustic and optical media, often in configurations especially designed to convert the 'inputs' of one into 'outputs' of the other: in one 1924 study, for example, spoken vowels were 'electrically recorded' by a sound receiver and the resultant electric currents then transposed to 'photographic film,' on which visible curves were produced 'showing the relative intensities of all the vibration frequencies present in [each] spoken vowel'.[36] A near-contemporaneous study harnessed celluloid to phonograph recordings via a technique called 'phono-photography' – this time, to visually encode the characteristic singing styles of 'Negroes'.[37] As the twentieth century progressed, research was increasingly geared to (or even driven by) the imperatives of nation states and other interests: the authors of a 1947 volume entitled *Visible Speech* nicely capture this when they invoke the influence on their own work of the Second World War (when optical imaging was advanced for military purposes), the commercial telecommunications industry (in which the authors were employed) and campaigns on behalf of the disabled (the immediate context for the

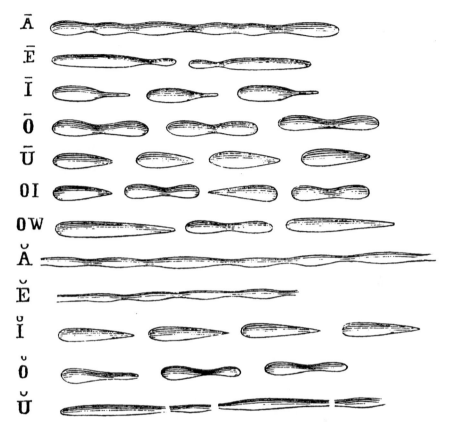

Figure 3.5 Woodcut showing vowel sounds, as recorded on phonograph foil, from Persifor Frazer, Jr, 'Some Microscopical Observations of the Phonograph Record', *Proceedings of the American Philosophical Society* 17:101 (1878), pp. 531–6

authors' own efforts, which were to make telephones and radio useful to the deaf).[38]

None of these developments, in isolation, may have had a decisive influence on modernist culture. But all contributed to a broad alignment of which that culture is a part, evident not only in these specific cases but also in at least three wider trends. The first of these relates to what I first said in this book's 'Introduction' about the senses functioning (sometimes) as an ensemble, and might here be called the 'underlying unity' theory of sensation. For the Austrian musicologist Erich M. von Hornbostel, writing in 1927,

> what is essential in the sensuous-perceptible is not that which separates the senses from one another, but that which unites them; unites them

among themselves; unites them with the entire (even with the non-sensuous) experience in ourselves; and with all the external world that there is to be experienced.[39]

The protagonist of Alfred Kubin's novel *The Other Side* (1908) agrees, reporting: 'More and more I felt the common bond uniting everything. Colours, scents, sounds and tastes were interchangeable.'[40] Clearly, such views contrast with Adorno and Eisler's thesis, also featured in this book's 'Introduction', according to which the senses have become historically de-coupled; moreover, they contrast with our own more recent commentary on 'silent' cinema, in which sight and sound appear as 'mutually exclusive'. However, rather than seeing such claims as necessarily competitive and incompatible, we should re-emphasise a point first made in discussion of Adorno and Eisler's thesis, and say instead that they form a single complex, in which each part is conjoined to its apparent refutation.

The second trend, connected to the first, returns us to Münsterberg's analogy between cinema and music. This may be called the practice (as opposed to 'simply' theory) of 'musicalising' vision. But whereas Münsterberg's analogy – like many others in the period, in fact, often linking music to painting – functions, precisely, analogically, this tendency instead takes music as something to be actually instantiated, '*made*', by visual rather than sonic means (clearly, there is an echo here of Symbolist poetics).[41] In cinema, this trend is exemplified by Hans Richter and Viking Eggerling, whose works use stop-frame animation to generate abstract sequences of shapes and patterns. In Richter's *Rhythmus 21* (1921), rectangles and squares are made to wax and wane in size, suggesting musical crescendos and diminuendos. Eggerling's *Symphonie Diagonale* (1921–4) mobilises more elaborate figures to approximate musical counterpoint and (as in Richter's title) rhythm. An equivalent in painting to these films is *Mechano-Faktura, Contrasting Elements* (1924), by Richter and Eggerling's colleague Henryk Berlewi. Here, several Richter-like series of shapes are laid out side by side upon a single canvas, where they do not so much succeed each other in time as do so spatially, in ascending (or descending) size order.[42]

The third trend by which sound and sight were equated, finally, returns us to previous chapters' discussions of Wagner, and his idea of the complementarity of arts and senses. This was in part a reinvention, in part a revival, and in part a critical revision of Wagner's theory of the *Gesamtkunstwerk*, taking forms Wagner would not necessarily have expected or approved. At the risk of further taxonomy's leading to fatigue, we may subdivide this trend into a further four subcategories – always remembering that such categorisations are not absolute or insular. Firstly, there were works which, rather than coordinating different media in the service of a single, 'higher' goal (as in Wagner's original formulation), instead use one medium to discharge the offices of others within the framework of its own: Apollinaire's 'Lettre-Océan', whose production of musical and painterly effects within the medium of poetry we have looked at already, exemplifies this tendency. Secondly, there were what we might think of as 'second-order' *Gesamtkunstwerks*, made out of works that are themselves self-sufficient and distinct. The informal and, as it were, 'inessential' union formed by another poem we have looked at, Loy's 'Brancusi's Golden Bird', and the Brancusi sculpture inspiring it, might be thought of in this light. Thirdly, there are single-media works that ostensibly transcend the phenomenal particularities of the media they adopt, to access an underlying principle many, again ostensibly, share: both the Richter and Eggerling films we have just considered might be said to illustrate this, especially given the pair's shared authorship of a text entitled 'Universal Language' (*Universelle Sprache*, 1920), which argues that a basic set of abstract forms constitutes a group of percepts all people may understand (as far as one can gather: the original text has now been lost).[43] And finally, there are *Gesamtkunstwerks* that partly fall outside the category of art altogether, either because they are formed of sensory phenomena artworks may *refer* to without necessarily producing, or because they emerge in an intermediate zone between artworks themselves and perceiving subjects. The 'burning whiteness' which Baudelaire attributes to passages in Wagner's *Lohengrin*, but which that music cannot really be said to 'contain' as an objective quality, may be considered as an example of the latter.

But to pursue this matter further, we must turn directly to what were often crucial 'hinges' between music and the visual arts in such discussions, as indeed in this last instance: light and colour.

LIGHT AND COLOUR

These two things are aligned to significant effect in D. H. Lawrence's *Aaron's Rod*, when the protagonist looks at his house, at night, from his back garden:

> he saw a curious succession of lighted windows, between which jutted the intermediary back premises, scullery and outhouse, in dark little blocks. It was something like the keyboard of a piano: more still, like a succession of musical notes. For the rectangular planes of light were of different intensities, some bright and keen, some soft, warm, like candle-light, and there was one surface of pure red light, one or two were almost invisible, dark green. So the long scale of lights seemed to trill across the darkness, now bright, now dim, swelling and sinking. The effect was strange.[44]

As in certain other examples already looked at in this chapter, this passage moves from a simple visual analogy (the house looks like a piano keyboard) to a more complex one, aligning visible features of the keyboard/house with their implied sonic counterparts: 'bright' notes as opposed to 'soft' ones, and so on. Here, however, the analogy is deepened by the introduction of two more specific qualities: colour ('red' and 'green') and 'light'. These qualities function through and upon each other, up to the point of mutual constitution, as when a window appears not just 'green' but '*dark* green'. It is this interdependence, and the fact that both qualities appear multiply and diversely, creating the possibility of contrasts and other relationships, apparently, that allows them to be recognised as 'musical'.

As both a complement and contrast to this episode, we may now consider an earlier Lawrence novel, *The Trespasser* (1912) – a text, significantly, replete with references to Wagner. In the novel's opening episode, a character turns from two musicians towards a fire, 'to watch the flames poise and dance with the music': an echo of Tyndall's 'singing flames'.[45] With reference to another light-source, the protagonist, Siegmunde – his name constitutes one of those Wagnerian references, being shared with an important character in the *Ring* cycle – asks Helen, '"What music do you think holds the best interpretation of sunset?"', presupposing an inverse kind of musico-ocular relation to the one we have just seen *Aaron's Rod* elaborate (p. 27). Just before his own body is likened to a 'piece of colour' (p. 21), meanwhile, Siegmunde see-hears this:

> Below, in the street, a military band passed glittering. A brave sound floated up, and again he laughed, loving the tune, the clash and glitter of the band, the movement of scarlet, blithe soldiers beyond the park. People were drifting brightly from church.
> [...] Everywhere fluttered the small flags of holiday. Every form danced lightly in the sunshine.
> [...] [S]carlet soldiers, and ludicrous blue sailors, and all the brilliant women from church shook like a kaleidoscope down the street. (p. 20)

Unlike Aaron in the later novel, looking at his house, Siegmunde does not so much regard his optical impressions as *analogues* of music as *complements* of actual music being played at the same time, as in Wagner's musical dramas (or, indeed, many mixed-media productions for the stage). All the various artistic and extra-artistic elements that make up this scene – the music being played by the band, the movements of the soldiers, even the colours of the clothes of passers-by, and so on – form a single (if ad hoc and unselfconscious) 'work of art': in the fourth and final sense defined in the preceding section of the present chapter, a *Gesamtkunstwerk*.

It is between the various possibilities rehearsed in these two novels that the history of so-called 'colour music' is played out. As the name suggests, this is an art designed to create 'musical' effects with coloured lights or other materials, either as an accompaniment to sounded music or as a stand-alone art in its own right. Its first clear manifestation is represented by the efforts of Louis Bertrand Castel (1688–1757) to devise an 'ocular harpsichord', featuring many small windows of coloured glass, each connected to a different key on a conventional harpsichord keyboard. This was often criticised by English-speaking commentators, including Sir David Brewster (1781–1868), who claimed that his own invention, the kaleidoscope – the very optical toy cited by Lawrence in *The Trespasser* – was a vast improvement in producing Castel's own desired effects.[46] As the kaleidoscope's appearance in this context indicates, the history of colour music is entangled with that of many other practices, technologies and art forms. This is nicely instanced by the career and writing of Adrian Bernard Klein, whose *Colour-Music* (1926) explains how he was first led to his topic as a painter, before concluding that 'Painting is no longer a vital art' and that music is now the 'most important art' instead.[47] In the book's preface, Klein sets out a range of further contexts for colour music and its contemporary vogue:

> The number of individuals actively engaged in the development of the art [. . .] is rapidly increasing, and there can be no question as to the widening interest in the general subject of colour. The remarkable experiments during and immediately following the [First World] War in connection with the treatment of nerve cases by exposure of the patient to specially coloured interiors illuminated by coloured light [a reference to the work of H. Kemp Prosser, a fellow painter, who developed a treatment for First World War causalities suffering from shell-shock involving specially painted rooms], the direction of taste exhibited by modern interior decoration, contemporary dress, the colouring of fabrics, stage production, the ballet, painting, the art of the hoardings, are all indications of a general pleasure in 'colour for colour's sake'.[48]

To this impressively diverse list, we may add another item, afforded by hindsight: Klein later worked in, and wrote a book on, colour cinematography.[49]

Theoretically, colour music drew on several traditions, some of which we have considered already. The notion of 'vibration' was cited frequently, though Alexander Wallace Rimington (1854–1918), at least, cautioned against moving beyond what we have just seen to be its Newtonian and Hartleyan basis to assume 'some underlying physiological law of sensation common to the organs of seeing and hearing'.[50] Less cautious was Edmund George Lind, who had Newton's division of the colour spectrum into seven colours in mind when proclaiming a relation between these colours and the seven notes of the diatonic scale.[51] Technically, colour musicians working after the advent of electric light and power were able to take advantage of these in their own inventions, as in Rimington's own 'colour organ' (1893), which updated Castel by having its keyboard govern banks of electric coloured lights. Meanwhile, a congenial context for several practitioners was cinema, as in the films of Oskar

Fischinger (1900–1967), made on either side of the 'silent'/sound divide, some of which interpret pre-existing, sonic music.

It is to an 'actual' musician, though, that perhaps the most well known experiment in 'colour music' of the modernist period is owed. In *Prometheus – The Poem of Fire* (1908–10), Aleksandr Scriabin sets music for a large orchestra and choir alongside that of a 'light keyboard', 'notated on the top line of the score in conventional music notation'.[52] With this instrument – a colour organ, much like Rimington's – it was intended that colours be 'played' in tandem with sounded music according to a set of pitch-colour correspondences (for example, C was paired with red). Like his contemporary Lind, Scriabin drew up this schema in the wake of Newton, though his more immediate source was theosophy, whose central texts similarly correlated colours with musical pitches, on the basis of their allegedly innate affinity.[53] Though technical constraints meant that *Prometheus* was usually performed without its visual component, a performance was given in New York in 1915 that realised at least some of Scriabin's ambitions for the work. As one audience member described the way that tones and coloured light combined: 'With the drift of the music, the colors changed and dissolved by superposition, juxtaposition and otherwise.'[54]

How does all of this relate to Wagner? Scriabin admired the other composer, and shared the latter's regard for ancient Greece – Prometheus is after all the God responsible for giving fire to humans in ancient Greek mythology – though he took issue with Wagner's theatrical designs, believing that these imposed an unfortunate barrier between musicians and their audience.[55] A similarly critical comparison is made by Leonid Sabaniev in his essay on *Prometheus* in *Der Blaue Reiter Almanac* (1912), the seminal anthology of art and art theory edited by the painters Franz Marc and Wassily Kandinsky (Wagner, Sabaniev contends, expresses the goal of reunifying the arts only 'vaguely'; Scriabin, 'much more clearly').[56] And here, we may take leave of 'colour music' to consider *Der Blaue Reiter* as a de facto *Gesamtkunstwerk* in its own right. The anthology consists of fourteen essays, one poem and a stage piece, interleaved with over 140 reproduced paintings, designed to highlight inter-art, cross-generic and trans-chronological comparisons (children's, folk and 'primitive' art, for example, are presented alongside acknowledged classics of the western academic canon). Embedded in Sabaniev's article, for instance, is a reproduction of Kandinsky's *Composition IV* (1911), alongside passages from Scriabin's score. Kandinsky's essay 'On Stage Composition' echoes and references Wagner at several points, while voicing what we might call the 'Greenberg' or 'Lessing' principle, according to which 'Each art has its own language' and is 'complete in itself'.[57] Another Kandinsky essay in *Der Blaue Reiter*, 'On the Question of Form', sweeps together references to and echoes of other figures considered in the present book, such as Hegel (sound 'works from the inside out'), Pythagoras (number is the '"essence of all things"'), and the Baudelaire of 'The Painter of Modern Life' ('The child [. . .] looks at everything with fresh eyes, and he still has the natural ability to absorb the thing as such').[58]

It is, however, for his stage piece *The Yellow Sound*, together with his theory and practice of abstraction, that Kandinsky has the greatest claims on our attention. These things are connected, not least by Kandinsky's idiosyncratic view of sound, which he counterintuitively uncouples from the acoustic. In 'On the Question of Form', he explains that all things are divided into an 'outer shell' and an 'inner sound', and that the task of visual, contemporary art is to make 'the *spirit* audible': that is, exteriorise 'inner sound' or sounds as vision.[59] In abstraction, as opposed to mimesis, such sounds are 'intensified by blotting out reality'; moreover, each abstract form (a circle, say, or a square) 'is a fixed symbol for a specific sound'.[60] *The Yellow Sound* extends this logic, combining coloured lights, music, scenography, recitative, and singing, in the service of a 'total' overall effect (at least in theory: in practice, sadly, the piece was unperformed in Kandinsky's lifetime). The close relation between sound and colour indicated by the piece's title is reminiscent of Scriabin; in this respect, Kandinsky, too, was much influenced by theosophy.

Even more emphatically, Kandinsky's *Concerning the Spiritual in Art* (1912) proclaims: 'Colour is the keyboard [. . .] The artist is the hand which plays [. . .] to cause vibrations in the soul.'[61] Again, according to this argument, colour is the royal road to musicality in vision. In agreement is the fellow painter Robert Delaunay, who in the late 1930s recalled his own paintings of 1912 by claiming: 'In the painting of *pure color*, it is color itself which, by its play, its ruptures, its contrasts', resembles 'the musical composition of Bach's time, or, in our own era, good jazz'.[62] Robert's wife and co-theoretician Sonia Delaunay implemented similar principles in her painted accompaniment to Blaise Cendrars's poem *La Prose du Transsibérien et de la Petite Jehanne de France*, a work whose very title ('Prose', here designating poetry) announces its *Gesamtkunstwerk*-like intent to be many things at once.[63] Perhaps against expectation, however (at least according to Marjorie Perloff), 'Delaunay's painting, far from matching the verbal text to be illustrated, undermines its meanings: her vision is everywhere brighter, sunnier, more positive', than Cendrars's words.[64] And it is this that qualifies the work as something genuinely subversive, as opposed to simply revisionary, of Wagner's model: what we might call an 'anti-*Gesamtkunstwerk*', made up of elements that not only do not 'match', but are deliberately designed not to. Kandinsky speaks to this when he declares that every element in a multimedia work may 'keep its own external life, even if it contradicts the external life of another element'.[65] More recently, Daniel Albright has identified a whole strain that works against as well as within the *Gesamtkunstwerk* tradition, cultivating interference and incommensurability between media in multimedia artworks, instead of coherence.[66] As we shall see in Chapter 5, Adorno and Eisler theorised a similar relation between music and the moving image in sound film.

PSYCHIATRY AND 'NEURO-GRAMMATOLOGY'

Here, however, we may turn away from inter-art relations for the meantime, and turn instead towards to the psychosensory phenomenon often treated as a component, if not a 'cause', of colour music: synaesthesia. In *The New Laokoon* (last cited in Chapter 1), Irving Babbitt rails against supposed literary manifestations of this condition on the grounds that 'Color-audition and similar phenomena have little bearing on the higher and more humane purposes of art [. . .] They concern more immediately the student of psychology and medicine, and in some cases the nerve-specialist.'[67] Such pathologisation of what, after all, would seem fairly harmless aesthetic experiments may seem intemperate, but has at least some historic justification in the fact that colour music's peak years broadly coincide with synaesthesia's own: both are predominately things of the late nineteenth and early twentieth centuries. A recent survey shows a clear surge of interest in synaesthesia in medical and other scientific contexts between 1881 and 1935.[68] In a longer but overlapping period, between 1837 and 1925, over 300 works were published for 'colour organs'.[69]

Substantively, scientific studies of the period fell, broadly speaking, into two camps. On the one hand, many believed synaesthesia to be pathological, especially in the early phase of its intensive study: in the opinion of American physician Isador Coriat (1875–1943), for example, it is 'a congenital defect or lack of differentiation in the individual nervous system such that stimulation of one projection area of the cortex passes over to another area'.[70] On the other hand, contending authorities considered synaesthesia to be 'a perfectly normal mental process [. . .] analogous to, if not identical with psychological phenomena that occur in all of us'.[71] In the latter camp are Raymond H. Wheeler and Thomas D. Cutsforth, whose pointedly-titled 'Synaesthesia, A Form of Perception' (1922) is of particular interest both for its exceptionally vivid phenomenology of the condition (Cutsforth, who perhaps not incidentally was blind, was a synaesthete himself, and here acts as his own subject) and for the radical conclusions it draws on that basis. Analysing his perception of a bell's ringing as a 'small, silvery cloud', the subject finds that

> what meant the sound to me was in reality this persisting, silvery, visual image. I was conscious of the metallic, mellow ring of the bell in terms of the silvery quality of the visual image; the intensity of the bell-sound was the brightness of the visual image; the changing quality and intensity of the bell came to me only in terms of changing quality and brightness of the silvery image. At no time was I getting away from visual qualities; they followed me no matter where I turned or what I did.[72]

The authors thus deduce that the conversion of sound into 'image' in Cutsforth's experience is but an idiosyncratic instance of what enables the transition from 'sensation' to 'perception' in everyone: a transition accompanying *all* impressions – or at least, all those that eventuate in the identification of sensory data with or as a given thing (p. 216). Synaesthesia, then, is not an aberrant or special case, but rather one that points toward the 'truth' of all perception: that 'the simplest possible mental process, or at least the simplest describable mental process is a dual phenomenon implying an attention shift' (p. 220). In effect, this argument represents both a reinterpretation and trans-valuation of the Nietzschean and Bergsonian critique of sensation discussed in Chapter 1, according to which commonplace impressions are travestied by 'translation'. For Wheeler and Cutsforth, in opposition to this better-known tradition, it is just such a process that we should welcome as 'the basis of knowing [. . .] of all forms of interpretation' (p. 218).

In literary contexts, synaesthesia is usually identified with the pleasures, and sometimes perils, of the aesthetic. The aforementioned 'Voyelles', by Rimbaud, and the 'nose music' featured in Joris-Karl Huysmans's *À Rebours* (1884) are relatively well known; far less so are James Huneker's stories, several of which feature individuals whose scientific and/or occult knowledge grants them access to sight-sound equivalences they otherwise could not have accessed.[73] In 'The Spiral Roar' (1905), a mysterious gas is used by an experimenter-visionary to produce spectacular and ultimately deadly fire-work displays: in the process, the narrator's eyes are 'sated by the miracles of harmonies', involving 'strange scales of chromatic pigments'.[74] In 'Dusk of the Gods' (1902), the protagonist falls into an apparently hypnotic trance induced by the playing of a distinguished pianist, during which he has a vision of

> what man had never seen before – the tone-color of each [musical] instrument [. . .] He saw strings of rainbow hues, red trumpets, blue flutes, green oboes, garnet clarinets, golden yellow horns, dark-brown bassoons, scarlet trombones [. . .] That the triangle had always been silver he never questioned; but this new chromatic blaze, this new tinting of tones – what did it portend? Was it a symbol of the further degradation and effeminization of music?[75]

Like Wheeler's and Cutsforth's 'small silvery cloud', these percepts fuse a specific sound source with a specific colour, resulting in what we might think of as 'colour music' without any of the usual apparatus. And whereas a triangle really *is* 'silver' in its manifest appearance, there is no other correlation here between the visual aspects of the instruments invoked and the colour of the sounds these instruments produce: rather, the latter are mooted as inherent in the sounds themselves (of course, Babbitt would say, as Huneker seems himself to hint here, that claims for such inherence really are symptomatic of 'degradation').

A somewhat different experience is reported in the autobiographical fictions of Bryher (Winifred Ellerman), better known as a founder and editor of the film journal *Close Up* – of which more in Chapter 5 – and as the lover of H. D. Here are two excerpts from *Development* (1920):

> From earliest remembrance certain phrases, names especially of places or of persons, were never free from an association of colour, fashioned of a tone, written in it; and as she grew, this feeling developed, unconsciously expanding until her whole vocabulary became a palette of colours, luminous gold, a flushed rose, tones neither sapphire nor violet, but the shade of southern water [. . .].[76]

> It was impossible to think of the alphabet as colourless. [. . .]
> Natural objects apart, which kept their actual hue, the initial letter gave the word its colour [. . .]; it was the consonants that made a page as vivid as a sunset [. . .] W was crimson; H, M, and Y were various shades of gold and primrose. B changed from raspberry to umber, N was the rich tint of a red squirrel, F and J were a deeper brown.[77]

In *Two Selves* (1923), similarly, Bryher states, 'She had always seen words as colour', and cites an Arabic lesson in which 'A sentence splashed and fell like the black and white kingfishers darting from one side to the other of the Nile.'[78] In both novels, then, the association of what might otherwise appear two quite distinct strands of sensory phenomena is immediate and ineluctable; moreover, it gains strength and is commensurately savoured more intensely over time.

What Bryher's novels also feature, on this evidence, meanwhile, is a rather different experience from that imagined in Huneker's short stories: a form of perception in which colours are associated not so much with music (which *Development*'s narrator says she does not like) as *language*.[79] This distinction is acknowledged in the scientific literature of the period, sponsoring spin-off categories such as 'pseduo-chromesthesia' (to designate the experience of those who report 'sensations of color when they *see* words, and not when they *hear* them enunciated').[80] With respect to the distinction between 'coloured' music and 'coloured' language generally, the seeming attitude of Woolf is interesting. In *Jacob's Room* (1922), she devotes a rather waspish piece of satire to an amateur researcher in the British Museum, who in the library's holdings forever seeks confirmation of 'her philosophy that colour is sound – or, perhaps, it has something to do with music. She could never quite say, though it was not for lack of trying.'[81] But in *To the Lighthouse*, she strikes a far more credulous and sympathetic note in the following account of Mrs Ramsay's recollections:

slowly those words they had said at dinner [. . .] began washing from side to side of her mind rhythmically, and as they washed, words, like little shaded lights, one red, one blue, one yellow, lit up in the dark of her mind, and seemed leaving their perches up there to fly across and across, or to cry out and to be echoed [. . .]. (p. 129)

In a related passage, Woolf shifts from the relation between spoken words and colour to that between sense impressions generally and *recollection*; this time, as the latter works within the mind of Mrs Ramsay's son James:

He began to search among the infinite series of impressions which time had lain down, leaf upon leaf, fold upon fold softly, incessantly upon his brain; among scents, sounds; voices, harsh, hollow, sweet; and lights passing, and brooms tapping; and the wash and hush of the sea [. . .]. (p. 184)

And in a yet-again related passage, *Jacob's Room* posits the ability of speech to translate itself, so to speak, into forms more durable than sound and thus amenable, again, to recollection: 'The voice continued, imprinting on the faces of the clerks in Whitehall [. . .] something of its own inexorable gravity, as they listened, deciphered, wrote down.' (p. 240). Here, the writing down of *what* the voice is saying by the clerks is duplicated by a shadow text 'written' on their faces, encoding *how* the voice being attended to is 'saying'. Voice, hands, consciousness and faces are connected by a single metaphor: inscription. And significantly, this inscription is identified as occurring not only within the minds and bodies of individuals, but also between such persons, socially; as also earlier in *Jacob's Room*, 'when mind prints upon mind indelibly' (p. 59).

Here, then, we are led to a new topic, distinct from though related to our earlier discussion of writing's use to represent sound typographically: the status of sound *as* 'writing', inscribed directly on the face or, especially, inside the brain. Woolf aside, the great exponent of this idea in the early twentieth century is the American psychologist Morton Prince.[82] In *The Unconscious* (1914; revised 1921) (a work that does not, incidentally, adopt the Freudian understanding of that term), Prince claims that 'with every passing state of conscious experience, with every idea, thought, or perception, the brain process that goes along with it leaves some trace, some residue of itself, within the neurons and in the functional arrangements between them'.[83] He then connects this idea to those of reading and writing, arriving at a what one might call 'neuro-grammatological' understanding of the brain as a giant, ever-augmenting text:

If our knowledge were deep enough, if by any technical method we could determine the exact character of the modifications of the dispositions of the neurons that remain as vestiges of thought and could decipher their meaning, we could theoretically read in our brains the record of our lives, as graphically inscribed on a tablet. (p. 133)[84]

'[T]heoretically' at least, knowledge of the brain is thus synonymous with the technique whereby knowledge of any kind, traditionally, is encoded: writing; or more precisely *reading*, the technique that accompanies writing, allowing texts of any kind to be 'decipher[ed]'. (Incidentally, something like this 'reading' of a person's brain is fantasised in E. T. A. Hoffmann's story, 'Master Flea', 1822, where a special magnifying glass allows the protagonist to look through other people's eyes and thus ascertain the contents of the brains behind.[85]) And how does Prince imagine 'neurograms' to be created? One analogy he uses is especially deserving of our attention:

> though our ideas pass out of mind, are forgotten for the moment, and become dormant, their physiological records still remain, as sort of vestigia, much as the records of our spoken thoughts are recorded on the moving wax cylinder of the phonograph. When the cylinder revolves again the thoughts once more are reproduced as auditory language. (p. 132)

The phonograph's conversion of sound into 'writing' thus provides a model of the brain's functioning. Just as Woolf imagines speech to dwell in memory as writing, so Prince imagines the work of recollection, conversely, to resemble a phonograph's turning of inscriptions into sound.

The phonograph's identification with writing here may seem surprising, given its now more typical identification with music. But in the late nineteenth and early twentieth centuries, this view seemed more or less self-evident. Earlier in this chapter, we saw how phonograph recordings were examined to see what vowel sounds 'looked' like, and may now consider the more general principle this mirrors, according to which phonographic cylinders (and gramophone discs) were not so much sound recordings that happened to be visible as written records capable of being heard. As Lisa Gitelman observes, Edison saw his invention primarily as 'a textual device', and in so doing, echoed an earlier nineteenth-century system of shorthand notation – also called 'phonography'.[86] This helps explain the fairly widespread use of the device for notetaking and related purposes, for instance, by the fictitious Dr Seward in Bram Stoker's *Dracula* (1897), and the real-life Prince, whose use of the phonograph to keep case notes is documented in *The Dissociation of a Personality* (1906). A more lurid variation on this theme is found in *Double Indemnity* (dir. Billy Wilder, 1944), a film noir centred on the insurance industry, where the protagonist commits his confession of murder to phonographic cylinders. And as we have already seen, Wittgenstein considers 'language' to reside in phonograph recordings, allowing for the 'translation' of these recordings into other languages, such as musical notation.

For a final example of phonography's identification with writing, we may consider Adorno's 'The Form of the Phonograph Record' (1934). Here, Adorno, like Wittgenstein, compares phonography to musical notation. However, whereas Wittgenstein stresses these two 'language's' equivalence, Adorno stresses instead what he sees as their qualitative difference. As we saw in Chapter 1, Adorno elsewhere in his writings follows Benjamin in viewing languages as 'fallen' insofar as these are composed of signs only arbitrarily linked to the things they designate. And in his essay on the phonograph, it is precisely in this way that Adorno conceives the relation between musical notation and music itself. Characterising musical notation as 'mere signs for music', he sees the 'groove[s]' in phonograph recordings by contrast as 'inseparably committed to the sound' that they encode.[87] Phonography thus holds open the utopian possibility that 'music, previously conveyed *by* writing, suddenly itself turns *into* writing' (p. 279; emphasis added). Like Chladni's sound figures – to which Adorno specifically compares them – phonograph recordings instantiate a 'natural' language, written organically, as it were, by the phenomena they represent (p. 280).

On Musical Notation

What, then, in conclusion, of musical notation, the pre-phonographic medium in which music may be written down? Insofar as music is the sonic art par excellence, as we have said before, its written form can be regarded as quintessentially the sight of sound, and thus a fitting topic with which to close the present chapter. Adorno's critique notwithstanding, we may therefore briefly address the topic under three headings: the role of notation in literary texts where it appears; notation's status in, and as a form of, visual culture; and the effects of notation on musical history.

Several examples come to mind under the first heading, including *Ulysses*, which 'quotes' the beginning of a hymn, in notated form, in 'Scylla and Charybdis'.[88] But perhaps the most famous, as well as consequential, such citing of notation features in W. E. B. Du Bois's *The Souls of Black Folk* (1903). At the head of each chapter of this text, Du Bois places several bars from a different 'sorrow song', his name for the musical genre African American spiritual.[89] Those that read music may thus 'sound' this music for themselves, either mentally or physically, an activity analogous to the 'soundtracking' in Fitzgerald's *Tender in the Night* discussed in the last chapter. But in the absence, or better, irrespective of this skill, the notation may more compellingly be better taken as *un*-sounded, 'mute' – and all the more eloquent for that fact. The notation can thus be taken as a kind of frozen music, standing as an apposite if perhaps hermetic statement in its own right. And in this respect, the music might be said to instantiate a characteristic move of black American aesthetics in general, stressing the paradoxically expressed inexpressibility of the black historical experience, so conditioned as this is by the manifold and interlocking horrors of slavery, poverty and racial victimisation (I am thinking here especially of Toni Morrison's phrase 'unspeakable thoughts, unspoken', to designate the psychic fallout from instantiations of all these things, in her 1987 novel *Beloved*).[90] In its very 'silence', then, notation gestures towards an expressive content only obliquely represented in the accompanying verbal text.

A different relation between sound (or soundlessness) and vision, meanwhile, is centrally the concern of Alfred Tolmer's *Mise en Page* (1931), which leads us to our second heading: notation's status as a form of visual culture. As Tolmer writes, the visual order that may characterise notation is in the first instance a side-effect of 'the convention necessary to translate sound into written notes. As, however, it is simply a transposed geometry, an aesthetic arrangement is produced automatically and is inherent in the musical page.'[91] Thus music's example to and use within graphic design – the discipline for which Tolmer's is virtually the founding text. A similar point is made by the music teacher Wendell Kretschmar in Thomas Mann's *Doctor Faustus*, in the course of a lecture significantly entitled *Music and the Eye*. As Mann's narrator reports, Kretschmar 'sketched for us the enchanting pleasure which even the visual picture of a score by Mozart afforded to the practised eye [. . .] A deaf man, he cried, quite ignorant of sound, could not but delight in these gracious visions.'[92]

And so finally, to our final subcategory in this section: the effects of notation on music; which, at least since the early twentieth century, musical historians have adjudged momentous. For Max Weber, whose *The Rational and Social Foundations of Music* (1921) is a relatively little-known though emblematic elaboration of his general socio-historic theory, it is in part the invention and practice of notation that creates the figure of 'the composer proper and guarantee[s] to the polyphonic creations of the Western world, in contrast to those of all other peoples, permanence, after-effect, and continuing development'.[93] Notwithstanding the cultural (and perhaps racial) chauvinism of these remarks, it is almost certainly true, as Weber also states, that the complex, multi-part, and multi-instrumental music that characterises much of the 'classical' tradition is 'neither producible nor transmittable nor reproducible without the use of notation'.[94] Picking up this theme, composer and musical theorist Carlos Chávez (1899–1978) writes that with the composers Wagner, Schoenberg and Stravinsky, especially,

> notation as a means of reproducing musical creation has come, because of its improvement and relative perfection, to be a decisive factor determining musical creation itself. Notation, born and perfected as a way of making musical reproduction possible, has been converted into a means for production also, for the creation of music.[95]

One consequence of this, as the critic Edmund Dehnert writes, was the pursuit of music as an entirely textual activity, indifferent to or even incapable of performance, as in the works of certain later composers that utilise pitch values legible on paper but beyond the range of human hearing.[96] Pursuing a slightly different tack, Schoenberg, one of the composers named by Chávez, argues that musical notation tends to privilege certain harmonic possibilities at the expense of others, in ways that skew the western tradition and restrict its tonal palette.[97] The growing importance of notation to this tradition has thus served to naturalise preferences that, Schoenberg argues, in strictly musical terms, are arbitrary.

The appearance of Schoenberg's critique of western music at this juncture is congenial to our wider purpose. For it is to Schoenberg's theory, and the self-conscious pursuit of 'modernising' music generally, that we now turn.

NOTES

1. Charles Baudelaire, 'Richard Wagner and *Tannhäuser* in Paris' (1860), in *Selected Writings on Art and Literature*, translated with an introduction by P. E. Charvet (Harmondsworth: Penguin, 1992), pp. 325–57; p. 331 cited; emphases in original. Subsequent references to this edition are given in the text.
2. Arthur Rimbaud, *Collected Poems*, translated with an introduction and notes by Martin Sorrell (Oxford: Oxford University Press, 2001), pp. 134–5.
3. This is not to contrast the substantive content of Baudelaire's essay with that of his poem: so far from being contrastive, indeed, the original text of the former reproduces two stanzas from the latter (see the full French text, reprinted as an appendix to Margaret Miner's *Resonant Gaps: Between Baudelaire and Wagner*, Athens, GA: University of Georgia Press, 1995). For more on the Baudelaire–Wagner–Symbolism nexus generally, see David Michael Hertz, *The Tuning of the Word: The Musico-Literary Poetics of the Symbolist Movement* (Carbondale: Southern Illinois University Press, 1987); Heath Lees, *Mallarmé and Wagner: Music and Poetic Language*, with extracts from the French translated by Rosemary Lloyd (Aldershot: Ashgate, 2007).
4. Mina Loy, *The Lost Lunar Baedeker*, edited by Roger L. Conover (Manchester: Carcanet, 1997), pp. 79–80.
5. For an interesting discussion of the latter point, see Susan Stewart, *Poetry and the Fate of the Senses* (Chicago: University of Chicago Press, 2002), pp. 171–5.
6. Loy, *The Lost Lunar Baedeker*, p. 157.
7. Hart Crane, *The Complete Poems of Hart Crane*, edited by Marc Simon, with a new introduction by Harold Bloom (New York: Liveright, 2001), p. 11.
8. Fernando Pessoa, *Selected Poems*, 2nd edn, translated by Jonathan Griffin (Harmondsworth: Penguin, 2000), p. 100.
9. Virginia Woolf, *Mrs Dalloway*, edited by Stella McNichol, with an introduction and notes by Elaine Showalter (Harmondsworth: Penguin, [1925] 1992), p. 75.
10. Virginia Woolf, *To the Lighthouse*, edited by Stella McNichol, with an introduction and notes by Hermione Lee (Harmondsworth: Penguin, [1927] 1992), p. 188. Subsequent references to this edition are given in the text. Isabel A, Pollock, *Lip-Reading, What it Is, and What it Does for the Partially Deaf* (London: J. J. Perfitt, 1901), p. 9; emphasis in original.

11. I am thinking here, of course, of Plato's famous account of writing, in the *Phaedrus* (c. 360 BC).

12. Johanna Drucker, *The Visible Word: Experimental Typography and Modern Art, 1909–1923* (Chicago: University of Chicago Press, 1994), p. 58.

13. Stéphane Mallarmé, *Collected Poems*, translated with a commentary by Henry Weinfield (Berkeley: University of California Press, 1994), p. 122.

14. Drucker, *The Visible Word*, p. 51.

15. Roger Shattuck, *The Innocent Eye: On Modern Literature and the Arts* (New York: Farrar, Straus and Giroux, 1984), p. 259.

16. This is not to deny the importance of onomatopoeia and other sound effects in the poem, on which see also Shattuck, *The Innocent Eye*, p. 259.

17. See, however, Michael Kaufmann, *Textual Bodies: Modernism, Postmodernism, and Print* (London: Associated University Presses, 1994).

18. William Faulkner, *As I Lay Dying: The Corrected Text* (New York: Vintage Books, [1930] 1987), p. 4.

19. Cf. Kaufmann, *Textual Bodies*, p. 43.

20. Cf. Marjorie Perloff, *The Futurist Moment: Avant-Garde, Avant Guerre, and the Language of Rupture*, with a new preface (Chicago: University of Chicago Press, 2003), p. 38.

21. Shattuck, *The Innocent Eye*, p. 259.

22. Steven Connor, *Dumbstruck: A Cultural History of Ventriloquism* (Oxford: Oxford University Press, 2000), p. 11.

23. Richard Leppert, *The Sight of Sound: Music, Representation, and the History of the Body* (Berkeley: University of California Press, 1993), p. xxi.

24. This 'commentator' is Charles Davy; who, in an article of 1934, argued that whilst painting is exclusively a 'spatial' art, and literature exclusively a 'temporal' one, cinema inhabits both space and time at once: see Laura Marcus, *The Tenth Muse: Writing about Cinema in the Modernist Period* (Oxford: Oxford University Press, 2007), p. 186.

25. This is not to say that Vertov saw cinema as intrinsically or 'rightly' soundless. He made sound films once the technical ability to do so became available to him, and saw *Man with a Movie Camera* itself as anticipating a 'sound' aesthetic. See Dziga Vertov, 'From Kino-Eye to Radio-Eye' (1929), in *Kino-Eye: The Writings of Dziga Vertov*, edited with an introduction by Annette Michelson, translated by Kevin O'Brien (Berkeley: University of California Press, 1984), pp. 85–92.

26. Hugo Münsterberg, *The Film: A Psychological Study* [first published as *The Photoplay: A Psychological Study*], with a foreword by Richard Griffin (Mineola: Dover, [1916] 1970), p. 45. Subsequent references to this edition are given in the text.

27. Ludwig Wittgenstein, *Tractatus Logico-Philosophicus*, translated by C. K. Ogden, with an introduction by Bertrand Russell (Mineola: Dover, [1921] 1999), p. 46.

28. Crane, *The Complete Poems*, pp. 103, 105; emphases in original. Subsequent references to this edition are given in the text.

29. James Joyce, *Ulysses: The 1922 Text*, edited with an introduction by Jeri Johnson (Oxford: Oxford University Press, 1993), p. 267.

30. James Joyce, *Ulysses*, p. 267; John Gage, *Colour and Culture: Practice and Meaning from Antiquity to Abstraction* (London: Thames and Hudson, 1995), p. 233.

31. Frederick Vinton Hunt, *Origins in Acoustics: The Science of Sound from Antiquity to the Age of Newton* (New Haven: Yale University Press, 1978), p. 32; Gillian Beer, *Open Fields: Science in Cultural Encounter* (New York: Oxford University Press, 1996), p. 298.

32. Beer, *Open Fields*, ch. 13.
33. Leigh Eric Schmidt, *Hearing Things: Religion, Illusion, and the American Enlightenment* (Cambridge, MA: Harvard University Press, 2000), p. 24.
34. John Tyndall, *Sound: A Course of Eight Lectures* (London: Longmans, Green and Co., 1867), p. 242.
35. Persifor Frazer, Jr, 'Some Microscopical Observations of the Phonograph Record', *Proceedings of the American Philosophical Society* 17:101 (1878), pp. 531–6.
36. Richard Paget, *Human Speech: Some Observations, Experiments, and Conclusions as to the Nature, Origin, Purpose and Possible Improvement of Human Speech* (London: Kegan Paul, Trench, Trubner, 1930), p. 88.
37. Milton Metfessel, *Phonophotography in Folk Music: American Negro Folk Songs in New Notation*, with an introduction by Carl E. Seashore (Chapel Hill, NC: University of North Carolina Press, 1928).
38. Ralph K. Potter, George A. Kopp and Harriet C. Green, *Visible Speech* (New York: D. Van Nostrand, 1947).
39. Erich M. von Hornbostel, 'The Unity of the Senses' (1927), in Willis D. Ellis (ed.), *A Source Book of Gestalt Psychology*, with an introduction by Kurt Koffka (London: Kegan Paul, Trench, Trubner, 1938), pp. 210–16; p. 214 cited.
40. Alfred Kubin, *The Other Side*, translated by Mike Mitchell (Sawtry, Cambridgeshire: Dedalus, [1908] 2000), p. 135.
41. On musico-painterly analogies, see Christopher Butler, *Early Modernism: Literature, Music and Painting in Europe, 1900–1916* (Oxford: Oxford University Press, 1994).
42. Gladys Fabre, 'A Universal Language for the Arts: Interdisciplinarity as a Practice, Film as a Model', in Gladys Fabre and Doris Wintgens Hötte (eds), *Constructing a New World: Van Doesburg and the International Avant-Garde*, consultant editor Michael White (London: Tate Publishing, 2009), pp. 46–57; pp. 49–51 cited.
43. See Richter's retrospective gloss on *Universelle Sprache* in Hans Richter, 'My Experience with Movement in Painting and in Film', in Gyorgy Kepes (ed.), *The Nature and Art of Motion* (London: Studio Vista, 1965), pp. 142–57.
44. D. H. Lawrence, *Aaron's Rod* (Harmondsworth: Penguin, [1922] 1950), p. 51.
45. D. H. Lawrence, *The Trespasser* (Harmondsworth: Penguin, [1912] 1960), p. 5. Subsequent references to this edition are given in the text.
46. David Brewster, *The Kaleidoscope: Its History, Theory and Construction, with its Applications to the Fine and Useful Arts*, 2nd edn (London: John Murray, 1858), pp. 158–9.
47. Adrian Bernard Klein, *Colour-Music: The Art of Light* (London: Crosby Lockwood and Son, 1926), pp. xv, 31, 33; emphasis removed.
48. Klein, *Colour-Music*, p. vi.
49. Adrian Bernard Klein, *Colour Cinematography* (London: Chapman and Hall, 1936).
50. A. Wallace Rimington, *Colour Music: The Art of Mobile Colour*, with prefatory notes by Hubert von Herkomer and W. Brown (London: Hutchinson, 1912), p. 29.
51. Lind recorded these ideas in a manuscript deposited in the British Museum, but since destroyed. For a reconstruction of his thinking, see Jeremy Kargon, 'Harmonizing These Two Arts: Edmund Lind's *The Music of Colour*', *Journal of Design History* 21:1 (2010), pp. 1–14.
52. Simon Shaw-Miller, *Visible Deeds of Music: Art and Music from Wagner to Cage* (New Haven: Yale University Press, 2002), pp. 65–6.
53. Shaw-Miller, *Visible Deeds of Music*, pp. 59–60.
54. Harry Chapin Plummer, 'Color Music – A New Art created with the Aid of Science', *Scientific American* 15:112 (10 April 1915), pp. 343–51; p. 343 cited.

55. Shaw-Miller, *Visible Deeds of Music*, p. 63.
56. Leonid Sabaniev, 'Scriabin's "Prometheus"', in Wassily Kandinsky and Franz Marc (eds), *The Blaue Reiter Almanac*, edited and with an introduction by Klaus Lankheit, translated by Henning Falkenstein with Manug Terzian and Gertrude Hinderlie (London: Tate Publishing, [1912] 2006), pp. 127–40; pp. 130–1 cited.
57. Wassily Kandinsky, 'On Stage Composition', in Wassily Kandinsky and Franz Marc (eds), *The Blaue Reiter Almanac*, pp. 190–206; p. 190 cited.
58. Wassily Kandinsky, 'On the Question of Form', in Wassily Kandinsky and Franz Marc (eds), *The Blaue Reiter Almanac*, pp. 147–87; pp. 149, 189, 174 cited.
59. Kandinsky, 'On the Question of Form', pp. 161, 154; emphasis in original.
60. Kandinsky, 'On the Question of Form', pp. 164, 165.
61. Wassily Kandinsky, *Concerning the Spiritual in Art*, translated by Michael T. H. Sadler, with an introduction by Adrian Glew (London: Tate Publishing, [1912] 2006), p. 52.
62. Robert Delaunay, 'Notes on the Development of Robert Delaunay's Painting' (1939–40), in *The New Art of Color: The Writings of Robert and Sonia Delaunay*, edited with an introduction by Arthur A. Cohen, translated by David Shapiro and Arthur A. Cohen (New York: Viking Press, 1978), pp. 16–19; p. 17 cited; emphases in original.
63. Perloff, *The Futurist Moment*, p. 15.
64. Perloff, *The Futurist Moment*, p. 29.
65. Kandinsky, 'On Stage Composition', p. 201.
66. Daniel Albright, *Untwisting the Serpent: Modernism in Music, Literature, and Other Arts* (Chicago: University of Chicago Press, 2000).
67. Irving Babbitt, *The New Laokoon: An Essay on the Confusion of the Arts* (London: Constable, 1910), p. 183.
68. Lawrence E. Marks, 'On Coloured-Hearing Synaesthesia: Cross-Modal Translation of Sensory Dimensions', in Simon Baron Cohen and John E. Harrison (eds), *Synaestheisa: Classic and Contemporary Readings* (Oxford: Blackwell, 1997), pp. 49–98; pp. 52–6 cited.
69. Shaw-Miller, *Visible Deeds of Music*, p. 70.
70. P. E. Vernon, 'Synaesthesia in Music', *Psyche* 10:4 (1930), pp. 22–40; p. 37 cited.
71. Vernon, 'Synaesthesia in Music', p. 22.
72. Raymond H. Wheeler and Thomas D. Cutsforth, 'Synaesthesia, A Form of Perception', *Psychological Review* 29:3 (1922), pp. 212–20; p. 213 cited. Subsequent references to this edition are given in the text.
73. I am grateful to Graham Taylor, of the University of Nottingham, for directing me to Huneker. See also Kevin T. Dann, *Bright Colors Falsely Seen: Synaesthesia and the Search for Transcendental Knowledge* (New Haven: Yale University Press, 1998).
74. James Huneker, *Visionaries* (London: T. Werner Laurie, [1905] 1906), pp. 106–7.
75. James Huneker, *Melomaniacs* (London: T. Werner Laurie, [1902] 1906), pp. 290–1.
76. Bryher, *Development* (London: Constable, 1920), p. 57.
77. Bryher, *Development*, pp. 163–4.
78. Bryher, *Two Selves* (Paris: Contact Publishing, 1923), pp. 9, 14.
79. Bryher, *Development*, p. 165.
80. William O. Krohn, 'Pseudo-Chromesthesia, or the Association of Colors with Words, Letters and Sounds', *American Journal of Psychology* 5:1 (1892), pp. 20–41; p. 20 cited; emphasis in original.
81. Virginia Woolf, *Jacob's Room*, edited with an introduction by Kate Flint (Oxford:

Oxford University Press, [1922] 1999), p. 143. Subsequent references to this edition are given in the text.

82. Though see also Richard Semon, *Mnemic Psychology*, translated by Bella Duffy, with an introduction by Vernon Lee (London: George Allen and Unwin, [1909] 1923).

83. Morton Prince, *The Unconscious: The Fundamentals of Human Personality Normal and Abnormal*, 2nd revised edn (New York: Macmillan, [1914] 1921), p. 119. Subsequent references to this edition are given in the text.

84. Prince himself uses the term 'neurogram' as a chapter title.

85. E. T. A. Hoffmann, 'Master Flea' (1822), in *The Golden Pot, and Other Tales*, translated with an introduction and notes by Ritchie Robertson (Oxford: Oxford University Press, 2000), pp. 239–375.

86. Lisa Gitelman, *Scripts, Grooves, and Writing Machines: Representing Technology in the Edison Era* (Stanford: Stanford University Press, 1999), pp. 1, 24.

87. Theodor W. Adorno, 'The Form of the Phonograph Record' (1934), translated by Thomas Y. Levin, in *Essays on Music*, selected with an introduction, commentary, and notes by Richard Leppert (Berkeley: University of California Press, 2002), pp. 277–82; pp. 279, 280 cited. Subsequent references to this edition are given in the text.

88. James Joyce, *Ulysses*, p. 189.

89. W. E. B. Du Bois, *The Souls of Black Folk* (New York: Dover, [1903] 1994).

90. Toni Morrison, *Beloved* (New York: Plume/Penguin, [1987] 1988), p. 199.

91. A. Tolmer, *Mise en Page: The Theory and Practice of Lay-Out* (London: The Studio, 1931), ch. 4, unnumbered page.

92. Thomas Mann, *Doctor Faustus*, translated by H. T. Lowe-Porter (Harmondsworth: Penguin, [1947] 1968), p. 62.

93. Max Weber, *The Rational and Social Foundations of Music*, edited and translated by Don Martindale, Johannes Riedel and Gertrude Neuwirth (Carbondale: Southern Illinois University Press, [1921] 1958), p. 88.

94. Weber, *Rational and Social Foundations*, p. 84.

95. Carlos Chávez, *Toward a New Music: Music and Electricity*, translated by Herbert Weinstock (New York: De Capo, [1937] 1975), p. 40.

96. Edmund Dehnert, 'The Consciousness of Music Wrought by Musical Notation', in Joseph W. Slade and Judith Yaross Lee (eds), *Beyond the Two Cultures: Essays on Science, Technology, and Literature* (Ames: Iowa State University Press, 1990), pp. 99–116.

97. Arnold Schoenberg, *Theory of Harmony* [*Harmonielehre*], translated by Roy E. Carter (London: Faber and Faber, [1911; 3rd edn 1922] 1978), p. 317.

Chapter 4

MODERNISING MUSIC

That music should exist at all is one of the most remarkable things about the world. To those who are moved by it intensely, it can seem both expressive of intimate urges and yet otherworldly, as if its making were more like a discovery of something outside of us than a product of pure human agency (as we saw in Chapter 1, this idea can be identified with Schopenhauer). For Arnold Schoenberg, one of the towering figures of twentieth-century music, something like the tension between the two 'halves' of this experience is inherent in all musical creation. In *Harmonielehre* (1911; 3rd edn 1922; translated into English 1978), his most celebrated work of theory, Schoenberg writes of the composer as a *craftsman*, working up materials, one imagines, like any other artist. And yet in seeming contrast to these others, who work on such relatively inert materials as, say, canvas, wood, or stone, the composer works upon an 'organism' – that is, something *living*, with its own autonomous plastic and developmental tendencies.[1] Thus, Schoenberg cautions, if alterations made to a composition are 'alien to the nature of this organism, then the majority of its consequences will be harmful' too (p. 53). If, however, the composer strives resolutely towards 'effects inherent' in an organism's 'nature', compositional success will be ensured, for 'it will always turn out that one has at the same time been obeying a necessity of this organism, that one has been promoting its developmental tendencies' (p. 53). Artistic excellence, in this context, then, consists in acting as nature's midwife – not its rival. Good composition entails subordinating the

---

creative will to forces of which it might otherwise fancy itself the master and creator.

This intriguing mix of metaphors – or calculated equivocation, if it is not a full-blown dialectic (throughout *Harmonielehre* as a whole, it is arguably all three) – between 'nature' and the organic, on one hand, and 'culture' and the man-made, on the other, is no mere surface ripple on Schoenberg's argument. Rather, it animates his claims about musical history in general. Speaking of tonality, the principle ubiquitous throughout much of western musical history, whereby each piece of music is governed by or written 'in' a given key or sequence thereof, he argues that contrary to long habituation, this system is neither more nor less 'natural' than any other.[2] For while 'nature admits of such diverse interpretations' that tonality can indeed be identified with it, a hard look at the facts compels the view that 'still other systems could surely be inferred from nature just as naturally' (p. 93). More specifically, he contends that precisely through its long ubiquity, tonality has obscured this fact, to the extent that it now appears 'a second nature. At present we can hardly, or just gradually, escape the effects of this artificial, cultural product' (p. 48). And it was precisely in order to 'escape' this 'product' that, in fact, Schoenberg embarked on the wider musical project for which *Harmonielehre* is a de facto manifesto: that of overhauling, working through, if not ultimately transcending tonality, through systematic use of 'dissonant' intervals considered 'foreign' by conventional harmonic theory. Here, he finds both precedent and justification for this project in the role that 'vagrant' or illicit chords have, allegedly, performed in western musical history:

> It is remarkable: the vagrant chords do not appear directly by way of nature, yet they accomplish her will [. . .] They are the issue of inbreeding, inbreeding among the laws of [the tonal] system. And that precisely these logical consequences of the system are the very undoing of the system itself, that the end of the system is brought about with such inescapable cruelty by its own functions, brings to mind the thought that death is the consequence of life [. . .] [I]t was precisely these vagrant chords that led inexorably to the dissolution of tonality [. . .]. (p. 196)

In other words, though vagrant chords are, strictly speaking, 'cultural,' their effect is to inadvertently expose the system they disrupt as no less cultural as well, rather than the inviolable and unchangeable edifice its mis-recognition as 'nature' would suggest. Or, to put this another way: vagrancy is the repressed 'truth' of tonality, in that its appearance points towards the existence of systems beyond tonality itself, for which such chords are not an aberration but entirely 'natural'. So it is that according to Schoenberg's view of musical history, tonality (in its conventional form) is set on an inexorable course towards destruction, as culture's stays are first eroded, then swamped by nature's wider empire. Culture grows by nature's gift, but then, extending this same process, is exploded from within.

The intricacy, if not inextricability, of nature's relation to culture here should come as no surprise. For late nineteenth-century theorists of music such as Edmund Gurney, as we have seen in Chapter 1, the question raised by music was above all to which part of nature this particular strand of culture owed its origin (Gurney's answer, sexual selection, is interestingly both close and at a signal slant to Schoenberg's 'inbreeding'). In the twentieth century, Adorno characterised music as 'the immediate manifestation of impulse and the locus of its taming', arriving at a similar conclusion by a different route; here, music is both expressive of primordial energies (so 'natural') and, as such, dependent on the 'cultural' attainments of technique and moderation.[3] But perhaps the key articulation of the 'nature'/'culture' opposition in our period is Claude Debussy's composition *Prélude à l'après-midi d'un faune* (1894); a work which, *pace* Schoenberg, is treated by some writers as the first decisive break with tonality in the western 'classical' tradition.[4] As its title indicates, the work concerns a faun, one of those creatures of ancient myth whose combination of animal and human features represents a dream of natural bliss without cultural constraints. Debussy's literary source, Mallarmé's poem *L'après-midi d'un faune* (1876), evokes a lack of sensual constraint especially; Vaslav Nijinsky's notorious 1912 ballet setting of the score capitalises on (if not exaggerates) this by having the faun first dance suggestively with nymphs and then masturbate. Within the score itself, Debussy deploys a range of adventurous techniques: lush orchestration; shifting metres; and, not least, unorthodox harmonic structures such as the whole-tone scale (formed of six consecutive tonal 'jumps' rather than the combination of tonal and semi-tonal steps that make up conventional major and minor scales), and the tritone (two notes separated by three whole tones). And it is the congruence of these techniques with the *Faun*'s thematic burden that explains the work's particular historical significance. For though the score does not exactly seek to represent the ideational content of this burden, term for term, neither does it shrink from broad suggestions of this burden when possible: to cite the most obvious instance, the flute played by the faun in Mallarmé's poem is echoed by the tonally ambiguous flute solo with which Debussy's score begins. In other words, Debussy's harmonically adventurous and other avant-garde effects – the very things that constitute his modernity, in strictly musical terms – are pegged to an archaising idea of 'faun-ness'. The link from text to score thus depends on an implicit wager, according to which the most primordial or ancient 'content' is best served by the most 'modern' technique or form. 'Culture' – and here we find a twist on Schoenberg – in the guise of atonality and so on, represents the royal road to 'nature'.

It will readily be seen how in addition to the nature/culture opposition,

Debussy's *Faun* engages others the first one opens out upon – ancient and modern, sensuous and sensually restrained, animal and human – just as Schoenberg's involves the related yet distinct pairing of 'craftsmanship' and 'organism'. In both respects, in fact, these cases are exemplary, because nothing is more characteristic of the modernist musical imaginary in general than to confound, bestride and simply mobilise such oppositions at almost every turn. For once we are primed to see this sort of thing, it helps connect the most diverse array of contexts. Jazz, for instance, regarded by many as the *sine qua non* of musical modernity, was identified just as often with 'primitive' expressive traits as with modernity itself – and sometimes, was identified with both at the same time. Researchers into 'folk' music, while being crucially reliant on new recording devices like the gramophone and phonograph for the collection and analysis of material, regularly identified the same machines with a trend whereby the very future of such music was endangered. And as the case of Schoenberg already intimates, the desire for radical innovation amongst avantgarde composers was sometimes allied with a deep respect for musical tradition. Oppositions here are not mutually exclusive but interwoven and attuned.

This interwoven-ness of contrasting values is an abiding theme throughout this chapter, each section of which treats a different set of trends, ideas or genres. The chapter as a whole aspires to cover most if not all major developments in musical history of the first half of the twentieth century, though this coverage is often partial and condensed – necessarily so, in a non-specialist volume such as this. And it is both for this and for connected reasons that this chapter, more than any other in this book, requires certain disclaimers at its start. Because it is far better for a study of this nature, in my view, to focus on the ground that music shares with other disciplines, I have tended to draw most on sources that aid this process, by treating music as socially and philosophically located, rather than as a law unto itself (I accept, however, that it is as just saw a 'law' that music may need to be discussed in other contexts). Relatedly, though I do discuss musical theory, I have tried to keep this to a minimum wherever this does not seem essential to some wider point. If the net result of these decisions is to make the chapter emphasise ideas *about* music rather than the thing itself, then so be it: ideas about music, I would say, are extremely interesting; and in any case, other sources may be consulted by the reader if more extensive coverage of intra-musical technicalities or detailed musical history is required.[5] Finally, rather than bombard the reader with great names, the chapter focuses on a relatively small, slender clutch of figures whose ideas and work help 'quilt' the chapter's own concerns together. No figure is more opportune in this respect than Schoenberg, whose views on musical history and dissonance we now return to. For no theme in modern music's history, arguably, is of more importance than musicians' understanding of historicity itself.

HISTORICITY AND DISSONANCE

In music, almost more than in any other subject which is at all controlled by the mind of man, there is a ceaseless and inevitable progress.

Herbert Antcliffe, *Living Music* (1912)[6]

Belief in 'progress' came naturally to many composers nurtured in the nineteenth century, that epoch of conviction of the inexorable march of history, whether in Hegelian, Marxist, nationalist or other forms. Nobody illustrates this better than Schoenberg, who saw his personal challenge to tonality in terms of supra-personal if not supra-human laws. As we have already seen, Schoenberg identifies tonality's demise with 'vagrant chords', those signs or seeds of dissolution allegedly thrown up by tonality itself; we can now see how insistently he links such phenomena of the musical past not only to the present as represented by his own career but also to the future towards which he thinks both this past and this present point. 'My aim is [. . .] to show that one *must* arrive at these results' he says at one point, sufficiently indicating his view that there is now simply no other path for reputable composers to follow than his own, away from conventional tonality (p. 70; emphasis in original). Mounting the same argument from the opposite historical direction, as it were, he analyses passages by Bach to show how the same outré, ostensibly illicit harmonies typical of 'ultramodernists' like himself are present (albeit in disguised form) in even the most hallowed music of the past (pp. 70, 324).[7] Returning to the bio-generative or hereditary metaphors he favours most, Schoenberg insists: 'Everything alive contains the future within it. Living means begetting and giving birth. Everything that now is strives toward what is to come' (p. 369). Thus music's history describes a single path, from which no step of any moment deviates.

Schoenberg's emphasis on nature as both the model for and ultimate ground of art was clearly passed on to his students, to judge from Anton Webern's *The Path to the New Music* (1932–3) (a text and title we will return to later on). Here, the younger composer invokes Goethe's 'primeval plant' – an archetype supposedly implicit in all varieties of plant extant, however superficially dissimilar – to explain music's core identity across a range of periods and genres.[8] However, Schoenberg's own key theoretical coordinate (as Webern well knew, judging from his own allusions to it) was not bio-morphology but nineteenth-century acoustics: specifically, what Schoenberg calls 'overtone theory', whereby fundamental tones – the lowest-pitched and most distinct of certain sound sources, such as strings, as used in musical instruments – are distinguished from 'overtones' (which in turn are higher-pitched in the harmonic series and less easily discerned).[9] Though musicians had long-known of this distinction, *Harmonielehre* gives it a distinctive twist, arguing that 'the evolution of music [. . .] has drawn into the stock of artistic resources more and more of the harmonic possibilities inherent in the tone' (p. 21). In other words, musical history consists in a progressive 'tuning' of the collective ear to an ever greater number and variety of overtones accompanying each and every (or some archetypal) fundamental. Moreover, since overtones may in fact occur at intervals 'foreign' to conventional tonality, as well as otherwise, the distinction between 'dissonance' and 'consonance' is here, as in other instances – remembering especially how 'vagrant chords' betray tonality as 'cultural,' rather than 'natural' – exposed as arbitrary. Rather than one subset of overtones being deemed 'natural,' and the other not, then, 'It all simply depends on the growing ability of the analyzing ear to familiarize itself with the remote overtones, thereby expanding the conception of what is euphonious' (p. 21). Thus, Schoenberg's post-*Harmonielehre* stated 'hope that in a few decades audiences will recognize the *tonality* of this music called *atonal*' and not acknowledge 'any other difference than a *gradual* one between the tonality of yesterday and the tonality of today'.[10] As we have seen before in a slightly different context, Schoenberg thus insists that 'nature', not any 'culture'-bound harmonic 'system', sets limits to which musicians are ultimately accountable.

For Schoenberg, then, musical progress is above all a matter of first properly distinguishing nature from culture, and then fully embracing all the gifts the former brings. He thus exemplifies the 'metanarrative of resource extension' which, as Daniel Albright notes, governs many early twentieth-century interpretations of musical history – one of two such metanarratives to which we may now turn.[11] In the first of these, 'resource' may designate any set of musical building-blocks composers or performers may make use of, and 'extension', the proliferation of these over time – a proliferation many early twentieth-century observers regarded as self-evident. Thus the French composer and teacher Nadia Boulanger (who in the course of her career taught many more renowned composers, such as Aaron Copeland, 1900–1990, and Oliver Messiaen, 1908–1992), in her 'Lectures on Modern Music' (1926), identifies the sheer range of musical intervals deployed by contemporary composers as the key factor distinguishing them from their historic counterparts (in 'Antiquity', she specifies, chords tend to involve up to just three harmonic intervals; by contrast, in the present, chords may involve anything up to thirteen).[12] Turning to a different set of 'resources', the contemporaneous British musical historian Adam Carse, in 1925, explains the history of orchestration (if not music as such) in terms of technological developments such as the changing means available for making musical instruments, suggesting further that these factors to some extent subsume more 'purely' compositional matters: 'Intimately and inseparably connected with the history of orchestration are: progress in the art and technique of musical composition; improvements in the construction of musical instruments, both of which are [. . .] associated with the growth of instrumental technique'.[13]

'Resources', then, for Carse, are more diverse than in either Boulanger's or Schoenberg's accounts – and, as such, are both more interdependent and distinctly *social*. What Boulanger, Carse and Schoenberg share, however, is a sense of their own present as close to if not coincident with history's 'progressive' apex. In this respect, they recall another British writer on music, Herbert Antcliffe, as quoted in the epigraph to this book's present section, to the effect that music's progress is 'ceaseless' and inexorable.

The second 'metanarrative' of music's historic trajectory, meanwhile, may be related to the first, insofar as this, too, relates to intramusical 'resources'. But here, the resources concerned are much more abstract, while the narrative is conveyed – insofar as this is possible – by music itself. As Karol Berger writes, music from the late eighteenth century onwards tends to make 'time's arrow, the experience of linear time, its essential subject matter'; to dramatise time's passing by 'filling' it with clearly delineated episodes and longer stretches of climax, suspense and resolution.[14] Recalling that (at least according to evidence considered in Chapter 1) time is an essential precondition of all music, then we may see how this particular historic shift might be interpreted as self-reflexive – how music of and since the late eighteenth century might be seen as 'about itself' in a somehow more thorough-going way than that of previous eras. For our second metanarrative, therefore (which we are by no means necessarily endorsing, just describing), music changes not just though the extension of resources, but also through increased self-consciousness of this very fact – that is, self-consciousness of what its formal and technical resources *are*. To hear this from an historical (if fictional) protagonist: Adrian Leverkühn, in Mann's *Doctor Faustus*, declares that in the work of Beethoven, especially (a key figure in late eighteenth- and early nineteenth-century music if ever there was one), 'the development, or working out' of sonata form, hitherto but an incidental detail of that form, 'becomes universal, becomes the centre' of music in this idiom.[15] The sustained elaboration of material over time, in other words, becomes a pivot around which other features of a composition turn – not only within those works explicitly identified as 'sonatas', but also others, including those representing the 'classic' nineteenth-century symphony, that follow the sonata's developmental protocols.[16] This, then, is one important reason *why* 'belief in progress' came 'naturally' to composers (as I put it earlier) nurtured in the nineteenth century. To such composers, 'progress' is not extrinsic but intrinsic to music's very substance.

Might these two historic metanarratives, or their objects, interact? Building on the claim that in the second, the resources of the first becomes self-conscious, we can conceive a situation whereby such self-consciousness becomes a resource in its own right – which then in turn becomes self-conscious, and so on. The objects of each metanarrative thus feed into one another, creating a kind of positive-feedback loop whereby change is steered more forcibly than by either object working independently. Though no such claim is made directly, an argument exhibiting this basic 'structure' (if, admittedly, not quite this specific content) can be gleaned from Max Weber's *The Rational and Social Foundations of Music*, whose views on musical notation we examined in the last chapter. Here, harmony and melody are identified as opposing principles at work within any given piece of 'chordal' music: 'Although harmonically conditioned and bound, melody, especially in chordal music, is not reducible to harmonic terms'; thus, 'chordal rationalization lives only in continual tension with melodicism which it can never completely devour'.[17] Thus too, the first step of what is, for us, effectively a two-step argument. For in the second step, the same opposition is identified as the progressive force *between* individual pieces, as in the following account of the demise of ancient Greek musical conventions – and incidentally, of the emergence of 'chordal' harmony itself:

> It appears that in Hellenic art music during the period of its greatest creativity the very striving for expressiveness led to an extremely melodic development which shattered the harmonic elements of the system. Since the end of the Middle Ages in the Occident, the same striving led to an entirely different result, the development of chordal harmony.[18]

Just as 'nature' continuously erodes the stays of 'culture' according to Schoenberg, then, so melody 'shatters' harmonic protocols for Weber. However, whilst Weber's thinking on the shift 'from chord to chord' locates this process on a microcosmic scale, he now locates the same process macrocosmically, switching his focus from the individual piece to the totality of such pieces, in their historical relations. The interplay of harmony and melody, in other words, is simultaneously what 'progresses' works from start to finish and what Antcliffe and other historicist commentators might consider wider-scale historic 'progress'.

It is with all of the above in mind that we should return to Wagner – as, indeed, at other points throughout this book. As we saw in Chapter 2, his music-drama *Tristan and Isolde* is known across a swathe of culture for its concern with transgressive sexuality. But we can now add that amongst musicians, particularly, it is best known both for its extreme chromaticism and for the so-called '*Tristan* chord': on the one hand, a compositional technique of using all twelve notes of the chromatic scale; on the other, a distinctive assemblage of four such notes, featured at points throughout the score, that (from the perspective of conventional harmonic theory) is strongly dissonant. With respect to our earlier discussion, these features are significant principally for their help articulating thematic content: as Jim Samson comments, the use of chromaticism especially acquires 'dramatic symbolism, underlying as it does the contrast between "passion" as a disruptive force and the order and stability of "civilization"' in *Tristan*'s plot.[19] But with respect to the present chapter's discussion, these features are significant also for their combined effects of tonal uncertainty, due to the facts that chromaticism bends and stretches tonality by definition, and that the *Tristan* chord, especially, suggests several key signatures (for instance, A minor) without being immediately identifiable with either.[20] Putting these two things together, we may see how *Tristan* might be mapped on to the distinction between microcosmic and macrocosmic forms of progress just drawn with respect to Weber. For in the first respect, the work's chromaticism, in an 'intra-work' sense, can be said to help drive Wagner's themes to their 'logical' conclusion (the titular couple's *Liebestod*, as glossed above in Chapter 2). And in the second respect, the same chromaticism, in an 'extra-' or 'inter-work' sense, allied to the *Tristan* chord, might be held to 'announce' the historic shift of music generally towards atonality.

The second part of this claim, in particular, has often been advanced: witness none other than Schoenberg's identification of the *Tristan* chord in *Harmonielehre*, as – inevitably – an exemplar of 'vagrancy' (p. 257). But a perhaps more vivid case can be made for the first part of this claim, according to which dissonance has strong if not innate links to transgressive subject matter. A key coordinate for this idea is Nietzsche's *The Birth of Tragedy*. As we also saw in Chapter 2, Nietzsche here pits the Apolline, the principle of individuation, against the Dionysiac, the principle of 'one-ness' (and also, music). However, in what may seem a countervailing gesture, Nietzsche also identifies the Dionysiac with *horror*: specifically, the thrilling and ultimately rejuvenating sense of horror said to characterise audiences contemplating Greek tragedy. It is in this context that Nietzsche writes: 'The pleasure produced by the tragic myth has the same origin as the pleasurable perception of dissonance in music'; moreover, music and tragedy itself are 'to an equal extent expressions of the Dionysiac capacity of a people, and they are inseparable'.[21] So when Nietzsche also states that highly crafted dissonance – here, we may think especially of *Tristan* – provokes responses analogous to those of tragedy, we may see why he identifies Wagner (along with other German composers) with a revival of the Dionysiac spirit '*in our contemporary world!*'[22] Thus the fact that *The Birth of Tragedy* is actually dedicated to Wagner, in addition to being (as we have commented before) substantially the most 'Wagnerian' of all his works (it is in this book too that *Tristan*'s third act is credited with literally annihilating power, as again we saw in Chapter 2). Dissonance, then, according to this argument, has a privileged relation to emotions perhaps otherwise untapped since the works of Aeschylus and Sophocles. Insofar as these emotions are commensurate with 'horror', dissonance, in music, thus represents an auditory stare into the abyss.

This, at least, is the impression given by many, if not all of the dramatic works written by composers in the post-Nietzsche (and also post-*Tristan* and atonal) era. In Schoenberg's *Erwartung* ('*Expectation*', 1909), highly unconventional harmony is harnessed to a scenario whose climax is the dis-covery by a woman of her dead husband. In *Wozzeck* (1925), by Schoenberg's pupil Alban Berg, the protagonist murders his wife and ultimately drowns. In Berg's *Lulu* (1937), the serial amorous entanglements of another protagonist end with Lulu's murder by Jack the Ripper. And in Richard Strauss's *Salome* (1906), the beheading of John the Baptist is trumped, dramatically speaking, by yet another protagonist's death, this time at the hands of her (in previous scenes, incestuously aroused) stepfather. Though such topological 'encoding' may ultimately be contingently and not intrinsically attached to dissonance, the latter's links to 'tragic' subject matter in such works are so forcefully artic-ulated that one can easily see how a more binding association, at least amongst some audiences, might persist.[23]

All the works surveyed above, apart from Strauss's, are by Schoenberg or a pupil, and we may conclude this section with some further observations about the 'school' these composers represent. As is well known, the elder composer later upped the ante on his campaign against conventional tonality by inventing a particular compositional method: the so-called serial, twelve-note, twelve-tone or tone-row system, whose key stipulation is that all twelve notes of the chromatic scale must be used in any given composition, before any one of these can be repeated (once a basic sequence involving all twelve notes is established, according to Schoenberg's instructions, this can be repeated, reversed, turned head-to-foot or transposed to a different starting note, in practically boundless combinations). The very title of Webern's *The Path to the New Music* encodes a partisan evaluation of this system, with Schoenberg as the heroic 'path'-finder, and 'New[ness]' a qualitative step beyond the old. We have seen how this text follows the teacher's 'naturalising' rhetoric already, and may now note how it even surpasses its model in this respect, Webern writing: 'there is no essential contrast between a product of nature and a product of art'; thus, accordingly, the twelve-note system itself has not been 'invented' but (as if it were a 'natural' law or species) 'discovered' (pp. 10, 32). Since belief in nature's sanction, here as in Schoenberg, goes hand in hand with a commensurate belief in history's, self-confidence about the latter is ramped up as well, Webern contending that 'ever since music has been written, all the great composers have instinctively had [the twelve-note system] before them as a goal' (p. 42). And in relation to that system, Webern makes a fascinating link between tonality and *repetition* – a link that ultimately yields a distinc-tion between the twelve-tone system and its predecessors in terms of what we might call 'narrativity'. In the following passage, a programmatic contrast is drawn between the 'old' music – represented, once again, by Beethoven – and the 'new' music of the Schoenberg school including Webern himself (the fol-lowing passage concludes in the past tense, with Webern recalling how he and his colleagues came to understand their mission):

What happens when I try to express a key strongly? The tonic ['key-' note of any given key] must be rather over-emphasised – so that listeners notice, otherwise it won't be enough to give satisfaction. It's just in Beethoven that we find this very strongly developed; the tonic is constantly reiterated, especially toward the end [of a piece], in order to make it stand out enough [. . .] *Now*, however, the exact opposite became a necessity; since there was no tonic any more [. . .] we felt the need to *prevent* one note being over-emphasised, to prevent any note's 'taking advantage' of being repeated. (p. 39; emphases in original)

For 'new' musicians, there is 'no tonic anymore' – for reasons that have, I hope, been made apparent since the beginning of this chapter. The 'end'-directedness of tonal works (especially, as we have seen, since the triumph of sonata form), therefore, must now be actively resisted, else any note in the chromatic scale illicitly assume the tonic's now-exploded privilege. Momentum, in sequential terms, is thus at loggerheads with tonal 'justice': 'All twelve notes have equal rights'; yet 'If one of them is repeated before the other eleven have occurred it would acquire a special status' (p. 52). In other words, the key justification for the twelve-note system, at least for Webern, lies in preventing just the 'satisfaction' undue repetition brings, for it is under this – and only this – condition that a whole new world of harmonic possibility can be revealed.

None of this should be taken to suggest, of course, that work by Schoenberg's school lacks any sense of drama, or indeed other forms of aesthetic satisfaction. This work's refusal to conform to harmonic expectations creates (if nothing else) its own frisson. But there is an irony to be noted here, revealed by juxtaposing the musico-historic theories we have considered throughout this section against the sort of works Webern implicitly describes. For if 'vagrancy' inexorably drives music forward at what we have called the macrocosmic level – to identify the Schoenbergian category we have now invoked repeatedly with one we have identified with Weber – then, by Webern's account, it culminates in works from which palpable, if not conceptual inexorability has been systematically stripped out. The very force identified by Schoenberg with the relentless march of progress at the 'macro' level leads, at the 'micro' level, to (a certain) 'progress's' suspense.

Pitch division, Rhythmic Chords and Synthesisers

Not everyone, of course, agreed with Schoenberg's means of 'modernising' music. Even those who shared his interest in unorthodox tonalities often took quite different paths towards that end, while others turned to different 'structural' variables in music as a focus for their innovations (sometimes, these tendencies coincided).[24] Four such foci will be considered in this section: pitch, rhythm, timbre and instrumentation.

Concern with pitch, of course, was Schoenberg's own preserve, insofar as he thought western tonality's original sin consisted in its repression of certain notes (assuming any given key) within the chromatic scale. But to other modernists, the chromatic scale was itself the problem, chopping into arbitrary 'bits' a range of phenomena naturally spanning a continuum. For Ferruccio Busoni, therefore, in *Sketch of a New Esthetic of Music* (1907), music of the future must liberate itself from all idea of fixed notes, and the notation system that serves to conceptually lock these into place – for 'Nature created *an infinite gradation*' of pitches, not merely twelve, whilst notation represents but 'part of a fraction of one diffracted ray from that Sun, "Music"', in its entirety.[25] Similarly, the Futurist painter and musician Luigi Russolo, in 1914, argues that the 'empty or filled dots' of conventional notation should be replaced by a continuous line, better suited to the progressive slides and slurs of pitch he desired for his particular form of new music (on which more later).[26] Pursuing a similar agenda, though without rejecting scalar divisibility as such, Harry Partch (1901–1974) devised a scale involving no less than forty-three named notes, building instruments to match, in the interest of better capturing in music the tonal subtleties of speech.[27]

Meanwhile, pitch's relation to seemingly quite different musical variables also came under intense scrutiny. Perhaps surprisingly, a notable figure in this respect is Ezra Pound, who ranked an idiosyncratic but ultimately prescient theory of musical rhythm amongst his most cherished achievements. In *The Treatise on Harmony* (1924), and sporadic utterances subsequently, Pound draws on nineteenth-century acoustics' discovery that pitch is an expression of the number of vibrations made by a sound source over the course of one second (hence the term 'frequency'). Since this discovery establishes pitch's relationship to time and its division, Pound argues for a fundamental identity between pitch and other temporal parameters of music – most obviously, rhythm itself. Thus, what we tend to consider 'note'-based phenomena such as melody and harmony are best conceived as permutating rhythmic variables, whilst 'the percussion of the rhythm can enter the harmony as exactly as another note would'.[28] Of sadly negligible influence, these ideas were anticipated as early as 1919 by Henry Cowell, whose *New Musical Resources* (1930) perhaps had more success than Pound's text in informing subsequent avant-garde practice. Here, Cowell argues not only that pitch is akin to rhythm, but also that the latter might be elaborated with something like the former's multiplicity, rhythms being stacked upon each other in a single piece, producing metrical 'chords'.[29] Though technical constraints prevented clear realisation of Pound and Cowell's basic principles at anything but the theoretical level, this become relatively easy after the Second World War with the development of tape and other technology, making the manipulation of both pitch and rhythm possible beyond the range of more 'normal' instrumentation. A piece like Karl-Heinz

Stockhausen's *Kontakte* (1960) makes this programmatic. Here, a certain note is slowed electronically until it becomes imperceptible as anything other than a set of 'beats'; it is then speeded up until it once again becomes a clear 'pitch'.

And what of rhythm as more conventionally understood? Amongst musical audiences in the early twentieth century, this was associated most with two things: the work of Igor Stravinksy, in a 'classical' context; and the variously exhilarating or unconscionable rhythms of jazz, outside of it (as we shall see, these contrasting values represent the sort of extremes around which opinions of jazz tended to polarise). As a writer for the British journal *Music and Letters* wrote in 1930 (ironically, in the course of an argument intended to demonstrate that rhythm is *not* the most significant aspect of Stravinsky's work): 'Stravinsky is perhaps the only composer who has raised rhythm in itself to the dignity of an art. He has shown us that rhythm is not merely the division of time into equal beats, but a pulse animating the whole of time in music'.[30] The composer's *Le Sacre du printemps* (*The Rite of Spring*, 1913), especially, became canonised in this respect, frequently changing time-signature from bar to bar; Nijinsky's accompanying choreography sometimes required dancers to execute one 'count' with one part of their bodies while a different count was executed by another.[31] The latter represents a clue to the affinity with jazz – or rather, jazz's 'feeder' genre, ragtime, which one commentator (in 1915) associated with 'a special sort of dance in which the rhythm of the arms and shoulders conflicts with the rhythm of the feet'.[32] The same commentator, speaking more specifically of syncopation – the signatory rhythmic feature of ragtime, whereby accents are displaced from 'on' to 'off' beats – speaks to Cowell's concerns, as much as Stravinsky's, when stating that this music characteristically features 'a persistent syncopation on one [instrumental] part conflicting with exact rhythm in another'.[33]

All of these developments have analogues in timbre (or its associated innovations), the sonic 'character' peculiar to different instruments, instrumental combinations and playing techniques. Several composers from the 1940s onwards devised 'scales' for this and other non-pitched variables, before arranging these in 'series', à la Schoenberg.[34] Most popular genres evolved distinct timbral, no less than harmonic or rhythmic vocabularies, often materialised in distinct equipment, including the mutes used by brass players in jazz bands, or the knife or bottle-neck slides sometimes used by guitarists playing the blues (the latter, not coincidentally, enable 'slides' between semitones, recalling Busoni's and others' interest in microtonal pitch). From distinct use of existing instruments, it was but a short step to the invention of new ones, including Thaddeus Cahill's 'Telharmonium' (patented in 1897), a vast machine, broadcast via telephone, that has some claim to being the first synthesiser, or John Hanert's 'Electrical Orchestra' (1945), whose operating principles echo modernist composition itself in first breaking tones into constituents such as 'growth', 'duration' and 'intensity,' and then allowing these to be 'reassembled into coherent musical structures'.[35] In this context we may also note the use of 'non-'musical devices as de facto instruments, such as the aeroplane propellers and siren featured in George Antheil's *Ballet Mécanique* (1925). Pound echoes this in 'Machine Art' (1927–30), a posthumously published meditation on the musical possibilities of factory machinery; we may also here remember Pound's laudation of Antheil from the present volume's 'Introduction'.[36]

All these strands converge with Russolo, whose *The Art of Noises* (1913; revised edn 1916) is thus in some ways the most representative as well as most famous manifesto of musical modernism. As we have seen, he echoes Busoni's call for 'liberated' pitch; he also anticipates Pound and Cowell by seeing harmony and rhythm (and also timbre) as radically connected, underwriting his call for innovation across all these fronts in music simultaneously (pp. 28–9). But his most celebrated demand is that the very category of music be expanded to include its apparent 'other', noise, revealing whole new fields of art to those who would perceive them. 'Let us cross a large modern capital with our ears more sensitive that our eyes', he counsels: 'We will amuse ourselves by orchestrating together in our imagination the din of rolling shop shutters, the varied hubbub of train stations, iron works, thread mills, printing presses, electrical plants and subways' (p. 26). The task of modern music, therefore, is to give this 'hubbub' less fugitive and more substantial form – to immemorialise and valorise as 'art' what has hitherto been seen as merely (and usually, an unwelcome) part of 'life'.

But this is only part of Russolo's project. Though he is rightly seen as seminal for a whole tradition in music, associated with the likes of Pierre Schaeffer (1910–1995) (coiner, we remember, of the term 'acousmatic'), using 'found', environmental sound as raw material, more central to his own ambitions were the invention and construction of new instruments, producing sounds distinct from those encountered in other contexts. These were called *Intonarumori* ('noise instruments') and subdivided into further categories such as 'roarers', 'cracklers' and 'gurglers' (the latter apparently 'produce[d] a complex timbre, like water running through a rain gutter') (p. 80). Insofar as these emulated existing sounds, these too, like Cahill's Telharmonium, can be considered amongst the first synthesisers – a class of instruments that are after all defined by emulation of sound sources other than themselves. However, Russolo insisted that 'the *Art of Noises should not limit itself to an imitative reproduction*' of existing sounds, but aspire instead to make 'new' sounds, unparalleled elsewhere (pp. 27–8; emphasis in original). 'Beethoven and Wagner have stirred our nerves and hearts for many years', he concedes; but '[n]ow we have had enough of them' (p. 25). Conceptually, if not yet materially (no other composers seem to have taken up *Intonarumori* in Russolo's lifetime), the age of machine-made music was born.

PRECISION AND PRESERVATION

This would, however, have been a dire prospect to Béla Bartók, the more renowned composer whose thoughts on another form of 'mechanical music' (entirely automatic, without any 'live' performative or even compositional element) conclude with this appeal: 'May God protect our offspring from this plague!'[37] Notwithstanding this distaste, though, Bartók's broader commentary on new sound technology's involvement in music represents a good entrée to that topic generally, and to the use of nominally 'reproductive' technology in musical 'production' in particular. Especially useful is his distinction between fully machine-made, automated music and two other kinds, both considerably more advanced than the first in 1937, when he wrote the essay quoted from above. These are, firstly, music made by instruments for 'fixing' performances executed upon them 'for future times', and secondly, music emitted by devices that 'radiate music [. . .] into the air' (as Bartók further comments, these principles 'are sometimes combined').[38] Under the first heading, we may group player pianos and other instruments harnessing a conventional keyboard to punch-roll technology to 'capture' performances committed to their keys; under the second, devices by now familiar from other portions of the present book, the gramophone and phonograph (especially), and radio.

Literary sources help document the first category. In T. S. Eliot's 'Portrait of a Lady' (1917), 'a street-piano, mechanical and tired / Reiterates some worn-out common song' – itself reiterating a fairly commonplace if not tired association of mechanism with meretriciousness: music robbed of all vitality.[39] A more equivocal evaluation runs through Conrad's *The Secret Agent* (1907), where a mechanised piano provides ironic commentary on terrorists' plotting in a London bar (a similar conceit features in Joyce's 'Circe'). Both these instances feature popular music, presumably capable of being played by 'live' performers; however, composers of 'classical' music like Stravinsky seized upon mechanised instruments as a means of liberation from constraints that are (in Bartók's words) 'an outcome of the structure of the human hand'.[40] Specifically, Stravinsky prized the 'unlimited possibilities of precision, velocity, and polyphony' represented by mechanical pianos, and exploited these in redactions of his own orchestral works, commissioned by the Playola instrument manufacturing company.[41] More radically, the admittedly obscure American composer Conlon Nancarrow (1912–1997) wrote works 'directly' for mechanised piano, further pushing past the limits set by manual musicians' technique.[42] Finally, in a move aligning Cowell's ideas with the futurology of Russolo, Carlos Chávez, in *Toward a New Music* (1937) (first quoted above in Chapter 3), looks forward to 'prodigies of polyphony and polyrhythm' to be realised by 'orchestra[s]' made up of many mechanised instruments playing simultaneously.[43] By the time Chávez wrote this, in fact,

Antheil had considered but rejected as impractical such a collocation for *Ballet Mécanique*.

Neither 'velocity' or 'polyphony', however, was uppermost in Stravinsky's mind (at least by his own account) when writing for Playola; instead, he privileged the seemingly least glamorous item on his list of virtues of mechanised instruments, quoted above: precision. Thus, of his initial interest in player pianos, he writes: 'I had always been anxious to find a means of imposing some restriction on the notorious liberty, especially widespread to-day, which prevents the public from obtaining a correct idea of the author's intentions', vis-à-vis the latter's compositions.[44] In other words, what player pianos as well as gramophones and phonographs promised to composers was precisely a means of imposing such 'restrictions' on a given piece of music's performative interpretation. This, then, leads us to those machines for 'radiat[ing] music into the air' identified above, gramophones and phonographs themselves - which several other writers also welcomed for the precise, imperishable record of any given performance (and thus, its precipitant 'intent') these apparently ensured. In 'The Mechanization of Music' (1925), for example, H. H. Stuckenschmidt draws a flattering contrast between the gramophone and musical notation – that now-familiar target of modernist musicians' ire – in which the latter is castigated for allowing all manner of variations to creep in between a composer's ideas and subsequent interpretation. Thus the future significance of gramophones lies 'in the possibility of authentically writing for them': that is, composing directly on gramophone records in 'relief script [. . .] with all conceivable nuances, with mathematically precise tempos, dynamic symbols, and phrasing'.[45] To the anticipated objection that writing of such detail would be impossible on such relatively small objects as gramophone discs, Stuckenschmidt replies with an ingenious proposal drawn from the Bauhaus artist László Moholy-Nagy (1895–1946): simply compose on 'a huge disc, approximately five meters in diameter, with correspondingly large lines' and then photomechanically reduce it 'to the size required' for playback.[46] Thus both Morton Prince's model of the mind and Adorno's conception of phonography as 'writing' (considered in the previous chapter) are rewritten as an artistic technique.

Stuckenschmidt's prediction did not, of course, come true, at least not in any wholesale sense (partly for a reason also glanced at in the previous chapter: that whatever its disadvantages, conventional notation provides a certain 'grammar' for music, in a sense helping to *produce* music, not merely encode it). But other, essentially no less outlandish, claims about the gramophone and phonograph did. Chavez's vision of what is now called 'world' music – that 'by means of the record, we can [. . .] preserve the music of all countries' and thus spread music 'from one country to another' – may be utopian, but is not fundamentally inaccurate.[47] Moholy-Nagy's call to turn the 'apparatuses' of phonographs or gramophones 'used so far only for reproductive purposes into ones that can be used for productive purposes as well' irresistibly suggests the emergence of DJ culture many decades later.[48] Moving on to other changes associated with sound recording, we may note the entrance of gramophone-inspired, and even gramophone-produced sounds into musicians' vocabularies, as in Edgar Varèse's *Intégrales* (1924–5), which imitates 'the effect of playing recorded sound backwards' with its orchestra, and John Cage's 'Imaginary Landscape No. 1' (1939), in which recordings are played at variable speeds.[49] Stravinsky is at the forefront of yet another trend, the writing of music specifically to 'fit' the time available on contemporary discs, with his *Sérénade en la* (1925).[50]

All of this would have seemed strange to folklorists, whose use of phonographs and gramophones to record the music of 'primitive' people from the late nineteenth century onwards helped create the discipline of ethnomusicology in its modern form.[51] Here, the intent was not to help produce 'new' music, but rigorously and without subjective bias capture music already in existence. A Stravinskyesque passion for precision was thus aligned with a curatorial – and often, elegiac and romanticising – concern with *preservation*, as in Bartók's many writings on the use of sound recording technology in the collection of eastern European folk music (in addition to being a composer, Bartók had a parallel and sometimes intersecting career doing just this). Recalling Rilke (see Chapter 1, above), Bartók likens gramophony's ability to highlight otherwise imponderable details to microscopy: 'Different kinds of trills, vibrations, clucking sounds, glissandos [continuous 'slides' in pitch], which are perhaps important characteristics of certain districts [where music is produced], can be examined and studied with the greatest care'.[52] As the tell-tale reference to 'glissandos' here hints, sound recording's 'writing'-like capacities are of particular utility where folk music is concerned, as this music typically involves features 'repressed' within the 'classical' tradition, for which no adequate symbols exist in conventional notation.[53] Making the romantic tone mentioned above explicit, Bartók thus acclaims the gramophone and phonograph as exceptions amongst machines that otherwise imperil the very modes of life on which folk music depends:

> This splendid invention, unlike those others which have been responsible for the destruction of beautiful things, has seemingly been given us by way of compensation for the immensely great devastation that has been the consequence of this age of inventions.[54]

The curiously 'double' attitude of folklorists to sound recording noted above, in this chapter's 'Introduction' – and identified there with a still more general tendency in twentieth-century musical discourse to interfold conceptual or axiological oppositions – is here openly acknowledged.

Folklore's material investment in technology thus sits uneasily within a more broadly based 'folk' aesthetic, promulgated by experts and non-specialists alike. This aesthetic is grounded in an antithesis between modernity and 'tradition', as well as knock-on oppositions – as in Bartók's definition of folk music itself as 'the spontaneous expression of the musical feelings of [. . .] a community which is more or less isolated from the higher and artificial civilization, especially from the civilization of the towns'.[55] Thus his further specifications that folklorists should collect 'among the simplest and poorest people, inhabiting regions as far removed from the "iron horse" [i.e. railway] as possible', and ignore all songs 'learned at school or from the radio, since these were implanted in the peasant environment by means of exterior intervention'.[56] Clearly, these stipulations privilege rural, impoverished and relatively insular milieus as loci of 'authenticity'. In a North American context, such privileging coincides with an implicit theory of modernity as contrary to *racial* authenticity, specifically. The (white) writer R. Emmet Kennedy, for example, considers it fortunate that 'there remain a few primitive folk who have not got away from being natural and who hold fast to racial characteristics': 'the Negroes of the South', whose characteristic religious music (African American spiritual) thus constitutes an antidote to the more un-'natural' lifestyle now characteristic of the North.[57] John Lomax (1867–1948), no stranger to essentialising racial views himself (but of more estimable achievements though the Archive of American Folk Song and other agencies, for whom he collected hundreds of blues and other recordings), favoured convicts amongst his black recording subjects, as their incarceration supposedly left them less 'contaminated', musically speaking, by contact with whites.[58] In the same year as Kennedy's book on spirituals, Dorothy Scarborough's *On the Trail of Negro Folk Songs* (1925) laments the way that amongst southern blacks, 'the old songs are being crowded out of existence by the popularity of phonographs and the radio'.[59] For all these writers, then, 'folk' music could virtuously be an object for, but not an object *of*, sound recording.

But what did folklorists' own recordings actually document? As Bartók concedes, the very qualities of music most interesting to him – glissandi, trills and others itemised above – are those that tend to change between performers and performances, so that any given recording will feature things impossible to reproduce, in every way, in any other. He therefore states: 'We can therefore obtain, at best, a fairly true, average recording which ultimately preserves the melody in a form that had never actually existed before'.[60] In other words, recording *makes* as much as documents its objects, for at least two, interconnected reasons: the first, that no two performances involving 'live' performers can ever, in principle, be entirely the same; the second, that sound recording exerts a perhaps incalculable but always assumable influence on performances' substantial content. This does not invalidate Bartók's own or anyone else's efforts at preservation, but does mean distinguishing between what they thought of themselves as doing and what, perhaps, they actually did. For by recording something, one ineluctably changes it, along with – if only infinitesimally – the world in which that recording takes a place. Far from rescuing folk music from the oblivion represented by recording culture, then, folklorists arguably did more to contribute to the growth of, and change within, that culture itself.

THE 'PHONOGRAPH EFFECT' AND JAZZ

As other recent commentators have also noted, then, early ethnomusicologists and others can be faulted for assuming that sound recording had no effect on what it documented. A more nuanced and self-reflective view is that actually, such documentation is conditioned by the presence of the recorder, equipment, and – not least – the expectation amongst those being recorded that whatever they do will be replayed at another time and place.[61] This can be linked to what Mark Katz calls the 'phonograph effect', which he sees as taking diverse forms across all genres of recorded music – from Stravinsky's tailoring of a certain work to fit the time available on contemporary gramophone discs, already noted, to such more specifically studio-conditioned developments as 'crooning', a manner of singing expressively at low volumes, originating in the need to circumvent the technical constraints of early microphones.[62] A possibly even more profound effect of sound recording is discussed by Michael Chanan, vis-à-vis the way 'classical' music has, since the beginning of the phonographic era, been interpreted, on disc, by performers. Whereas Stravinsky and others, as we have seen, may understandably have welcomed recording for apparently 'fixing' such interpretation for all time, the actual history of recording instead reveals a 'paradox' whereby the differentiation of interpretations from each other is 'accelerated [. . .] reducing the idea of a traditional style of performance to a chimera'.[63] The fact that *one* performance can be recorded, that is, entails the possibility of others being recorded too – and of the latter self-consciously cultivating its difference from the first, and so on. There is no reason to suppose that this effect is confined to classical music. On the contrary, it helps explain all post-recording music's rapid pace of change.

Certainly, it helps explain the history of jazz – or at least, certain strands within that multiplex, capacious genre prevalent in the first half of the twentieth century.[64] As pioneering jazz critic Robert Goffin wrote in 1934, 'The most extraordinary achievement' of jazz, at least in certain forms, 'has been the dissociation of interpretation from the "stenographical" execution of the work', typical of 'classical' performances, 'resulting in a finished musical creation which is as much the work of the performer as of the composer'.[65] Though there may be less reason to believe his accompanying claim that 'Up to the time of jazz, it is safe to say that the performer was no more than the faithful representative of the composer' – a claim made in apparent ignorance of Stravinsky's and others' contemporaneous grievances – Goffin is surely right to think that jazz is, in important ways, characterised if not defined by improvisation.[66] This improvisatory element and jazz's historic overlap with sound recording (both genre and machinery originate in the late nineteenth century, though the first self-declared 'jazz' recording was not made until 1917) are connected at a deep substantive level. For as a recent commentator writes, sound recording was 'essential for the development of jazz', capturing improvisations which otherwise 'could not – or only to a limited degree – be written down'.[67] Jazz's unwritten element and its recordability, in other words, are two sides of a single coin.[68] And though some have always seen recording as inimical to jazz's 'spirit' – on the grounds that 'live' performance is jazz's native element, for performers and their audiences alike – the prevailing aesthetic that grew up around such recordings prized their uniqueness as musical iterations, even of the 'same' core material available elsewhere. Bartók's observation that all recordings capture music that 'that had never actually existed before' was thus trans-valued.

This link between jazz and sound recording can be extended to other genres, both similarly rooted in the late nineteenth and early twentieth centuries and as developed ever since. Burnet Hershey's 1922 report on the global diffusion of jazz in its more commercial forms, for example, may serve as a gloss on recordings' status as trans-national commodities throughout the twentieth century, regardless of their specific content: 'In India,' he writes, 'the frequent streams of returning [imperial] officials from England all bring with them new cargoes of tunes – direct from New York via [London's] Lescester [sic] Square'.[69] Similarly, the arranger Lee Orean Smith's (1874–1942) analysis of what we might call the dialectical relation between innovation in recording and in 'live' performance – '"There is no doubt"', he says, that the demand for '"better and more interesting"' arrangements within recording situations drove those outside the studio to seek similar arrangements, which then fed back into the original demand – rings true for the relation between 'reproduction' and 'production' in twentieth-century popular music generally.[70] The specificity of jazz, therefore, is only partly accounted for by its relation to the gramophone and phonograph. Besides its rhythmic quality, discussed above, three other features were also cited by contemporaries to explain this specificity: nationality, economics and 'race'.

The nationality of jazz has rarely been in doubt. Though some early critics grumbled that its syncopations merely rehashed material from European masters such as Beethoven, this was generally regarded as the first if not only autochthonous music of the USA, by enthusiasts and opponents alike.[71] In the 'enthusiast' camp, then, one commentator wrote in 1917 that 'here and nowhere else are the beginnings of American music, if American music is to be anything but a pleasing reflection of Europe', a line of thought later associated with composers such as George Gershwin (1898–1937) and Leonard Bernstein (1918–1990).[72] In the opposing camp, however, another writer grumbled one year later that this music betrays a national 'attitude toward life only too familiar to us all, an attitude shallow, restless, avid of excitement, incapable of sustained attention, skimming the surface of everything, finding nowhere satisfaction, realization, or repose'.[73] Both observations relate specifically to ragtime, the precursory or early form of jazz whose accompanying discourse represents a little-known continuity with that of *neurasthenia* ('nervous exhaustion'), the late nineteenth-century medical complaint, similarly pegged to national mores and conditions.[74] Thus in 1902, ragtime was said to constitute a 'musical outlet for the extreme nervousness of American youth', and for 'national nervousness' generally.[75] Putting the causal shoe, as it were, on the other foot, another commentator called ragtime 'a direct encouragement' to another somato-psychic illness, 'hysteria'.[76] Earlier, we noted jazz's tendency to polarise opinions, and can here gauge the extreme hostility reactions to the music sometimes took. For in such testimony, jazz is not just 'symptomatic' of something in the by now familiar historiographic or sociological sense, but actually produced by – or productive of – disease.

The neurasthenic paradigm also helps explain jazz's association with economic processes, its second putative precipitant or component. As its seminal theorist George Miller Beard wrote in 1881, neurasthenia was linked to 'The increase in the amount of business of nearly all kinds in modern times' – a link increasingly sloughed on to jazz throughout the 1920s, at the same time as the term and genre 'ragtime' were being displaced by 'jazz' itself.[77] This is evident in a range of periodical and other commentary, now thankfully anthologised in volumes such as Karl Koenig's *Jazz in Print (1856–1929)* (2002), to which I am particularly indebted throughout this section (as my references will already have made clear). Ruth Pickering's 'The Economic Interpretation of Jazz' (*The New Republic*, 1921), for instance, rehearses an ingenious if facetious account of jazz as a response to increased population density in urban centres, and the associated squeeze on space: 'The life of trade moves population into the cities, rents soar, space is cramped', she writes; thus the '"shimmy"' and other dance-moves associated with jazz represent the body's reconciliation of its expressive urges with the close proximity of others.[78] In a similar vein, Clive Bell, in the same year and journal, associates jazz with a 'typically modern craving for small profits and quick returns', broadly anticipating Adorno's critique, evolved throughout the 1930s, according to which jazz is both externally conditioned and inwardly defined by the commodity form and its imperatives.[79] Anne Shaw Faulkner's 'Does Jazz put the Sin in Syncopation?' (*Ladies' Home Journal*, 1921) answers its titular question with a resounding 'yes'. Not only does jazz menace 'laws and order' generally, Faulkner states, but it more specifically hampers workplace productivity; thus, 'in almost every big industry where music has been instituted it has been found necessary to discontinue jazz because of its demoralizing effect [. . .] This was noticed in an unsteadiness and lack of evenness in the workmanship of the product after a period when the work-men had indulged in jazz music.'[80] Again, hostility to jazz, as in some 'national' interpretations, is grounded in the music's alleged extra-musical effects.

Others, however, welcomed jazz with great enthusiasm. Outside the USA, this was nowhere more evident than in France, where (as briefly noted above in this book's 'Introduction') it became linked to aesthetic and social innovation of all kinds. James Reese Europe's (1881–1919) concerts in the country were rapturously received, doubtless keying into the relatively exalted mood created by Allied victory in the First World War (Europe and his band members were originally sent to fight alongside France on the Allied side as US soldiers, but were then seconded to play music both before and after armistice).[81] Throughout the 1920s, 'classical' composers such as Debussy, Erik Satie (1866–1925) and Darius Milhaud (1892–1974) wrote music influenced by jazz, as did the francophone Stravinsky.[82] Summing up the latter trend (while also broadening it to include composers outside France), Antheil reminisced: 'Counting out Kodaly and Bartok [sic: Zoltán Kodály (1882-1967), and Bartók, both Hungarian], every other European composer, pretending to being even partially alive at that time became mulatto'; that is, a mix of black and white 'racial' elements.[83] This leads us, then, to the category of 'race' itself, and claims for jazz as 'black', or more specifically, as African American. Long before the twentieth century, European commentators had seen Africans as possessed of a particular facility for rhythm; by the later period, North Americans of African descent were also linked to blood of the 'highest temperature known' (though this blood was said to 'lose' that 'fire in America'), and, albeit more circumspectly, to particularly constructed vocal chords, corresponding to distinct musical endowments.[84] For the African American Alain Locke, such ideas coexist with a seemingly more class-based or contextual account of what is 'black' about black music. Here is his account of 'Original Jazz', which he insists is distinct from both syncopation and 'close eccentric harmony':

> it is inborn in the typical or folky type of Negro. It can be detected even in a stevedore's swing, a preacher's sway, or a bootblack's flick; and heard equally in an amen-corner quaver, a blue cadence or a chromatic cascade of Negro laughter.[85]

Does this describe an inner 'essence', working its way outwards, or something more contingent, borne of specific ways of working (the 'stevedore's', and so on)? Locke seems poised equivocally between these possibilities – perhaps symptomatically, given the career-long tension in his work between championing 'Negro' culture as found, and wishing this culture to be 'raised' to a more academic, less 'folky' level.[86] The advantage of the first position is, of course, to cast jazz as a treasury all of black African ancestry are endowed with; its disadvantage (and thus a recommendation for the second position), the suggestion that all such people 'innately' cleave to a particular aesthetic.

If, in our own present, it is the latter position that prevails – the former having of course long since been discredited through association with the most malign and (though ostensibly materially grounded) metaphysical of racial doctrines – the former held great sway throughout the early twentieth century, significantly, amongst celebrants of jazz no less than critics, black and white. In this chapter's introduction, I observed that jazz was sometimes identified with 'primitive' expressive traits at the same time as with modernity; here is what I specifically had in mind, a description of jazz-inflected 'blues' from Afro-Caribbean Claude McKay's novel *Home to Harlem* (1928):

> The piano-player had wandered off into some dim, far-away, ancestral source of music. Far, far away from music-hall syncopation and jazz [i.e. from commercial, implicitly lesser forms of jazz], he was lost in some sensual dream of his own. No tortures, banal shrieks and agonies. Tum-tum ... tum-tum ... tum-tum ... tum-tum. ... The notes were naked acute alert. Like black youth burning naked in the bush. Love in the deep heart of the jungle. ... The sharp spring of a leopard from a leafy limb, the snarl of a jackal, green lizards in amorous play, the flight of a plumed bird, and the sudden laughter of mischievous monkeys in their green homes. Tum-tum ... tum-tum ... tum-tum ... tum-tum. ... Simple clear and quivering. Like a primitive dance of war or of love ... the marshalling of spears or the sacred frenzy of a phallic celebration.
>
> Black lovers of life caught up in their own free native rhythm, threaded to a remote scarce-remembered past, celebrating the midnight hours in themselves, for themselves, of themselves, in a house in Fifteenth Street, Philadelphia ... [87]

At first sight, this may look like a page torn from the same book as R. Emmet Kennedy's testament to spirituals, which similarly deploys the key-word 'primitive' as an antonym of contemporaneity. But far from looking to the past nostalgically, McKay asserts that for 'Black lovers of life', at least, there is no need to counterpose the ancient and the modern: on the contrary, the former is accessible *right now*, 'in a house in Fifteenth Street, Philadelphia'. Music of a certain sort is thus a kind of time machine, dragging the 'ancestral' past into the present, where it provides existential as much as aesthetic nourishment. And though the references to animals and such-like here may dismay, McKay's reference to 'phallic celebration' indicates that for him, the 'primitive' is a source of potency, not a stigma.[88]

We have, of course, encountered this sort of thing before. In Chapter 1, we identified texts by Lawrence (whom McKay admired), Eliot and Yeats with 'depth' modernism, similarly identifying sound, including music, with access to the otherwise impalpable and distant past. Similar ideas obtain as well in my final example of a celebrant approach to jazz, by one of the music's greatest practitioners, Duke Ellington (1899–1974). Here, the 'racial' theory of jazz provides a means by which the 'national' one is amended:

> The music of my race is something more than the 'American idiom'. It is the result of our transplantation to American soil, and was our reaction in the plantation days to the tyranny we endured. What we could not say openly we expressed in music, and what we know as 'jazz' is something more than just dance music [. . .] It expresses our personality, and, right down in us, our souls react to [its] elemental but eternal rhythm [. . .][89]

Like jazz's critics, though to diametrically opposed ends, Ellington locates jazz's ultimate significance (and origin) in the extra-musical. Thus, jazz is not 'American' but *African* American, a music born of transatlantic crossings, indelibly marked by the experience of slavery. We may now note that for Locke, too, 'jazz' is broadened as a category to include a 'lived' or social element, as if to make this extra-musicality emphatic (specifically, for Locke, we may now make explicit, 'jazz' includes not only other sound produced by 'negroes' besides music, but also non-sound-centred forms of bodily activity). What 'jazz' means to the musical imaginary more broadly still, then, is the prospect of music being more than itself, without sacrificing or ceasing to elaborate its own distinctive mode of being.

JAZZ AND THE EXTRA-MUSICAL, AND BLUES

With this said, we may consider the effect of jazz on other media besides music, including those of visual culture, and (especially) literature. This is a fashionable topic in contemporary scholarship, but has its roots in 'The Jazz Age' (to invoke F. Scott Fitzgerald's famous phrase) itself.[90] Witness Clive Bell's commentary on 'ragtime literature', here focused on the then most recent work of Joyce (to judge by the dates, Bell has in mind those sections of *Ulysses* serialised in *The Little Review*):

> In his later publications Mr. Joyce does deliberately go to work to break up the traditional sentence, throwing overboard sequence, syntax, and, indeed, most of those conventions which men habitually employ for the exchange of precise ideas. Effectually, and with a will, he rags the literary instrument: unluckily, this will has at its service talents which though genuine are moderate only.[91]

'Rag[ging]', in other words, is ruination – at least insofar as literature aspires to 'precise' conveyance of ideas (clearly, not everyone accepts this characterisation, just as posterity has not generally shared this estimate of Joyce's 'talents'). Thus the sort of criticisms exemplified by Anne Shaw Faulkner, above – jazz causes 'evenness' in 'workmanship', and so on – are displaced from the social to the artefactual; a charge of aesthetic rather than economic dereliction.

Notwithstanding this negative account of Joyce, Bell's discussion yields some usefully more value-neutral and general observations. His declaration that 'In literature jazz manifests itself both formally and in content', for instance, turns on a distinction also evident in visual culture.[92] On the 'formal' side, at least in aspiration, can thus be located painter Aaron Douglas's (1899–1979) recollection that amongst his colleagues in the 1920s, '"pleas could be heard on all sides for a visual pattern comparable to, or rather expressive of, the uniqueness found in the gestures and bodily movements of the Negro dance, and the sounds and vocal patterns as found in the Negro song"' (as we saw in Chapter 3, an analogue for the latter 'pattern' was ostensibly ensured by 'phonophotography').[93] Jerome Lachenbruch's 'Jazz and the Motion Picture' (1922) finds jazz responsible for the way then-recent films, beyond specific plot points, are 'filled with sudden surprises and compressed emotional excitement', and further links this to a 'Deleting [of] the obvious' in such films' editing.[94] Turning to 'content', Douglas is again significant, as one of many African American painters whose images of musicians and their audiences help document as well as constitute the Harlem Renaissance, that pan-cultural movement whose other protagonists include McKay and Locke.[95] Finally, jazz also furnished subject matter to the movies (as indeed we know already via *L'Inhumaine*, discussed in this book's 'Introduction'); none other than Duke Ellington appeared in several films himself.

But it is in poetry that jazz's influence on form and content mesh most tightly. Witness the stupendous evocation of a couple dancing in Hart Crane's 'For the Marriage of Faustus and Helen' (1923):

A thousand light shrugs balance us
Through snarling hails of melody.
White shadows slip across the floor
Splayed like cards from a loose hand;
Rhythmic ellipses lead into canters
Until somewhere a rooster banters.

Greet naïvely – yet intrepidly
New soothings, new amazements
That cornets introduce at every turn –
And you may fall downstairs with me
With perfect grace and equanimity.

Or, plaintively scud past shores
Where, by strange harmonic laws
All relatives, serene and cool,
Sit rocked in patent armchairs.[96]

We know the music danced to here is jazz because Crane said so in a letter, and also because of intratextual evidence, a racial slur, 'nigger cupids scour the stars!', in the preceding lines (Crane was white).[97] But we could also guess the music's identity from the 'cornets' and 'rhythmic ellipses' specified – the latter of which is formally reflected in the sudden shift to rhymed from unrhymed couplets in the last lines of the first stanza quoted; a shift that causes the reader, as it were, to, like the dancers, quickly shift his or her feet. Later in the poem, a 'deft catastrophes of drums' echoes the likening of dancing to falling down the stairs 'With perfect grace': images of poise and chaos's impossible coincidence.[98] And though there may be other explanations for 'the incandescent wax / Striated with nuances' still later in the poem linked to music (John T. Irwin notes that wax was often used to 'grease' the floor in contemporary dancing venues), this just possibly relates to phonograph recordings, of waxen ancestry (Edison's early cylinder recordings were made of wax), and often considered as a 'Striated' surfaces, as we have seen.[99] If the latter is so, this entire experience of jazz, like so many others, is conditioned by phonography.[100]

How else have we seen form and content linked in poetry? By typography, in Apollinaire (see Chapter 3), whose work in this respect is less flamboyantly reflected by African American writer Sterling A. Brown in 'Cabaret' (1932), where the sounds of jazz are represented by 'nonsense' syllables and, inextricably, the way these syllables are arranged for print in either lower- or upper-case letters:

Bee – dap – ee – DOOP, dee – ba – dee – BOOP
[. . .]

Dee da dee D A A A A H[101]

The combination of phonemic and typographic variables within each verbal unit leads us to quickly understand a given sound's overall character: 'DOOP', after all, is not quite the same as 'doop'. Similarly, the elongated spacing used throughout the last 'word', 'D A A A A H', evokes a musically conclusive chord. In Langston Hughes 'Harlem Night Club' (1926), somewhat differently, the words 'Play, plAY, PLAY!' combine lower case and upper case within conventional words; this time, establishing contrasting sound levels, or other expressive values, inside verbal units, as well as in between them.[102] Hughes's 'The Big Timer' (1931) represents still another formal innovation: here, two strips of text are placed in parallel, one carrying the poem itself and the other a musically established 'Mood' (p. 153).

But though jazz is an abiding feature of Hughes's work, of arguably more integral importance to his *oeuvre* is jazz's sister-genre, the blues, whose signature features are verbal as well as musical. Hughes's 'Gal's Cry for a Dying Lover' (1927) has three verses in the characteristic form of a blues lyric: one couplet repeated twice; another to complete the verse (p. 104). 'The Weary Blues' (1925) incorporates the loneliness-lamenting lyrics of a singer accompanying himself on the piano (p. 50). And 'Blues Fantasy' (1926) ends by meditating on two things central to the blues aesthetic: firstly, the process whereby verbal utterances such as 'Hey!' take on a supra-verbal expressive function; secondly, partly through the first thing's office, the way 'sad' emotions proper to the blues are transformed into something like their opposites:

> And when I get on the train
> I'll cast my blues aside.
>
> Laughing,
> Hey! . . . Hey!
> Laugh a loud,
> Hey! Hey! (p. 92)

Here, the repeated 'Hey!' stands for an inflection not explicit in the word itself. (In this context, it is worth bearing in mind that two slightly later poems, originally joined as one and also treating the blues, were later split under the respective titles 'Hey!' and 'Hey! Hey!': here, it is as if the word itself, which does not appear within the text of either poem, were summative of the texts they head.) As has often been suggested, the point of airing 'blue' emotions, in the blues, is not to wallow in them, but in quasi-Hegelian fashion to sublate them – that is, preserve, transcend and overturn them, all at the same time.[103] Insofar as the repeated word 'Hey!' here simultaneously dispels the blues ('I'll cast my blues aside'), maintains the blues (because that ostensibly discarding gesture is insistently reiterated), and *is* the blues (or part of one, instantiated by the text), then, Hughes is reflecting on, and indeed enacting, just that.

Coda: Musical (un)Timeliness

And so, finally, to a poet whose reflections on music provide one of the most suggestive meditations in all modernism on an issue this chapter has obliged us to address (again): music's relationship with time. In 'Burnt Norton' (1936), T. S. Eliot uses this relationship to ground an identification between music and the spoken word, and claims that words and music owe time not only for their conditions of emergence, but also, by the same token, the conditions of their passing or demise. Like the mortal beings they thus resemble, words and music nonetheless resist the latter fate, by virtue of their capacity to be arranged in configurations of at least relative endurance. Accordingly, the poem's fifth section alternates invocations of time's passing-ness with those of apparently opposed, though no less temporal categories: permanence and stasis; lastingness and perpetuity. In so doing, the poem ultimately complicates all temporal oppositions, suggesting, amongst other things, that endings may precede beginnings, that endings may in some respects *be* beginnings, and that in any case, all such terminal or nodal points of time may be gathered up in a transcendent 'meta-' time, in which temporal differentiation is dissolved. During certain privileged moments, 'all is always now'.[104] While we are 'in' such moments, time's various dimensions coexist.

Certainly, music is not exhaustive or exclusively coincident with such moments; as well as music, Eliot is surely thinking here not only of words but also a non-medium-specific Christian sense of secular time as redeemable by God's eternity. But not for nothing does Eliot's paradigmatic image of these moments involve listening to the sustained note of a violin.[105] Correlatively, 'Burnt Norton's' famous opening three lines – 'Time present and time past / Are both perhaps present in time future, / And time future contained in time past[. . .]' – evoke nothing so much as Adorno's observation that 'To comprehend music adequately, it is necessary to hear the phenomena that appear here and now in relation to what has gone before and, in anticipation, to what will come after'.[106] Collating Eliot's text with Adorno's, then, we may say that music is necessarily 'with', 'against' and irrespective of time's flow, simultaneously. Meanwhile, such categories as 'Time present' and 'time past' are not the only ones Eliot's poem opposes: also in its fifth section, it juxtaposes 'stillness' and 'Mov[ing]', 'silence' and sound, and life and death, and hints at the opposing pairing's interrelations in every instance.[107] And so we are returned to one of this chapter's first contentions: that nothing is more characteristic of the modernist musical imaginary than to confound, bestride and mobilise conceptual oppositions at many turns. We can now see that one reason why this might be so is that music is *itself* such a 'confounding', simply through its relationship with time – whereby all 'pasts' are somehow present in the 'future', and all 'presents' mediate the two poles, 'past' and 'future', on its either side. (Of time itself, moreover, it may similarly be said that all 'futures' will become the 'past', given long enough, and the 'present's' mediation.) Eliot's contemporary, Stravinsky, wrote, in a text published in the same year as 'Burnt Norton', that as creatures 'doomed to submit to the passage of time – to its categories of past and future', music's great value resides for humans in its giving 'substance, and therefore stability, to the category of the present'.[108] One thing this may mean is that a medium as intensively conscious as music is of its own historicity – as the examples of Schoenberg and others discussed throughout this chapter have shown it as being – may also be the one that grants as close an experience as we may have of time's suspension, time's arrest.

NOTES

1. Arnold Schoenberg, *Theory of Harmony* [*Harmonielehre*], translated by Roy E. Carter (London: Faber and Faber, [1911; 3rd edn 1922] 1978), p. 53. Subsequent references to this edition are given in the text.

2. I am aware, in saying this, that I risk egregiously simplifying an enormously complicated subject. Tonality is by no means easily defined; much less was its status as (for instance) 'natural' or 'cultural' generally agreed upon in Schoenberg's lifetime – or indeed before. Nonetheless, my primary purpose here is expository, and by presenting Schoenberg's argument as I do, I hope to accurately convey the polemical thrust of his position. For discussion of the historical background to this position, see Carl Dahlhaus, *Studies on the Origin of Harmonic Tonality*, translated by Robert O. Gjerdingen (Princeton: Princeton University Press, 1990).

3. Theodor W. Adorno, 'On the Fetish-Character in Music and the Regression of Listening' (1938), translation modified by Richard Leppert, in *Essays on Music*, selected with introduction, commentary and notes by Richard Leppert (Berkeley: University of California Press, 2002), pp. 288–317; p. 288 cited.

4. See, for example, Paul Griffiths, *Modern Music: A Concise History*, revised edn (London: Thames and Hudson, 1994), p. 7. Other writers locate this break earlier, however, in such works as Liszt's late piano pieces of the 1880s: see, for example, Jim Samson, *Music in Transition: A Study of Tonal Expansion and Atonality, 1900–1920* (London: J. M. Dent, 1977), p. 16. My point is not to insist on an absolute break between tonality and its ostensible antithesis at any given point, but rather stress the way such breaks, wherever located, are framed in terms of other oppositions.

5. See, for example, Alex Ross, *The Rest is Noise: Listening to the Twentieth Century* (New York: Farrar, Straus and Giroux, 2007).

6. Herbert Antcliffe, *Living Music: A Popular Introduction to the Methods of Modern Music* (London: Joseph Williams, 1912), p. 3.

7. Schoenberg applies the term (translated as) 'ultramodernist' to himself on p. 70. In English, this was more commonly associated with composers such as George Antheil.

8. Anton Webern, *The Path to the New Music*, edited by Willi Reich, translated by Leo Black (Bryn Mawr: Theodore Presser, [1932–3] 1963), p. 40. Subsequent references to this edition are given in the text.

9. Schoenberg himself presents 'overtone theory' as contested, and emphasises that he thus uses it guardedly, heuristically, without mortgaging himself to the theory's ultimate confirmation or rejection: *Harmonielehre*, pp. 19–20.

10. Arnold Schoenberg, 'Problems of Harmony' (1934), in *Style and Idea: Selected Writings of Arnold Schoenberg*, edited by Leonard Stein, translated by Leo Black (London: Faber and Faber, 1975), pp. 268–87; p. 284 cited; emphases in original.

11. Daniel Albright (ed.), Commentary within *Modernism and Music: An Anthology of Sources* (Chicago: University of Chicago Press, 2004), p. 15.

12. Nadia Boulanger, 'Lectures on Modern Music', *Rice Institute Pamphlet* 13:2 (1926), pp. 113–95; p. 115 cited.

13. Adam Carse, *The History of Orchestration* (New York: Dover, [1925] 1964), p. 1.

14. Karol Berger, 'Time's Arrow and the Advent of Musical Modernity', in Karol Berger and Anthony Newcomb (eds), *Music and the Aesthetics of Modernity: Essays* (Cambridge, MA: Harvard University Press, 2005), pp. 3–22; p. 14 cited.

15. Thomas Mann, *Doctor Faustus*, translated by H. T. Lowe-Porter (Harmondsworth: Penguin, [1947] 1968), p. 185.

16. These developmental protocols themselves, meanwhile, are well described by another historical protagonist, the British music writer Donald Frances Tovey, in an *Encyclopaedia Britannica* article on 'sonata forms' originally published in 1911: 'In its early [historic] forms the sonata is a new kind of suite, complete in its contrasts. In its later developments the individual movements, while complete as designs, raise emotional issues which each movement is unable to satisfy without the others' (Donald Francis Tovey, *Musical Articles from the 'Encyclopaedia Britannica'*, with an editorial preface by Hubert J. Foss, London: Oxford University Press, 1944, p. 230).

17. Max Weber, *The Rational and Social Foundations of Music*, edited and translated by Don Martindale, Johannes Riedel and Gertrude Neuwirth (Carbondale: Southern Illinois University Press, [1921] 1958), pp. 8, 10.

18. Weber, *Rational and Social Foundations*, p. 65.

19. Samson, *Music in Transition*, p. 5.

20. Samson, *Music in Transition*, p. 5.

21. Friedrich Nietzsche, *The Birth of Tragedy, Out of the Spirit of Music*, edited with an introduction by Michael Tanner, translated by Shaun Whiteside (Harmondsworth: Penguin, [1872] 1993), pp. 115, 116.

22. Nietzsche, *The Birth of Tragedy*, pp. 115, 94; emphases in original.

23. Cf. Christopher Butler, *Early Modernism: Literature, Music and Painting in Europe, 1900–1916* (Oxford: Oxford University Press, 1994), p. 114.

24. Cf. Samson, *Music in Transition*, pp. 195–6.

25. Ferruccio Busoni, *Sketch of a New Esthetic of Music*, translated by Th. Baker (New York: G. Schirmer, [1907] 1911), pp. 24, 28; emphasis in original.

26. Luigi Russolo, *The Art of Noises*, translated with an introduction by Barclay Brown (Hillsdale: Pendragon Press, [1913–16] 1986), p. 69. The portion of this text I quote from here dates from 1914. Subsequent references to this edition are given in the text.

27. Harry Partch, excerpt from *Genesis of a Music* (1949), in Albright (ed.), *Modernism and Music*, pp. 30–6.

28. Ezra Pound, *Antheil, and the Treatise on Harmony* (Chicago: Pascal Covici, [1924] 1927), p. 27.

29. Henry Cowell, *New Musical Resources* (New York: Alfred A. Knopf, 1930), pp. 71–2.

30. Andrew J. Browne, 'Aspects of Stravinsky's Work', *Music and Letters* 11:4 (1930), pp. 360–6; pp. 360–1 cited.

31. Albright (ed.), Commentary within *Modernism and Music*, pp. 236–7.

32. Hiram K. Moderwell, 'Ragtime' (1915), in Karl Koenig (ed.), *Jazz in Print (1856–1929): An Anthology of Selected Early Readings in Jazz History* (Hillsdale: Pendragon Press, 2002), pp. 102–4; p. 103 cited.

33. Moderwell, 'Ragtime', p. 102.

34. Griffiths, *Modern Music*, p. 133.

35. Hans-Joachim Braun, 'Introduction', in H.-J. Braun (ed.), *'I Sing the Body Electric': Music and Technology in the 20th Century* (Hofheim: Wolke, 2000), pp. 9–32; p. 13 cited.

36. Ezra Pound, *Machine Art, and Other Writings: The Last Thought of the Italian Years*, selected and edited with an introduction by Maria Luisa Ardizzone (Durham, NC: Duke University Press, 1996).

37. Béla Bartók, 'Mechanical Music' (1937), in *Béla Bartók Essays*, selected and edited by Benjamin Suchoff (Lincoln, NE: University of Nebraska Press, 1978), pp. 289–98; p. 298 cited.

38. Bartók, 'Mechanical Music', p. 291.

39. T. S. Eliot, *Collected Poems, 1909–1962* (London: Faber and Faber, 1974), p. 10.
40. Bartók, 'Mechanical Music', p. 291.
41. Igor Stravinsky, *Chronicle of My Life* [translated anonymously from the French] (London: Victor Gollancz, 1936), p. 167.
42. See Jürgen Hocker, 'My Soul is in the Machine – Conlon Nancarrow – Composer for the Player Piano – Precursor of Computer Music', in Braun (ed.), *'I Sing the Body Electric'*, pp. 84–96.
43. Carlos Chávez, *Toward a New Music: Music and Electricity*, translated by Herbert Weinstock (New York: De Capo, [1937] 1975), p. 49.
44. Stravinsky, *Chronicle of My Life*, p. 166.
45. H. H. Stuckenschmidt, 'The Mechanization of Music' (1925), translated by Michael Gilbert, in Jost Herman and Michael Gilbert (eds), *German Essays on Music* (New York: Continuum, 1994), pp. 149–56; p. 154.
46. Stuckenschmidt, 'The Mechanization of Music', p. 155.
47. Chávez, *Toward a New Music*, p. 76.
48. László Moholy-Nagy, 'Production – Reproduction: Potentialities of the Phonograph' (1922–3), in Christoph Cox and Daniel Warner (eds), *Audio Culture: Readings in Modern Music* (New York: Continuum, 2006), pp. 331–3; p. 331 cited.
49. Griffiths, *Modern Music*, pp. 146, 110.
50. Stravinsky, *Chronicle of My Life*, p. 202.
51. See Erika Brady, *A Spiral Way: How the Phonograph Changed Ethnography* (Jackson, MS: University Press of Mississippi, 1999).
52. Béla Bartók, 'Some Problems of Folk Music Research in East Europe' (1940), in *Béla Bartók Essays*, pp. 173–92; p. 175 cited.
53. Béla Bartók, 'Hungarian Folk Music' (1929), in *Béla Bartók Essays*, pp. 3–4.
54. Béla Bartók, 'The Folklore of Instruments and their Music in Eastern Europe' (1911–31), in *Béla Bartók Essays*, pp. 239–86; p. 239 cited.
55. Bartók, 'Some Problems of Folk Music Research in East Europe', p. 173.
56. Bartók, 'Hungarian Folk Music', p. 4; Béla Bartók, 'Why and How Do We Collect Folk Music' (1936), in *Béla Bartók Essays*, pp. 9–24; p. 15 cited.
57. R. Emmet Kennedy, *Mellows: A Chronicle of Unknown Singers* (New York: Albert and Charles Boni, 1925), p. 4.
58. Marybeth Hamilton, *In Search of the Blues: Black Voices, White Visions* (London: Jonathan Cape, 2007), pp. 81–2.
59. Dorothy Scarborough, assisted by Ola Lee Gulledge, *On the Trail of Negro Folk Songs* (Cambridge, MA: Harvard University Press, 1925), p. 64.
60. Bartók, 'Why and How Do We Collect Folk Music?', p. 14.
61. See, for example, Brady, *A Spiral Way*; Hamilton, *In Search of the Blues*.
62. Mark Katz, *Capturing Sound: How Technology has Changed Music* (Berkeley: University of California Press, 2004), p. 3. On 'crooning,' see Braun, 'Introduction', in *'I Sing the Body Electric'*, p. 20.
63. Michael Chanan, *Repeated Takes: A Short History of Recording and its Effects on Music* (London: Verso, 1995), p. 11.
64. I am aware that, in what follows, I say little about the diversity of jazz, and thereby risk eliding differences between, say, commercial, 'tin pan alley' jazz of the 1920s, more 'authentic', esoteric forms, and so on. Nonetheless, the tendency to treat jazz as a single, monolithic thing is a tendency within much of the commentary I go on to quote, so it does not seem apt, when quoting it, to insist on distinctions evidently far from obvious to the commentators themselves.
65. Robert Goffin, 'Hot Jazz', in Nancy Cunard (ed.), *Negro: Anthology* (London: Wishart, 1934), pp. 378–9; p. 379 cited.

66. Goffin, 'Hot Jazz', in Cunard (ed.), *Negro: Anthology*, p. 379.

67. Braun, 'Introduction', in *'I Sing the Body Electric'*, p. 21.

68. This is not to say that *all* jazz is unwritten. Music played by large ensembles, especially, often makes extensive use of scores.

69. Burnet Hershey, 'Jazz Latitude' (1922), in Koenig (ed.), *Jazz in Print*, pp. 191–4; p. 193 cited.

70. Lee Orean Smith, quoted in Anon., 'The Boys who Arrange the Tunes you Play' (1922), in Koenig (ed.), *Jazz in Print*, pp. 204–5; p. 205 cited.

71. Anon., 'Ragtime' (1899), in Koenig (ed.), *Jazz in Print*, pp. 51–4.

72. Kelly Moderwell, 'A Modest Proposal' (1917), in Koenig (ed.), *Jazz in Print*, pp. 116–19; p. 119 cited.

73. Daniel Gregory Mason, 'Concerning Ragtime' (1918), in Koenig (ed.), *Jazz in Print*, pp. 121–4; p. 123 cited.

74. Perhaps the most comprehensive study of neurasthenia is Tom Lutz, *American Nervousness, 1903: An Anecdotal History* (Ithaca, NY: Cornell University Press, 1991).

75. W. F. Gates, 'Ethiopian Syncopation – The Decline of Ragtime' (1902), in Koenig (ed.), *Jazz in Print*, pp. 68–9; p. 69 cited.

76. Francis Toye, 'Ragtime: The New Tarantism' (1913), in Koenig (ed.), *Jazz in Print*, pp. 94–6; p. 95 cited.

77. George Miller Beard, *American Nervousness; Its Causes and Consequences. A Supplement to Nervous Exhaustion (Neurasthenia)* (New York: G. P. Putnam's Sons, 1881), p. 115.

78. Ruth Pickering, 'The Economic Interpretation of Jazz' (1921), in Koenig (ed.), *Jazz in Print*, pp. 151–2; p. 151 cited.

79. Clive Bell, 'Plus de Jazz' (1921), in Koenig (ed.), *Jazz in Print*, pp. 154–7; p. 154 cited; Theodor W. Adorno, 'On Jazz' (1936), translated by Jamie Owen Daniel, modified by Richard Leppert, in *Essays on Music*, pp. 470–95.

80. Anne Shaw Faulkner, 'Does Jazz put the Sin in Syncopation?' (1921), in Koenig (ed.), *Jazz in Print*, pp. 152–4; p. 152 cited.

81. See R. Reid Badger, 'James Reese Europe and the Prehistory of Jazz', in Reginald T. Buckner and Steven Weiland (eds), *Jazz in Mind: Essays on the History and Meanings of Jazz* (Detroit: Wayne State University Press, 1991), pp. 19–37.

82. Bernard Gendron, *Between Montmartre and the Mudd Club: Popular Music and the Avant-Garde* (Chicago: University of Chicago Press, 2002), pp. 83–7.

83. George Antheil, 'The Negro on the Spiral; Or, A Method of Negro Music', in Cunard (ed.), *Negro: Anthology*, pp. 346–51; p. 348 cited.

84. Kofi Agawu, 'The Invention of "African Rhythm"', *Journal of the American Musicological Society* 48:3 (1995), pp. 380–95; Henry E. Krehbiel, 'Lafcadio Hearn and Congo Music' (1906), in Koenig (ed.), *Jazz in* Print, pp. 78–9; p. 79 cited.

85. Alain Locke, *The Negro and his Music* (Port Washington, NY: Kennikat Press, [1936] 1968), p. 72.

86. See Paul Allen Anderson, *Deep River: Music and Memory in Harlem Renaissance Thought* (Durham, NC: Duke University Press, 2001), ch. 3.

87. Claude McKay, *Home to Harlem* (New York: Harper and Brothers, 1928), pp. 196–7.

88. See Tom Lutz, 'Claude McKay: Music, Sexuality, and Literary Cosmopolitanism', in Saadi Simawe (ed.), *Black Orpheus: Music in African American Fiction from the Harlem Renaissance to Toni Morrison* (New York: Garland, 2000), pp. 41–64.

89. Duke Ellington, 'The Duke Steps Out' (1931), in *The Duke Ellington Reader*,

edited by Mark Tucker (New York: Oxford University Press, 1993), pp. 46–50; p. 49 cited.

90. For an example of such scholarship, see David Yaffe, *Fascinating Rhythm: Reading Jazz in American Writing* (Princeton: Princeton University Press, 2006).

91. Clive Bell, *Since Cézanne* (London: Chatto and Windus, 1922), pp. 223–4.

92. Bell, *Since Cézanne*, p. 223.

93. Quoted in Graham Lock and David Murray, 'Introduction: The Hearing Eye', in Graham Lock and David Murray (eds), *The Hearing Eye: Jazz and Blues Influences in African American Visual Art* (Oxford: Oxford University Press, 2009), pp. 1–18; p. 1 cited.

94. Jerome Lachenbruch, 'Jazz and the Motion Picture' (1922), in Koenig (ed.), *Jazz in Print*, pp. 179–80.

95. See Richard J. Powell and David A. Bailey, *Rhapsodies in Black: Art of the Harlem Renaissance* (Berkeley: University of California Press, 1997).

96. Hart Crane, *The Complete Poems of Hart Crane*, edited by Marc Simon, with a new introduction by Harold Bloom (New York: Liveright, 2001), p. 29. Subsequent references to this edition are given in the text.

97. Crane, *Complete Poems*, p. 29. In this letter (to Gorham Munson), Crane identifies 'jazz rhythms' with the first verse of this poem's second section, just above the passages I quote; see Hart Crane, *The Letters of Hart Crane, 1916–1932*, edited by Brom Weber (New York: Heritage House, 1952), p. 89. I would argue that such 'rhythms', as well as jazz-related topical references, overspill this locus.

98. Crane, *Complete Poems*, p. 29.

99. Crane, *Complete Poems*, p. 30; John T. Irwin, *Hart Crane's Poetry: 'Apollinaire Lived in Paris, I Live in Cleveland, Ohio'* (Baltimore: Johns Hopkins University Press, 2011), pp. 311, 336.

100. It is also worth mentioning here that Crane habitually composed while listening to the phonograph: see Brian Reed, *Hart Crane: After His Lights* (Tuscaloosa: University of Alabama Press, 2006), ch. 4.

101. Sterling A. Brown, *The Collected Poems of Sterling A. Brown*, selected by Michael S. Harper (New York: Harper and Row, 1980), pp. 102–3.

102. Langston Hughes, *The Collected Poems of Langston Hughes*, edited by Arnold Rampersad, with David Roessel (New York: Vintage, 1994), p. 90. Subsequent references to this edition are given in the text.

103. See, for instance, Ralph Ellison's famous definition: 'The blues is an impulse to keep the painful details and episodes of a brutal experience alive in one's aching consciousness, to finger its jagged grain, and to transcend it, not by the consolation of philosophy but by squeezing from it a near-tragic, near-comic lyricism' (Ralph Ellison, 'Richard Wright's Blues', in *Shadow and Act*, New York: Vintage, [1945] 1972, p. 78).

104. Eliot, *Collected Poems*, p. 182.

105. Eliot, *Collected Poems*, p. 182.

106. Eliot, *Collected Poems*, p. 177; Theodor W. Adorno, 'Little Heresy' (1965), translated by Susan H. Gillespie, in *Essays on Music*, pp. 318–24; p. p. 319 cited.

107. Eliot, *Collected Poems*, pp. 181–2.

108. Stravinsky, *Chronicle of My Life*, p. 92.

Chapter 5

THE ART OF LISTENING

Humphrey Jennings's celebrated Second World War film *Listen to Britain* (1942) relates to listening in at least three, closely integrated ways. In the first place, the film's title serves as an exhortation to its viewers to 'listen' to its subject-matter: war-time Britain, as its people go about their business in a more or less normal and (so the film seeks to persuade us) good-humoured way. In the second place, by depicting this subject matter, the film itself 'listens', thus answering its own exhortation and embodying its title. And in the third place, the film depicts listening in a more conventional sense, as enacted by those it represents: for instance, workers listening to music played over tannoys in their factory; a group listening to someone accompanying her own singing on the piano. In one such scene, Jennings documents a performance by the orchestra of the Central Band of HM Royal Air Force and the pianist Myra Hess at the National Gallery in London – one of many famous concerts staged at lunchtime in that venue throughout the war.[1] As the music plays, the camera moves amongst the audience, revealing different auditory 'styles': rapt, amused and so on. This, the film suggests, is what the British people in a time of war are like: not fretful desolates (though doubtless, Jennings could have found evidence for this if he chose), but calm, collected aesthetes.

In a memoir written shortly after the war, Stephen Spender recalls these same lunchtime concerts and the impetus behind them. During the war, he says, there was a revival of interest in the arts. This arose spontaneously and simply, because people felt that [. . .] [these] were concerned with a seriousness of living and dying with which they themselves had suddenly been confronted. The audiences at the midday concerts [. . .] sat with a rapt attention as though they were listening for some message from the artist, who, though perhaps he had lived in other times, was close to the same realities as themselves [. . .].[2]

As an instantiation of this tendency,

One day [. . .] In the middle of the minuet there was a tremendous explosion. A delayed-action bomb had gone off in Trafalgar Square. In the trio of the minuet which they were playing, the musicians did not lift the bows from their strings. A few of the audience, who had been listening with heads bowed, straightened themselves for an instant and then resumed their posture.[3]

For both performers and their audience, then, music is too vital for attention to relinquish – at least, for longer than an 'instant' (if at all), despite the proximity of what might otherwise seem a rather more urgent object of attention. The very gravity of war, Spender suggests, deflects moral as much as intellectual energies away from itself, towards the 'higher' seriousness of music. Thus the speed with which attentive listeners resume their momentarily relinquished postures. Thus too, perhaps, the listening of Britain valorised by *Listen to Britain*; the same listening to which the film's audience is asked, in turn, to 'listen'.

It is between these two accounts that the topics of this chapter come into view. As both Jennings and Spender suggest, listening is distinct from 'mere' hearing, that more casual and indiscriminate activity, for all that the former is doubtless predicated on the latter (and indeed co-efficient with the latter, if we see the two things as representing poles of a continuum). For related reasons, both accounts define listening in terms of listeners' 'attention' – in Spender's case, explicitly – and thus as opposed to *in*-attention or distraction. Finally, both accounts suggest a privileged link between listening and music, though as we shall later in this chapter, other objects can present themselves as worthy objects for the attentive ear as well. For if music is emphatic in its claims on our attention, other sounds, less emphatic in this respect, may yield equal if not even greater perceptual yields. In order to perceive this, the listener must adopt a listening approach that is as agile and unprejudiced as possible.

It is for just this reason that the ideal of listening, for several commentators, as we shall see, involves the union of several if not all the senses. Listening, that is, in such commentary, absorbs other sensory organs besides the ear – or at least, ensures that these are not working at cross purposes. However, alternative models are also possible, sponsored by cultural trends such as the shift from 'silence' to sound in cinema, whose critics sometimes thought of listening as contrary to other senses' highest functioning. As befits the final chapter of this book, this chapter will address such issues while revisiting others looked at earlier, such as sound recording (here focused on tape technology, rather than that involving discs) and silence, the latter of which appears again here, as it did Chapter 1, as something to be listened *to*, rather than as something from which listening is excluded or repelled. The chapter will be led by turns back to the Second World War, a conflict often represented as a trial by, or stimulus to, listening. It begins, however, by looking at *attention*, as theorised in the nineteenth century, and in subsequent musical aesthetics.[4]

LISTENING AND/AS ATTENTION

Attention plays a key role in late nineteenth-century psychology. For William James, who is central to this tradition, it is the making as much as 'sorting' of experience; thus 'each of us literally *chooses*, by his way of attending to things, what sort of a universe he shall appear to himself to inhabit'.[5] For Gustav Spiller, in 'The Dynamics of Attention' (1901), 'attention does not deal so much with points as with fields', making it crucial to the dialectic of the one and many, or parts and wholes, that allows us to identify things as aspects or instantiations of each other.[6] For Bergson, in *Matter and Memory* (1896), attention has a specifically *temporal* dynamic, helping draw past impressions into relation with those of the present: thus, his account casts memory as an *éminence grise* within attention, the former 'strengthening and enriching perception, which, in its turn becoming wider, draws into itself a growing number of complementary recollections'.[7] Pushing this appeal to time still further, Mach's *Contributions to the Analysis of the Sensations* declares, 'we feel the work of attention *as* time': attention is the mental 'stretch' that makes time appreciable as such.[8]

Despite this somewhat acclamatory tone, attention discourse also harbours an admission of attention's internal limitations. As Jonathan Crary comments on this discourse: 'Attention as a process of selection necessarily meant that perception was an activity of *exclusion*, of rendering parts of a perceptual field unperceived'.[9] In other words, attention never was, or ever could be 'total': on the contrary, for it to be efficient in one domain, many thought, it had to be inefficient in at least some, if not a potentially indefinite range of others. Attention was thus grounded in its ostensible antithesis. And if this was true for attention at its 'purest', how much more so might it be for attention that was partial, split or intermittent?

Each of these ideas and queries finds echo or prefiguration in ideas of listening to music. For Hegel, lecturing in the 1820s, music concentrates attention primarily through the pleasing sense of regularity it imparts through rhythm:

thus, music's utility in drilling soldiers (the link here is to Bergson's sense of memory as piquing attention's sensitivity to percepts that 'enrich' one another by recurring).[10] Hegel's ardent if critical reader Adorno states that 'the capacity for musical understanding is equated, broadly speaking, with the ability to remember and anticipate', recalling Mach's idea that attention is what allows consecutive units of time to be perceived as a totality.[11] Hegel's own association of music and time, considered in Chapter 1, might also be examined in this light, as indeed might a whole range of late nineteenth- and early twentieth-century accounts of *melody*: for instance, the founding *Gestalt* psychologist Christian von Ehrenfels's (1859–1932) definition of melody as 'something other than the sum of the individual tones on the basis of which it is constituted'.[12] All such accounts may be identified with Spiller's distinction between 'points' and 'fields', and, more specifically, attention's mediation of the two. Similar accounts of melody appear in Gurney's *The Power of Sound* and Vernon Lee's *Music and its Lovers* (1932), the latter of which is in some respects an unacknowledged rewrite of the former.[13]

And Lee's study is also, perhaps, the most suggestive as well as far-reaching investigation of musical listening from the first half of the twentieth century in its own right. Encompassing an ontology of music as well as a phenomenology (ontologically, Lee says, music is an essentially if obscurely *motile* art, reactivating 'traces' of past movements left within our nervous systems both by ourselves and ancestors), the phenomenological part of Lee's discussion turns on a similar distinction to that drawn above between 'listening' and 'hearing', which Lee gives a distinctive twist by identifying with corresponding types of person: 'Listeners' are those who give 'complete attention to the music'; 'Hearers' are those 'whose attention is intermittent and diffluent'.[14] Another of our own earlier points is echoed by Lee's observation that 'there is usually some degree of "listening" in all "hearing" of music and a necessary substratum of "hearing" in all "listening"' (p. 108). A two-point understanding of listening is hereby underscored: it instantiates attention; it is never present wholly on its own, in 'pure' form.

More surprisingly, perhaps, Lee sees 'listeners' not only as those who *do* descend to 'mere' hearing, but also those who *know* they do – whose listening is self-consciously riddled by impurities and gaps. Furthermore, she sees 'hearers' as not entirely impervious to music, but rather as liable to have their interest in it take specific forms. Here, she contrasts the testimony of 'musical' answerers to questionnaires (these provide the evidential basis for Lee's study) with that of those who are 'less musical':

> the distinctly musical Answerers proved to be those who admitted without hesitation that their musical attention was liable to fluctuations and lapses. They were continually catching themselves thinking

of something else while hearing music. They complained of their own inattention and divagation [. . .] On the other hand, the less musical Answerers, those precisely who found in music a meaning beyond itself, seemed comparatively unaware of such lapses or interruptions [. . .] When asked whether the music suggested anything, they abounded in accounts of inner visions, trains of thought and all manner of emotional dramas, sometimes most detailed and extensive [. . .]. (pp. 30–1)

The turn to 'inner vision' in the minds of 'mere' hearers, then, appears commensurate with inattention – the same inattention that, more self-consciously, also betrays the musical experience of 'listeners'. But whereas the latter do or do not attend to music *as* music, 'hearers' tend to associate music with the extra-musical; moreover, they draw no fundamental distinction in their own experiential terms between the extra-musical and music itself. There is a link here to, but also a decided twist upon, something considered much earlier in the present book: theories that see music as non-mimetic and self-referential – the sort of theories privileged in 'high' aesthetic discourse (as we saw in Chapter 1) since the late eighteenth century – as opposed to those for which music 'think[s]' – to re-deploy Lee's words – of 'something else'. For whereas the normative ideal of non-mimetic or self-referential music, as that earlier consideration saw, originally served to distinguish one kind of music from another, it here serves to distinguish between ways in which music of any kind, potentially, may be perceived.

For Lee, then, music may be essentially non-mimetic or it may not be, but is far from being universally perceived as such in any case. Contrary perceptive modes are not without interest, and even dignity. Moreover, even those 'musical Answerers' who do, in large part, listen attentively may do so in a curiously oblivious or self-occluding way – for any piece of music's apprehension '*as a whole*', Lee further argues, depends on a 'special act of analysis' that 'blots out the awareness of the various and variously unified perceptive activities without which' the listener 'should not be aware of its existence' (p. 45; emphasis in original). Attention must thus conceal the very processes upon which it is predicated. This leads us on to those 'less musical Answerers' to Lee's questionnaires, who do little true 'listening' at all, but only 'hear'. Such people may be identified with the characters in E. M. Forster's *Howard's End* (1910) who here take in a performance of Beethoven's Fifth Symphony:

Whether you are like Mrs Munt, and tap surreptitiously when the tunes come – of course, not so as to disturb the others; or like Helen, who can see heroes and shipwrecks in the music's flood; or like Margaret, who can only see the music; or like Tibby, who is profoundly versed in counterpoint, and holds the full score open on his knee [. . .] in any case, the passion of your life becomes more vivid [. . .].[15]

All these characters, with the exception of Tibby (whose 'profound' knowledge of counterpoint marks him rather as 'musical', if not exclusively concerned with music *qua* sound), perceive music in terms of 'other' things: the 'passion' of their lives 'becomes more vivid'. In Helen's case, music is further understood as summing up 'all that had happened or could happen in her [own] career' – a formula that makes explicit her sense of music as referential (p. 29). And though most of these characters remain absorbed in music for the duration of the symphony (Helen's attention at one point, however, 'wander[s], and she gaze[s] at the audience, or the organ, or the architecture'; p. 27), this absorption is itself conspicuously 'other'-thing or extra-musically directed: notoriously, in Helen's case, it also encompasses 'gods and demigods', 'goblins' and dancing elephants (p. 28).

To sum up, musical listening, for both Lee and Forster, contains its 'others' in at least two ways: some of it is not really listening at all, and maybe much of it is more occasioned by music than genuinely attentive to it. But what of other objects to which the ear may attend, if in similarly patchy and self-negating ways? Three such objects may be considered in conclusion to the present section; the first, the analysand's speech in psychoanalysis. For Freud, in a paper on psychoanalytic technique from 1912, the secret of successful clinical psychoanalysis 'consists simply in not directing one's notice to anything in particular and in maintaining the same "evenly-suspended attention" [. . .] in the face of all one hears' when listening to patients.[16] To some extent subverting the central tenet of attention theory identified by Crary – that attention is above all *exclusive*, disregarding most of what might potentially concern it at any one time – Freud thus commends a style of listening that refuses to choose too quickly, so to speak, between what may ultimately prove more or less significant. Warming to this theme, Freud adds: 'as soon as anyone deliberately concentrates his attention to a certain degree, he begins to select from the material before him'; thus, this 'is precisely what must not be done' – for 'In making the selection, if [the analyst] follows his expectations he is in danger of never finding anything but what he already knows; and if he follows his inclinations he will certainly falsify what he may perceive' (p. 112). The Nietzschean and Bergsonian critique of sensory perception, outlined in Chapter 1, is thus echoed as a call to investigative open-mindedness. And just as artists were sometimes, as we have also seen, likened to technologies in the context of such critique, so Freud here concludes by saying of the 'good' psychoanalyst: 'He must adjust himself to the patient as a telephone receiver is adjusted to the transmitting microphone' (pp. 115–16). Telephony is exemplary here because it 'hears' without 'listening' – much like the phonograph for Douglas Kahn, discussed in the present book's 'Introduction'.

The second non-musical object of listening we may consider here is spoken prose, defined by William Morrison Patterson in *The Rhythm of Prose* (1916) as 'uttered language which, on a given occasion, produces a series of syllabic impressions, whose temporal arrangement is largely irregular, that is, haphazard, but which can be subjectively organized' as rhythmic.[17] Echoing Lee's division of her subjects into discrete 'types', Patterson distinguishes between '"aggressively" rhythmic' listeners, and those whose relatively feeble rhythmic sense prevents them discerning rhythm in much or even any spoken prose. Like Hegel, Patterson links rhythm to attention, stating that 'Rhythmic experience' itself may 'be roughly described as a complex of perception, emotion, and sensation, with all three elements subjected to the moulding processes of attention, both voluntary and involuntary' (p. 91). And though his emphasis on prose *as* prose perhaps prevents him saying much about music as an element within or model for prose itself, certain remarks indicate that racial theories of music might not be too far removed from Patterson's mind as he describes what listening to prose 'rhythmically' is like: invoking tropes familiar to us from Chapter 4, he writes that the 'aggressively' rhythmic subject spontaneously locates rhythm in whatever he or she hears in much 'the same way that a negro automatically improvises complicated syncopating melodies while he plies his hoe on the corn-field' (p. 74).

The final sonic object we may consider in this section is Proustian *mémoire involontaire*, as glossed by Samuel Beckett. In Beckett's study, *Proust* (1931), Proust's seminal and – we may now say – 'Pattersonian' distinction between voluntary and involuntary mental processes is reworked in terms of a distinction between attention and inattention. It is only when memory is both involuntary and inattentive that, Beckett says, it deserves our own or secures Proust's esteem, for only then is it untravestied by *habit*. Accordingly, whereas voluntary and attentive memory may 'be relied on to reproduce for our gratified inspection those impressions of the past that were consciously and intelligently formed', it 'has no interest' in an allegedly more precious thing, that 'mysterious element of inattention that colours our most commonplace experiences'.[18] It is the latter, in Beckett's view, on which Proust so signally dilates. Thus, Proust's demonstration that involuntary memory has 'in its flame [. . .] consumed Habit and all its works, and in its brightness revealed what the mock reality of experience never can and never will reveal – the real'.[19] 'The real', paradoxically, can only be discovered on the condition that it is not actively sought out.

It may be objected that nothing Beckett says here relates specifically to sound and listening – though in the 'seed-' text for Beckett's study, Proust identifies the sound of a spoon's knocking against a plate as one precipitant, amongst others, of *mémoire involontaire*.[20] But it surely helps illuminate a text that manifestly *does* relate to sound and listening, Beckett's own drama of both voluntary and involuntary recollection, *Krapp's Last Tape* (1958).

Memory and Silence

Beckett's play is one the most profound meditations on listening extant. As it opens, the protagonist, an old man, prepares to record a tape ('his last'), a kind of diary entry, on the occasion of his birthday. From the archive of tapes at his disposal, the audience are led to understand he has been doing this throughout his life. Towards the beginning of the play, Krapp selects one tape from this archive, and then begins to play this on a tape recorder, thus allowing the audience, too, to listen to his former self as he does, recorded on a long-gone previous occasion. Krapp's listening thus becomes an act of self-reflection, as the 'two' Krapps, so to speak, confront each other: the one on tape by speaking into a future he cannot foresee; the one on stage by listening into a past from which he is more or less estranged.

Then things get more complicated. As the audience listen to the tape-recorded, younger Krapp, it becomes clear that *this* Krapp, too, like his older self, has been listening to previously recorded tapes in preparing to record the one now playing. There are, then, 'three' Krapps implicit in the drama's *mise en scène* – or alternatively, a single Krapp, representing three successive stages of life. As the Krapp we see on stage listens to his younger self, the first starts, presumably, to remember things related by the second, themselves related in the form of a report on what the 'third', youngest Krapp has said in a still earlier tape (for example, the oldest Krapp listens while the younger one dilates upon a love affair averted to within the tape that *he*, the younger one, has listened to). At length, the oldest, on-stage Krapp becomes discomforted by what he hears and suspends his listening by switching off the tape recorder. Hereafter, listening is resumed and again suspended several times, before Krapp eventually records the 'last' tape of his and the play's own present. This recording is itself, however, abruptly terminated just before the play's conclusion, as Krapp feels compelled to instead retrieve and again re-play its predecessor.

Evidently, then, Beckett's drama turns on an identification between listening and memory, though the precise terms of this identification are not quite as straightforward as they may first appear. For instance, contrary to this conjuncture in some respects is the way listening sometimes points towards memory's absence, as when the oldest Krapp finds he has forgotten the meaning of the word 'viduity' (spoken by his younger self) and has to look it up in a dictionary.[21] Similarly, there are moments when memory runs ahead of listening, as when Krapp stops replaying his younger self's tape, having evidently remembered what that self is about to say and realised that he does not wish to hear it (in the event, the elder Krapp forward-winds the tape precisely in order that this hearing be avoided) (p. 16). However, the drama's overarching premise is both that listening enables memory, and that in so doing, more specifically, it also enables memory of how, within the past, one had remembered.

Thus, the on-stage Krapp's hears less about his younger self's 'contemporary' experience than of that younger self's own retrospection. We know from the 'Introduction' to the present book that sound recording is what enables the 'stock-piling' of time (to recall Jacques Attali's term) on which such recollective listening depends. But what we can now add is that for sound recording to facilitate remembrance as it does in Beckett's play, it must be deployed in rituals, themselves dependent on technical possibilities sound recording technology instantiates: the replaying of recordings one had earlier created (especially on designated anniversaries); the interruption and forward-winding of recordings (to better manipulate the memories one does or does not wish to evoke); the re- or backwards-winding of recordings in order to hear portions of them more than once (in Beckett's drama, this happens once the oldest, on-stage Krapp has aborted recording of his 'last' tape, at the drama's end; p. 19), and so on. These, after all, are the concrete uses of technology around which the action of *Krapp's Last Tape* (such as it is) revolves. And though such usage appears entirely 'voluntary' and deliberate, it here affords at least some purchase on the 'involuntary' memory that Beckett so admired in Proust. For however systematically he cultivates them, we can be fairly sure that Krapp's memories are of the kind that haunt or torture, rather than those that gladden and sustain. Memory, that is, for Krapp, appears as all-devouring and ineluctable, not as something that is circumscribed or governed.

It is this sense of an illimitable force to which opposed phenomena ultimately yield that leads us on to silence. As Krapp's present gives way to recollection, a stage direction indicates, *'The tape runs on in silence'* (p. 20; emphasis in original). Both the taped Krapp and his older self, this implies, are led by memory beyond the point where language stops. Earlier in the play, the on-stage Krapp spends much of his time listening in silence; meanwhile, silence also features prominently as a topic of the taped Krapp's spoken discourse (p. 12). The play's final stage direction, in particular, represents memory *as* 'silence', or at least as having a silencing effect. But what not only this but also all the other instances just cited also point towards is the centrality of silence, throughout Beckett's work, as a phenomenon in its own right. In a text often taken as a manifesto for his mature aesthetic, the so-called 'German Letter of 1937', Beckett conceives silence both as the cessation or antithesis of sound and as opposed to 'official' or conventionally written English:

> It is indeed becoming more and more difficult, even senseless, for me to write an official English [*sic*]. And more and more my own language appears to me like a veil that must be torn apart in order to get at the things (or the Nothingness) behind it [. . .] Let us hope the time will come, thank God that in certain circles it has already come, when language is most efficiently used where it is being most efficiently misused.

As we cannot eliminate language all at once, we should at least leave nothing undone that might contribute to its falling into disrepute. To bore one hole after another in it, until what lurks behind it – be it something or nothing – begins to seep through; I cannot imagine a higher goal for a writer today [. . .] Is there any reason why that terrible materiality of the word surface should not be capable of being dissolved, like for example the sound surface, torn by enormous pauses, of Beethoven's seventh Symphony, so that through whole pages we can perceive nothing but a path of sounds suspended in giddy heights, linking unfathomable abysses of silence?[22]

One should quote this passage at such length because each word, ironically – in what is thus a self-critical, as well as self-exemplifying gesture – adds weight to Beckett's central charge: that words themselves have fallen into 'disrepute' (or, if this process is judged as being not yet quite complete, should be made to do so).[23] Thus, the aspiring writer 'bore[s]' holes into language, critiquing his or her own medium. In so doing, this writer follows a procedure similar to Beethoven, in that composer's Seventh Symphony, a work in which 'enormous pauses' really do punctuate music, as Beckett's gloss suggests (in fact, these pauses feature prominently in the symphony's final movement). Though it may not be entirely clear what equivalent 'silences' might consist of in the context of a written text, like this – except insofar as a concern with what Beckett here calls the 'materiality' of language defines a whole tradition, extending at least as far back as Mallarmé and forward to Derrida – it is relatively easy to see how they might feature when a text is spoken. For once characters are put on stage, nothing is easier, it might be thought, than to have them speak elliptically, say very little, or even say nothing. Famously, the texts Beckett wrote for both the stage and other performative media (including radio, for which he wrote several times) are full of this. In Beckett's *oeuvre* as a whole, then, silence is not opposed to, but the very form and substance of, dramatic action.

This is not to say, however, that silence is alien to non-dramatic genres. In Virginia Woolf's *The Voyage Out*, Terence Hewet plans to write a novel entitled *Silence* about '"the things people don't say"' – a prospectus which might be said to anticipate at least one facet of Woolf's own subsequent novelistic career.[24] Much of T. S. Eliot's overtly Christian poetry is structured by an opposition between sound and silence; not coincidentally, it also casts the latter as necessary (though in this fallen world, all-too rarely met with) to believers' receptivity to God's word.[25] When the same writer speaks of 'silent withering of autumn flowers' in 'The Dry Salvages' (1941), we are all but compelled to strain our ears towards the very sound he says we cannot hear.[26] And in Walter de la Mare's *The Listeners, and Other Poems* (1912), silence plays what one may call a 'structural' role within each poem, many of which focus on occasions and locales of soundlessness, such as abandoned homes, and bedrooms in which people are asleep.[27] Implicitly, the wager here is that in the absence of sound, poetic evocations may be summoned more effectively. Silence, then, facilitates attention – a tacit claim here strengthened by the way each poem tends to offer 'synchronic' impressions, as it were, of any given scene, rather than 'diachronic' ones in which discrete events unfold over an extended period of time (the sort of period, of course, in which attention may drift away). Thus, an implied isomorphism, pervading the collection, between three things: the attention of protagonists as drawn by silence within each poem; the attention of each poem *to* these same silences; and the attention each poem asks of its ideal listeners or readers. Silence, then, for de la Mare, is what a poem 'wants' as much as or in addition to being what a poem may or may not be about.

Silence may also, of course, be considered as a social virtue, born out of solicitude, indicating sensitivity to what the other may, or may not, say. This is how it appears in Robert le Traz's *Silent Hours* (1934), a tribute to the word-less solidarity of patients at tuberculosis sanatoria, translated for an English-speaking readership by none other than Dorothy Richardson. In Richardson's own fiction, as we have seen in Chapter 2, silence is the medium of fellow feeling, protecting the individuality of those who share it in a way that sound may not. It comes as no surprise, then, to see *Pilgrimage* take a connoisseurial interest in silences, some of which are resonant with Eliot's 'The Dry Salvages' in their insistence on what one may call the 'soundless sounds' of flowers: the 'harebells, inaudibly tinkling as they sway' in *Dimple Hill* (1938), for instance, or 'the strange silent noise of the sunlight and the flowers' in *The Tunnel* (1919).[28] When a room 'darkle[s] in the silence' elsewhere in the latter novel, it is with a similar sense to this last-quoted passage's that light-effects (whether the light concerned is burgeoning or diminishing) make silence 'present' to senses other than the auditory (vol. 2, p. 69). And when the phrase 'almost audible' is used in *Dimple Hill*, it suggests a silence one might savour with the auditory sense itself (vol. 4, pp. 477, 481).

Silence may also, however, have desolate instantiations. To describe the alternation between George Harvey Bone's periods of relative sanity and those of his psychosis in *Hangover Square*, Patrick Hamilton writes:

> It was as though he had been watching a talking film, and all at once the sound-track had failed. The figures on the screen continued to move, to behave more or less logically; but they were figures in a new, silent, inde-scribably eerie world. Life, in fact, which had been for him a moment ago a 'talkie', had all at once become a silent film. And there was no music.[29]

In madness, then, Bone experiences something like cinematic history in reverse, passing from the 'talk[ing]' era to a silent one, where 'figures' are deprived of speech. Life here loses much of its coherence – even the 'super-added', merely incidentally connected kind regularly provided in screenings of actual silent films by 'live' musical accompaniment, an arrangement Hamilton's final line alludes to. But though Hamilton presents as self-evident an equation between 'talking' films and normalcy, many others, in an only slightly earlier period, saw silence as the norm – aesthetically: not in terms of sanity and its vicissitudes – and 'talkies' as uncanny or disturbing. To see why, we must turn now to the historical transition between 'silent' and 'sound' cinematic modes.

Against the 'Talkie'

Certain features of this history are known to us already. As noted in this book's 'Introduction', the vast majority of films produced before 1927 are 'silent', that is, they do not feature what Hamilton refers to as a 'sound-track'. In the wake of *The Jazz Singer*, however, filmmakers increasingly took advantage of the new technology showcased by that 1927 film in order to create such soundtracks, so adding to their films a sonic element, comprising either spoken dialogue or music, or both. This meant that over time, 'silent' cinema became increasingly rare, ultimately more or less disappearing as a commercial format. As a consequence, several features that had helped define film in its 'silent' era more or less disappeared as well: inter-titles, whose function, it seemed, was now more fluently fulfilled by audible speech; 'live' musical accompaniment, now rendered obsolete, many felt, by music pre-recorded on the soundtrack of any given film itself.

Despite such claims of 'obsolescence', however, not everybody thought that soundtrack technology rendered the techniques of 'silent' cinema redundant. For Richardson, whose journalism on cinema in the journal *Close Up* (1927–33) exhibits significant parallels with those features of her fiction addressed above, 'Vocal sound' in film is especially baleful, upsetting 'the balance between what is seen and the silently perceiving, co-operative onlooker' on which truly satisfying film spectatorship depends.[30] Thus, *Pilgrimage*'s preference for silent communion between subjects joined in time and space is refigured as one between subjects who are temporally and spatially disjunct. Another *Close Up* contributor better known for her 'literary' writing, H. D., also criticises synchronised speech, recalling one instance (evidently, this had involved witnessing an actor filmed at relatively close quarters while a soundtrack simultaneously replayed that actor's voice) with this, as it were, symptomatically agrammatical construction: 'The projection of voice and the projection of image were each in itself perfect and ran together perfectly as one train on two rails but the rails somehow functioning in perfect mechanical unison, remained a separate [*sic*] – separate entities, fulfilling different mechanical requirements.'[31] Synchronisation at the technical level thus fails to sponsor unity at the aesthetic one. It must be stressed that Richardson, especially, did not object to sound as such as an accompaniment to or even as an element within film: indeed, she praises musical accompaniment in particular for its ability to help the viewer 'manufacture' a 'reality' only synechdocally or associatively represented by the images projected on the screen.[32] Rather, what the *Close Up* writers collectively objected to was the way synchronised dialogue presented objects to two senses now corralled together that did not satisfy those senses taken separately, or in themselves. As a like-minded film theorist, Béla Balázs (1884–1949), puts this point in the context of a lament for the 'lost' art of expressive mouth movements made by 'silent' movie actors: 'a mouth that speaks intelligibly to the ear, can no longer remain intelligible to the eye'.[33]

It is the rationale behind this opposition to sound film that casts new light upon the guiding topics of the present chapter. For it is precisely listening (on which, of course, this chapter centres), that, extraordinarily, appears in these accounts not so much as a virtue but as a vice. As another commentator, Luigi Pirandello, complained in 1929: 'The succession of talking images on the screen tires the eye and detracts from the power of a dialogic scene'.[34] Listening, that is, has negative effects on *looking*. Richardson, again, is also explicit on this point, echoing a Mach-related claim that we have seen her make before – as we saw in Chapter 2, this is ventriloquised in *Pilgrimage*, by Hypo, in relation to Wagner's musical dramas – as follows: 'it is impossible both to hear and to see, to the limit of our power of using these facilities, at one and the same moment [. . .] [O]ne or the other will always take precedence in our awareness.'[35] For Pirandello amongst others, such arguments ultimately led to a defence of 'silent' film, rather than sound, on the grounds of medium specificity – a Lessing-ite or Greenbergian criterion according to which film, as properly concerned with 'images', should not be allowed to 'speak'.[36] Similarly, Balázs complains that in the wake of sound, film has become less an art form in its own right than a proxy form of 'theatre'.[37] The allegation here, then, is that in learning how to talk, film has somehow forgotten how to be itself.

This is not to say, however, that all those hostile to sound film as found were hostile to sound film in principle, or as it might become. For filmmakers such as Sergey Eisenstein, sound-syncing technology had great potential that might yet be released aesthetically if harnessed to a formal and technical principle already familiar from 'silent' film: montage. In a text translated and published by *Close Up* in 1928, Eisenstein and his fellow directors W. I. Pudovkin and G. V. Alexandrov theorise the possibility of montage involving sound as well as images, intercutting auditory and visual material in much the same way that filmmakers had long since learned to intercut images with one another. To describe the effects this new technique may make achievable, they, like Münsterberg before them (in the text on pre-sound film discussed above in Chapter 3), deploy a metaphor derived from music: in this case, 'counterpoint';

which here, as its musical provenance suggests, designates the relatively diverse and independent character of the things it nonetheless relates, rather than these things' strict parallelism or simultaneity.[38] Thus, images may be accompanied by sounds that do not correspond to them in a strictly 'realistic' or illustrative fashion, or juxtaposed to produce what the authors call a 'pronounced non-coincidence' of auditory and visual material.[39] The great potential of sound-sync technology, in other words, consists in the ability to pair sounds with images with which they do *not* have a self-evident affinity.

It is partly with Eisenstein in mind, then, that Eisler and Adorno, in *Composing for the Films*, evolve a theory of musical accompaniment as similarly out of joint with the images it attends. Rejecting the widespread tendency in commercial cinema to 'match' the supposed affective content of music to the dramatic thrust of any given film or scene (for example, by using 'sad' music to accompany sad scenes, 'happy' music for happy ones, and so on), the authors instead propose a form of music that 'can throw its meaning into relief by setting itself in opposition to what is being shown on the screen'.[40] In the example Adorno and Eisler go on to offer, Eisler's own score for Slatan Dudow's *Kuhle Wampe* (1931), the 'strict form and stern tone' of the music forms a pointed contrast to the 'depressing' situation dramatised within the screenplay (pp. 26–7). Further distancing themselves from cinematic norms, the authors oppose the use of leitmotifs as pioneered by Wagner (in Wagner's own works, leitmotifs are short melodic phrases that play 'symbolic' or scenario-explicative roles, recurring whenever a given character or theme features on the stage). Thus Wagner is in this, as in so many other respects, Adorno's bête noire; not coincidentally, we might reflect, given that, as we saw in Chapter 2, Adorno sees 'sound' cinema itself as descended from Wagner's theory and practice of the 'total work of art'. And if leitmotifs may not be used in cinematic music, what techniques should composers of such music adopt instead? Demonstrating their partisanship with the musical avant-garde, Adorno and Eisler recommend the use of what we know from Chapter 4 of the present book to have been that avant-garde's substantive signature, dissonance, here praised for its allegedly inherent 'dramatic' qualities (p. 41).

In sum, many of those who did not deprecate its use entirely thought that sound could play a positive role in film only insofar as it was critical, helping to ironise or otherwise interrogate images that the camera presented to the eye. We are left then only to consider film in Humphrey Jennings's sense (albeit briefly), as something that constitutes a form of 'listening', independently of whether it is something a spectator may choose or be compelled to listen *to*. Balázs speaks to this when, in one of his more receptive moments, vis-à-vis sync-sound technology, he contends: 'It is the business of the sound film to reveal for us our acoustic environment, the acoustic landscape in which we live [. . .] from the mutterings of the sea to the din of a great city'.[41] Film may thus raise to proper dignity what we may always have 'sensed' without hitherto aesthetically appreciating.

BLINDNESS AND CATHECTED SPACE

It is with this in mind that we may shift our focus to a topic that, at first blush, may appear to have nothing whatsoever to do with cinema: blindness. To take this 'first blush' first: if cinema is definitively visual – notwithstanding its use or otherwise of sound – it might be thought that blindness is no less definitively non- or 'counter-' visual, relating to vision solely under the auspices of loss or exile. However, just as theorists of film justified their welcoming or otherwise of sound in film in terms of the senses' effects on one another, so theorists of blindness considered the condition to involve potential consequences for senses other than the one directly concerned. Specifically, commentators on blindness held that in the absence of vision, touch and hearing might offer blind people some form of compensation for their disability. Putting this point now by way of contrast to, rather than congruence with, the tenets explored above in relation to the alleged primacy of 'silent' over 'talking' film, we may say that such commentary considers hearing and listening not as antithetical to vision but as capable of fulfilling vision's role in vision's absence.

A careful, hedged articulation of this thesis forms the centrepiece of Pierre Villey's *The World of the Blind: A Psychological Study* (1914; English translation, 1922). Here, the ability of blind persons to form a fully adequate conception of their surroundings is asserted against the contrary claims of those for whom a lack of vision renders all such conceptions irredeemably impoverished. By a happy providence of nature, Villey argues, those whose eyesight has been lost 'find, in exchange, resources in other senses which are neglected by most men [. . .] but which are most valuable to those who know how to use them and make them fructify'.[42] Specifically, hearing and touch, and to a lesser extent other undamaged senses, 'make up for the absent sense of sight' (p. 72). However, as the first of these two passages already intimates, Villey does not believe the senses 'make up' this absence solely in their own right: rather, supervening mental processes harness data from these senses that might otherwise have been ignored but which would in any case have been available. 'This is how substitution of the senses is to be understood', Villey contends (and thus implicitly, in no other way): 'The function of the mind is to unify the elements supplied to it by the senses, to co-ordinate them and to synthesise them for the purpose of action' (p. 98). Touch and hearing in the blind and in the sighted are fundamentally no different; what differs, between the two groups, is the way these senses are interpreted.

We are led back, then, to attention, that faculty or process bringing discrimination and coherence where there may otherwise be confusion and disparity. For as Villey insists, the blind are distinguished at least as much by their prodigiousness of attentiveness as by their actual disability: hence, one of the collateral hazards of blindness is 'excessive concentration' (p. 34). Recalling William James's commentary on attention, we may thus say that though the blind and sighted occupy a single world (the title of Villey's book notwithstanding), they may inhabit different 'universe[s]'. As we now know, what constitutes these different universes for James and his contemporaries is more the mind's selection from and understanding of sensation than sensation in itself. In effect transvaluing the Greenbergian appreciation of art 'unaided by the mind' set out above in Chapter 1, we may therefore take Villey as suggesting (again, in effect: this is not a locution he would have favoured) that blind persons negotiate their environments successfully precisely insofar as they do not resemble modernists.

If blindness cultivates attention, though, the particular forms of attention most distinctive of it may be strangely inattentive of themselves. Take 'The Sense of Obstacles', an ability whereby many blind people seem to 'know, without touching, that a closely proximate object is in one's way (p. 101). Though most earlier commentators had interpreted this phenomenon as a rarefied and distance-spanning form of touch, Villey considers hearing more likely to be responsible: one way he elucidates this claim is by comparison to the then still not fully explicated, but seemingly ear-related, echo-locational capacities of bats (p. 111). Thus, sounds that convey information about objects' positions in space are misrecognised, appearing not *qua* sound, reflected off these objects, but as 'tactile' properties emanating from those objects themselves. 'The blind perceive by ear', Villey sums up, 'what they believe that they perceive by the skin' (p. 104). Hearing is even more important to blind people than some blind people are aware.

And what of the way blind people orientate themselves in space more generally? Again, Villey thinks the ear responsible for this, stating that such sounds as 'footsteps on the floor, or the crackling of the fire' can 'give to the blind man [an adequate sense of] the dimensions' of a room (p. 252). Similarly, the blind detective in Baynard H. Kendrick's *The Odour of Violets* (1941) negotiates his way around buildings via hearing – and in so doing, moves our own agenda forward, by turning his sensory handicap to a more distinctly professional advantage, connected to the fact that detectives characteristically come into contact with those practising evasion or deceit. 'A room was always audibly alive' to this detective, Kendrick writes: 'People about him breathed in different tempos; marked themselves by tiny coughs and unnoticed sniffles.'[43] By means of these auditory clues, the detective infers not only people's presence but also their unconsciously communicated character and state of mind. Another novel, Henry Green's *Blindness* (1926), also dilates upon what we might call the 'naive' or unselfconscious auditory habits (and emissions) of sighted people as opposed to the more rigorous and probing listening of the blind. Recalling Balázs's interest in the 'reveal[ing]' of acoustic landscapes, Green writes of his protagonist:

> He was in the summer-house [. . .] Cries of rooks came down to him from where they would be floating, whirling in the air like dead leaves, over the lawn. The winds kept coming back, growing out of each other, and when a stronger one had gone by there would be left cool eddies slipping by his cheek, while a tree further on would thunder softly. Every wind was different [. . .].[44]

It is precisely 'Every wind[´s]' auditory difference from every other that a sighted person might not be expected to notice while a blind one does (that these differences *are* chiefly auditory, meanwhile, is confirmed when Green adds of the protagonist: 'as he listened to [these winds'] coming and to their going, there was rhythm in their play'; p. 435). The sightless thus throw the sighted's relative inattention into clear relief; a suggestion *Blindness* recapitulates 'structurally', as it were, by having its protagonist become blind only once the novel has started, and then become ever more acoustically discerning over the remainder of its course. 'There were so many things to do', Green sums up his character's reflections towards the novel's close: 'all the senses to develop' (p. 442). Sensation may thus be not just a means to other ends but an end in itself.

It is in this sense, then, that blindness may be aligned with that prospectus for sound cinema considered earlier: it too is a sensory regime raising to their true dignity phenomena that might otherwise be ignored. And it is in this sense also that blindness may be related to another thing discussed above, this time in Chapter 1: that 'existential ethos' according to which the self flourishes in proportion to its 'registration' (to recall Richardson's term) of sense impressions. This leads us to consider what we might call 'situational' or non-organic blindness, resulting not from chronic disability but something more temporary and contingent such as nightfall or inhabiting a darkened room. For according to fictional texts, at least, this may also cause listening to blossom – albeit seemingly less often in situations of disinterested aesthetic pleasure than of anxiety or fear. Consider David in *Call it Sleep*, here terrified by the presence of creatures apparently near him in a cellar:

> his ears had sharpened. He could hear sounds that he couldn't hear before [. . .] Against his will he sifted the nether dark. It was moving – moving everywhere on a thousand feet [. . .] His jaws began to chatter. Icy horror swept up and down his spine like a finger scratching a comb. His flesh flowed with terror.[45]

Now consider another child, Michael Fane, unsettled in a new bedroom having been put to bed for the night towards the start of *Sinister Street*:

far up the street, newsboys would cry hoarsely the details of a murder or suicide. As they passed beneath his bedroom window their voices would swell to a paralyzing roar, and as the voices died away round the corner, Michael would be left shaking with fear.[46]

And now finally consider Michael as an adult, towards the end of the same novel, entering another person's house to stand before another person's bedroom:

> Michael unlocked the front-door quietly and stood listening for a moment in the passage. He could hear a low snarling in the bedroom, but from where he was standing not a word was distinct and he could not bring himself to the point of listening close at the keyhole [. . .] [T]he darkness grew thicker and every instant more atramental, beating upon him from the steeps of the house like the filthy wings of a great bat: and still the snarling rose and fell. It rose and fell like the bubbling of a kettle, and then without warning the kettle overflowed with spit and hiss and commotion. Every word spoken by Barnes and the woman was now audible.[47]

Though the details differ in each instance, a single wager governs all three cases: that hearing is either 'sharpened' by, or sharpens, fear or trepidation (in the last instance, it may help to specify, Michael fears that one of those on whom he eavesdrops will be revealed by conversation to have committed murder, echoing the auditor's fears from childhood). Not coincidentally, all three episodes also feature various degrees of darkness, a fact contributing to the plausibility of this 'wager' in at least two connected ways – the first being that hearing may be considered as substitutive of sight in cases of impaired vision (which darkness paradigmatically represents), as we have seen; the second being that darkness is proverbially considered a stimulus to fear itself. All three episodes, moreover, situate auditors in relatively constricted spaces, putting into play still another pair of factors, the first on this occasion being that such spaces are more likely than others to present sounds to the ear with a minimum of interference; the second being that, by the same token, such spaces are also more likely than others to make auditors feel imperilled by what is heard within or closely proximate outside. Finally, two of out of the three episodes situate their protagonists either literally or figuratively at unpleasantly close quarters to fear-inspiring animals: in David's case, to rats; and in the elder Michael's case, to a particularly monstrous 'bat' – one of those creatures we have seen Villey invoke to elucidate the hearing prowess of the blind.

We are thus presented with three instances of 'cathected' space, in which affective energies are stoked by listening.[48] Cellars and bedrooms, especially, are paradigmatic of such places, being closely associated with qualities and functions often strongly cathected in their own right: identity, privacy and intimacy (amongst other things) in the case of bedrooms; the partial removal or avoidance of ambivalently regarded things, in the case of cellars. In all three passages just quoted, such spaces are domestic, suggesting that fear may penetrate most deeply when occasioned in a place that – at least normatively speaking – exists to give security and comfort. And it is this that gives a peculiar piquancy to accounts of cathected space occasioned by what is perhaps the most powerful and popularly resonant context in which fear and domesticity converged in British culture of the first half of the twentieth century: the Second World War; specifically, as manifested by the Blitz, and other bombing campaigns targeting British cities. For if we reflect that bombing, in such campaigns, almost always came at night-time, we may see how it coincided with that 'situational' or non-organic blindness just spoken of (indeed, the blackouts prescribed by defending authorities in an attempt to curb such bombings' efficacy intensified this blindness). And if we reflect further that such bombing threatened the homes and other buildings in which its human targets sheltered, we may see how the fear invested in cathected space might take on a new dimension, becoming focused not only on what might transpire *within* such space but also *to* such space, given these buildings' Blitz-revealed, bombing-relative physical fragility.

We are returned, then, to the present chapter's point of departure, via the testimony of those who, like Jennings and Spender, witnessed bombing raids at first hand. Here, for instance, is Robert Herring, like H. D. a member of the *Close Up* group, writing in a journal published by another member of that group, Bryher:

> This evening, home from office, there comes – *crash*! I decide to join the mattress below [a reference to the furnishing and location of the bomb shelter in Herring's building] [. . .] I skip the last three stairs, as *whizz-whew* goes a bomb [. . .] Crackle, crash – every thinkable noise, and some others. Then quiet, rimmed by fire-bells.[49]

And here is Herring's evocation of a meal at which he is hosted by a couple ('the surgeon' referred to below is one of this couple):

> 'Did you often see [Sarah] Bernhardt [the famous actress]?' says the surgeon (*bang.*) 'Only in her (*crash*) old days (*I'm so sorry*)'. 'Ah, she had a voice of –' (*whew, whizz, crinkle, zip*) 'I saw her in –' (*crash*)'.
>
> 'The garden, I think,' says my host, on the whole a practical man, and certainly the noise, as of a demented bus drawing up, sounded near. We agree, but don't say so. The surgeon continues his dissertation, the meal continues. I look at my hostess; she has never heard anything like this

before (neither have I), but she does not show it. She serves herself to plane-noises as she does to parsnips – with distaste, but with dignity.[50]

And here, finally, is Bryher, acclaiming H. D.'s forbearance under similar conditions:

> She has such a keen sense of hearing and was so sensitive to the slightest sound that I never understood how she not only managed to endure the noise but to write some of her finest poetry in spite of it.[51]

The bombing's sheer noisiness aside, the keynotes of these passages are, on one hand, bombing's utter violation of domestic normalcy, and on the other, countervailingly, the same bombing's weird co-option into a semblance of domestic routine.

It is H. D. herself, however, who perhaps responds to such events most profoundly, finding in them 'higher' philosophical significance. Here is part of 'The Walls Do Not Fall' (1944) – surely amongst the poems Bryher has in mind when speaking of her 'finest':

> [. . .] when the shingles hissed
>
> in the rain of incendiary,
> other values were revealed to us,
>
> other standards hallowed us;
> strange texture, a wing covered us,
>
> and though there was whirr and roar in the high air,
> there was a Voice louder,
>
> though its speech was lower
> than a whisper.[52]

Bombing reveals a 'Voice' that, paradoxically, its own far greater volume would seem more likely to conceal. And what is this voice? The answer is suggested earlier in the same poem:

> Thoth, Hermes, the Stylus,
> the palette, the pen, the quill endure,
> [. . .]
>
> But we fight for life,
> we fight, they say, for breath,
>
> so what good are your scribblings?
> this – we take them with us

beyond death; Mercury, Hermes, Thoth
invented the script, letters, palette;

the indicated flute or lyre-notes
on papyrus or parchment

are magic, indelibly stamped
on the atmosphere somewhere,

forever; remember, O sword,
you are the younger brother, the latter-born,

your Triumph, however exultant,
must one day be over

*in the beginning
was the Word.*[53]

The 'Voice' is thus the fount and matrix of the 'Word', itself exalted here as
a deathless and originary force, as in the creation narratives and sacralising
personifications of religion (the italicised allusion to the Gospel of John aside,
Hermes and Mercury are Gods of messages and their transmission in ancient
Greek and Roman myth, respectively, while Thoth is the ancient Egyptian God
responsible for alphabets and writing). Having acted at the world's 'beginning', this word has since been manifest in many media – in verbal form and
in that of music ('flute or lyre-notes'), inscribed by 'palette', 'pen' and 'quill',
fixed on 'parchment' and 'papyrus', and instantiate as H. D.'s own text. There
is even a suggestion here that newer media than those listed may be at the back
of H. D.'s mind, even as she contemplates the word's apparently medium-
or apparatus-less apotheosis. For in 'stamp[ing]' itself 'indelibly', this word
evokes nothing so much as those technologies that – as the present book has
noted so many times now – make words recorded and repeatable, the gramophone and phonograph.[54]

CODA: LISTENING AS LIFE

A final word on war leads to our conclusion. Listening in the Second World
War has been seen to harrow and oppress, mugging rather than entreating
the attention. But such listening does not disgrace or completely overshadow
other auditory modes – as, indeed, H. D. already has suggested. Virginia Woolf
captures this well when in her own account of bombing, she writes that once
immediate danger seems to have passed, in any given raid, the mind 'reaches
out and instinctively revives itself', by turning to more benign and exalting

stimuli.[55] One such stimulus is Wagner's music, accessed via memory, as heard at Bayreuth a previous year.[56] To the recalling ear, this music presents a salve to the terrors and discomforts of the present.

In this salving role, music typifies what appeals to and ennobles listening – and in doing so, suggests a certain regulatory ideal concerning not just objects of listening but also listening itself. In *Between the Acts*, Woolf writes that music 'makes us see the hidden, join the broken. Look and listen. See the flowers, how they ray their redness, whiteness, silverness and blue.'[57] To the attentive listener, music thus brings manifold illuminations, embedding listening per se in a wider field of sensory percepts (especially visual: music 'makes us *see*'), and these percepts themselves in a still wider field of cognitive and even spiritual comprehension. In 'The School of Giorgione' – the very text, we may recall, where it is said that 'All art constantly aspires towards the condition of music' – Pater effectively elaborates upon this argument, absorbing a broadened sense of listening into the still broader category of 'play':

> In [. . .] the favourite incidents of Giorgione's school, music or the musical intervals in our existence, life itself is conceived as a sort of listening – listening to music, to the reading of Bandello's novels, to the sound of water, to time as it flies. Often such moments are really our moments of play, and we are surprised at the unexpected blessedness of what may seem our least important part of time; not merely because play is in many instances that to which people really apply their own best powers, but also because at such times, the stress of our servile, everyday attentiveness being relaxed, the happier powers in things without are permitted free passage, and have their way with us.[58]

Released from 'servile' cares, 'life itself' becomes 'a sort of listening' – hence all things, we may extrapolate, become a proxy for or analogue of 'music'. In this extended sense, to listen is, with all one's senses, *to enjoy*; to be appreciative of all in life that can be savoured.

It is as an exemplar of this expanded sense of listening that we may now turn in conclusion to Stephen Graham, that connoisseur of city sounds met with above in Chapter 2, who, in *London Nights*, records a night-time car journey from the City, in the heart of London, to Epping Forest, on its outskirts. This journey is, it turns out, made for none but eminently 'playful' or aesthetic purposes. Here is how the first part of Graham's and his companion's drive plays out:

> We cross the fields of London, London Fields, and the wild heath, Cambridge Heath, without knowing it. No, perhaps the dreariness was Dalston, perhaps it was partly Hackney; there was clover under the asphalt, clover on Hackney Downs. The car impatiently jumps in

holes in the road. We pull up in a spacious empty place, looking at a Congregational Church, which, thanks to its Victorian buttresses, in the moonlight looks like a cathedral. It is Lower Clapton. We move from the inner to the outer suburbs. Clapton becomes Lea Bridge with majestical views of squads of poplar trees beyond reservoirs, and lights o' London on another side of town.[59]

Clover, a church, and city lights all engage the 'listener', in Pater's sense of things or their perceivers being bathed in 'unexpected blessedness'. Night-time exalts rather than curtails perception. And so, with sights now joined by more orthodox 'acoustic' objects, Graham draws the curtain on this episode in two paragraphs that also here serve to bring the present book to its close:

> The owls yell in the high trees, but the wind whispers reassuringly over the wide forest. *Her hour, her hour*, shriek the owls, as if announcing a spectre, and then *Peace, peace*! says the wind. Then *dell, dell, dell*, the silvery chime of an unforgetting clock telling the hour to the trees. *Dell, dell, dell, dell*, happy human music, refreshing the soul, stilling the mind in the midnight hour.
>
> So we stand there, and while the bell sounds two cigarette ends glow in a forest glade. We have no secrets there, however, but a love of beauty. Our end being attained, we return to the car – and passing through all the dark suburbs, reach the gay, enchanted City once again.[60]

NOTES

1. See Peter Stansky and William Abrahams, *London's Burning: Life, Death and Art in the Second World War* (London: Constable, 1994), pp. 98–9.
2. Stephen Spender, *World Within World* (London: Hamish Hamilton, 1951), p. 286.
3. Spender, *World Within World*, p. 287.
4. A final point worth making about Jennings and Spender, meanwhile, is that both encode listening primarily in terms of *visual* cues, such as the aspect of a face or 'bow[ing]' of one's head (in this respect, both echo Joyce's *Chamber Music*, as cited in our 'Introduction', where players play with ' head to the music bent'). This reflects the fact that whereas we can see seeing, we cannot hear listening. The cultural representation of hearing is often decisively inflected by this fact.
5. William James, *The Principles of Psychology*, 2 vols (New York: Dover, [1890] 1950), vol. 1, p. 424; emphasis in original.
6. Gustav Spiller, 'The Dynamics of Attention', *Mind* 10:40 (1901), pp. 498–524; p. 514 cited.
7. Henri Bergson, *Matter and Memory*, translated by Nancy Margaret Paul and W. Scott Palmer (New York: Zone Books, [1896] 1991), p. 101.
8. Ernst Mach, *Contributions to the Analysis of the Sensations*, translated by C. M. Williams (Bristol: Thoemmes, [1885] 1998), p. 111; emphasis altered.
9. Jonathan Crary, *Suspensions of Perception: Attention, Spectacle, and Modern Culture* (Cambridge, MA: MIT Press, 1991), pp. 24–5; emphasis in original.
10. G. W. F. Hegel, *Aesthetics: Lectures on Fine Art*, 2 vols, translated by T. M. Knox (Oxford: Clarendon Press, [1835] 1975), vol. 2, p. 907.

11. Theodor Adorno, *In Search of Wagner*, translated by Rodney Livingstone, with a new preface by Slavoj Žižek (London: Verso, [1952] 2005), p. 21.
12. Christian von Ehrenfels, 'On "Gestalt Qualities"' (1890), translated by Barry Smith, in Barry Smith (ed.), *Foundations of Gestalt Theory* (Munich: Philosophia Verlag, 1988), pp. 82–177; p. 90 cited.
13. Lee knew Gurney personally, and reviewed *The Power of Sound* in the *Contemporary Review* for December 1882. See Gordon Epperson, *The Mind of Edmund Gurney* (Madison: Fairleigh Dickson University Press, 1997), pp. 22–3. I am grateful to my colleague Catherine Maxwell for the second piece of information.
14. Vernon Lee, *Music and its Lovers: An Empirical Study of Emotion and Imaginative Responses to Music* (London: George Allen and Unwin, 1932), p. 19. Subsequent references to this edition are given in the text.
15. E. M. Forster, *Howard's End*, with an introduction and notes by David Lodge (Harmondsworth: Penguin, [1910] 2000), p. 26. Subsequent references to this edition are given in the text.
16. Sigmund Freud, 'Recommendations to Physicians Practicing Psycho-Analysis' (1912), in *The Standard Edition of the Complete Psychological Works of Sigmund Freud*, 24 vols, translated and edited by James Strachey, in collaboration with Anna Freud, assisted by Alix Strachey and Alan Tyson (London: Hogarth Press, 1948–74), vol. 12, p. 111. Subsequent references to this edition are given in the text.
17. William Morrison Patterson, *The Rhythm of Prose: An Experimental Investigation of Individual Difference in the Sense of Rhythm*, 2nd edn (New York: Columbia University Press, [1916] 1917), p. 74. Subsequent references to this edition are given in the text.
18. Samuel Beckett, *Proust* (London: Chatto and Windus, 1931), p. 19.
19. Beckett, *Proust*, p. 20.
20. Marcel Proust, *In Search of Lost Time*, 6 vols, translated by C. K. Scott Moncrieff and Terence Kilmartin, revised by D. J. Enright (London: Vintage, [1913–27] 1996), vol. 6, p. 219.
21. Samuel Beckett, *Krapp's Last Tape, and Embers* (London: Faber and Faber, 1965), p. 14. Subsequent references to this edition are given in the text.
22. Samuel Beckett, 'German Letter of 1937', translated by Martin Esslin, in *Disjecta: Miscellaneous Writings and a Dramatic Fragment*, edited by Ruby Cohn (New York: Grove Press, 1984), pp. 170–3; pp. 171–2 cited.
23. It must be emphasised, however, that Beckett wrote this text in German, not the 'official English' criticised within.
24. Virginia Woolf, *The Voyage Out*, edited with an introduction and notes by Lorna Sage (Oxford: Oxford University Press, [1915] 2001), p. 249.
25. See, for example, section V of 'Ash Wednesday' (1930).
26. T. S. Eliot, *Collected Poems, 1909–1962* (London: Faber and Faber, 1974), p. 193.
27. Walter de la Mare, *The Listeners, and Other Poems* (London: Constable, 1912).
28. Dorothy Richardson, *Pilgrimage*, 4 vols (London: Virago, [1915–67] 2002), vol. 4, p. 455; vol. 2, p. 253. Subsequent references to this edition are given in the text.
29. Patrick Hamilton, *Hangover Square*, with an introduction by J. B. Priestley (Harmondsworth: Penguin, [1941] 2001), p. 15.
30. Dorothy Richardson, 'A Thousand Pities' (1927), in James Donald, Anne Friedberg and Laura Marcus (eds), *Close Up, 1927–1933: Cinema and Modernism* (London: Cassell, 1998), pp. 166–8; p. 167 cited.
31. H. D., 'The Cinema and the Classics, III: The Mask and the Movietone' (1927), in Donald, Friedberg and Marcus (eds), *Close Up, 1927–1933*, pp. 114–20; p. 115 cited.

32. Dorothy Richardson, 'Continuous Performance, II: Musical Accompaniment' (1927), in Donald, Friedberg and Marcus (eds), *Close Up, 1927–1933*, pp. 162–3; p. 163 cited.
33. Béla Balázs, *Theory of the Film: Character and Growth of a New Art*, translated by Edith Bone (New York: Dover, [1945] 1970), p. 68.
34. Luigi Pirandello, 'Will Talkies Abolish the Theatre?' (1929), translated by Nina Davinci Nicols, in *Shoot!: The Notebooks of Serafino Gubbio, Cinematograph Operator* (1915), translated by C. K. Scott Moncrieff, with an introduction by Tom Gunning (Chicago: University of Chicago Press, [1915] 2005), pp. 215–22; p. 218 cited.
35. Dorothy Richardson, 'Continuous Performance: A Tear for Lycidas' (1930), in Donald, Friedberg and Marcus (eds), *Close Up, 1927–1933*, pp. 196–201; p. 197 cited.
36. Pirandello, 'Will Talkies Abolish the Theatre?', p. 218.
37. Balázs, *Theory of the Film*, p. 195.
38. S. M. Eisenstein, W. I. Pudowkin [Pudovkin] and G. V. Alexandroff [Alexandrov], 'The Sound Film: A Statement from the USSR' (1928), in Donald, Friedberg and Marcus (eds), *Close Up, 1927–1933*, pp. 83–6; p. 84 cited; emphasis removed.
39. Eisenstein, Pudowkin and Alexandroff, 'The Sound Film', p. 84; emphasis removed.
40. Theodor Adorno and Hanns Eisler, *Composing for the Films*, with an introduction by Graham McCann (London: Athlone Press, [1947] 1994), p. 26. Subsequent references to this edition are given in the text.
41. Balázs, *Theory of the Film*, p. 197.
42. Pierre Villey, *The World of the Blind: A Psychological Study*, translated by Alys Hallard (London: Duckworth, [1914; 1922] 1930), p. 14. Subsequent references to this edition are given in the text.
43. Baynard H. Kendrick, *The Odour of Violets* (London: Methuen, 1941), p. 90.
44. Henry Green, *Nothing, Doting, Blindness*, with an introduction by D. J. Taylor (London: Vintage, 2008), p. 435. Subsequent references to this edition are given in the text.
45. Henry Roth, *Call it Sleep* (Harmondsworth: Penguin, [1934] 1977), p. 91.
46. Compton Mackenzie, *Sinister Street*, 2 vols (London: Martin Secker, 1913), vol. 1, p. 40.
47. Mackenzie, *Sinister Street*, vol. 2, p. 1107.
48. I deploy the term 'cathexis' here with certain reservations, not the least of these being that Freud disapproved this translation of his *besetzung*. However, no English-language alternative has ever stuck. For discussion of these terms, and their translation, see Jean Laplanche and Jean-Bertrand Pontalis, *The Language of Psychoanalysis*, translated by Donald Nicholson-Smith, with an introduction by Daniel Lagache (London: Karnac Books, 1973), pp. 62–5.
49. Robert Herring, 'Delayed Action (A Diary of Recent Events)', *Life and Letters To-day* 27:39 (1940), pp. 89–107; p. 91 cited.
50. Robert Herring, 'Sheffield (Diary at a Distance)', *Life and Letters To-day* 27:41 (1941), pp. 211–35; pp. 214–15 cited.
51. Bryher, *The Days of Mars: A Memoir, 1940–1946* (London: Calder and Boyars, 1977), p. 115.
52. H. D., *Collected Poems, 1912–1944*, edited by Louis L. Martz (New York: New Directions, 1982), p. 520.
53. H. D. *Collected Poems*, pp. 518–19; emphases in original.
54. For more on sound technology and H. D., see Adalaide Morris, *How to Live/What to Do: H. D.'s Cultural Poetics* (Urbana: University of Illinois Press, 2003).

55. Virginia Woolf, 'Thoughts on Peace in an Air Raid' (1940), in *Collected Essays*, 4 vols (London: Hogarth Press, 1967), vol. 4, pp. 173–7; p. 176 cited.
56. Woolf, 'Thoughts on Peace in an Air Raid', p. 176.
57. Virginia Woolf, *Between the Acts*, edited by Stella McNichol, with an introduction and notes by Gillian Beer (Harmondsworth: Penguin, [1941] 2000), p. 73.
58. Walter Pater, 'The School of Giorgione' (1871), in *The Renaissance*, edited with an introduction and notes by Adam Phillips (Oxford: Oxford University Press, [1873] 1998), p. 96.
59. Stephen Graham, *London Nights* (London: Hurst and Blackett, 1925), pp. 263–4.
60. Graham, *London Nights*, p. 265; emphases in original.

BIBLIOGRAPHY

Adams, Henry, *The Education of Henry Adams*, with an introduction by D. W. Brogan (Boston: Riverside Press, [1907] 1961).

Adorno, Theodor W., *Essays on Music*, selected with an introduction, commentary and notes by Richard Leppert (Berkeley: University of California Press, 2002).

Adorno, Theodor, *In Search of Wagner*, translated by Rodney Livingstone, with a new preface by Slavoj Žižek (London: Verso, [1952] 2005).

Adorno, Theodor and Hanns Eisler, *Composing for the Films*, with an introduction by Graham McCann (London: Athlone Press, [1947] 1994).

Agawu, Kofi, 'The Invention of "African Rhythm"', *Journal of the American Musicological Society* 48:3 (1995), pp. 380–95.

Albright, Daniel, *Untwisting the Serpent: Modernism in Music, Literature, and Other Arts* (Chicago: University of Chicago Press, 2000).

Albright, Daniel (ed.), Commentary within *Modernism and Music: An Anthology of Sources* (Chicago: University of Chicago Press, 2004).

Anderson, Paul Allen, *Deep River: Music and Memory in Harlem Renaissance Thought* (Durham, NC: Duke University Press, 2001).

Anon., 'Ragtime' (1899), in Karl Koenig (ed.), *Jazz in Print (1856–1929): An Anthology of Selected Early Readings in Jazz History* (Hillsdale: Pendragon Press, 2002), pp. 51–4.

Anon., 'The Boys who Arrange the Tunes you Play' (1922), in Karl Koenig (ed.), *Jazz in Print (1856–1929): An Anthology of Selected Early Readings in Jazz History* (Hillsdale: Pendragon Press, 2002), pp. 204–5.

Antcliffe, Herbert, *Living Music: A Popular Introduction to the Methods of Modern Music* (London: Joseph Williams, 1912).

Antheil, George, 'The Negro on the Spiral; Or, A Method of Negro Music', in Nancy Cunard (ed.), *Negro: Anthology* (London: Wishart, 1934), pp. 346–51.

Antheil, George, *Bad Boy of Music* (London: Hurst and Blackett, [1945] 1947).

Aristotle, *De Anima (On the Soul)*, translated with an introduction and notes by Hugh Lawson-Tancred (London: Penguin, [c. 350 BC] 1986).

Armstrong, Tim, *Modernism, Technology and the Body: A Cultural Study* (Cambridge: Cambridge University Press, 1998).

Armstrong, Tim, 'Two Types of Shock in Modernity', *Critical Quarterly* 42:1 (2000), pp. 60–73.

Arnheim, Rudolf, *Radio*, translated by Margaret Ludwig and Herbert Read (London: Faber and Faber, 1936).

Attali, Jacques, *Noise: The Political Economy of Music*, translated by Brian Massumi, with a foreword by Fredric Jameson and an afterword by Susan McClary (Minneapolis: University of Minnesota Press, [1977] 1985).

Babbitt, Irving, *The New Laokoon: An Essay on the Confusion of the Arts* (London: Constable, 1910).

Badger, R. Reid, 'James Reese Europe and the Prehistory of Jazz', in Reginald T. Buckner and Steven Weiland (eds), *Jazz in Mind: Essays on the History and Meanings of Jazz* (Detroit: Wayne State University Press, 1991), pp. 19–37.

Bakhtin, Mikhail, *Rabelais and his World*, translated by Hélène Iswolsky, foreword by Krystyna Pomorska, prologue by Michael Holquist (Bloomington: Indiana University Press, 1984).

Balázs, Béla, *Theory of the Film: Character and Growth of a New Art*, translated by Edith Bone (New York: Dover, [1945] 1970).

Barkan, Elazar and Ronald Bush (eds), *Prehistories of the Future: The Primitivist Project and the Culture of Modernism* (Stanford: Stanford University Press, 1995).

Barnes, Djuna, *New York*, edited with a commentary by Alyce Barry (Los Angeles: Sun and Moon Press, 1989).

Bartók, Béla, *Béla Bartók Essays*, selected and edited by Benjamin Suchoff (Lincoln, NE: University of Nebraska Press, 1978).

Baudelaire, Charles, *Selected Writings on Art and Literature*, translated with an introduction by P. E. Charvet (Harmondsworth: Penguin, 1992).

Beard, George Miller, *American Nervousness; Its Causes and Consequences. A Supplement to Nervous Exhaustion (Neurasthenia)* (New York: G. P. Putnam's Sons, 1881).

Beckett, Samuel, *Proust* (London: Chatto and Windus, 1931).

Beckett, Samuel, *Krapp's Last Tape, and Embers* (London: Faber and Faber, 1965).

Beckett, Samuel, *Disjecta: Miscellaneous Writings and a Dramatic Fragment*, edited by Ruby Cohn (New York: Grove Press, 1984).

Beer, Gillian, *Open Fields: Science in Cultural Encounter* (New York: Oxford University Press, 1996).

Bell, Clive, *Since Cézanne* (London: Chatto and Windus, 1922).

Bell, Clive, 'Plus de Jazz' (1921), in Karl Koenig (ed.), *Jazz in Print*

(1856–1929): An Anthology of Selected Early Readings in Jazz History (Hillsdale: Pendragon Press, 2002), pp. 154–7.

Benjamin, Walter, *Illuminations*, edited and with an introduction by Hannah Arendt, translated by Harry Zohn (London: Fontana Press for HarperCollins, 1992).

Benjamin, Walter, *One Way Street, and Other Writings*, translated by by Edmund Jephcott and Kingsley Shorter, with an introduction by Susan Sontag (London: Verso, 1997).

Benjamin, Walter, *The Origin of German Tragic Drama*, translated by John Osborne, with an introduction by George Steiner (London: Verso, [1924–5] 1998).

Berger, Karol, 'Time's Arrow and the Advent of Musical Modernity', in Karol Berger and Anthony Newcomb (eds), *Music and the Aesthetics of Modernity: Essays* (Cambridge, MA: Harvard University Press, 2005), pp. 3–22.

Bergson, Henri, *Laughter: An Essay on the Meaning of the Comic*, translated by Cloudesley Brereton and Fred Rothwell (London: Macmillan, [1900] 1911).

Bergson, Henri, *Matter and Memory*, translated by Nancy Margaret Paul and W. Scott Palmer (New York: Zone Books, [1896] 1991).

Bergson, Henri, *Time and Free Will: An Essay on the Immediate Data of Consciousness*, translated by F. L. Pogson (Mineola: Dover Publications, [1889; 1913] 2001).

Berman, Marshall, *All That Is Solid Melts Into Air: The Experience of Modernity* (London: Verso, 1983).

Blesser, Barry and Linda-Ruth Salter, *Spaces Speak, Are You Listening? Experiencing Aural Architecture* (Cambridge, MA: MIT Press, 2007).

Boulanger, Nadia, 'Lectures on Modern Music', *Rice Institute Pamphlet* 13:2 (1926), pp. 113–95.

Bowen, Zack, *Musical Allusions in the Work of James Joyce: Early Poetry through 'Ulysses'* (Albany: State University of New York Press, 1974).

Brady, Erika, *A Spiral Way: How the Phonograph Changed Ethnography* (Jackson, MS: University Press of Mississippi, 1999).

Braun, Hans-Joachim, 'Introduction', in H.-J. Braun (ed.), *'I Sing the Body Electric': Music and Technology in the 20th Century* (Hofheim: Wolke, 2000), pp. 9–32.

Brewster, David, *The Kaleidoscope: Its History, Theory and Construction, with its Applications to the Fine and Useful Arts*, 2nd edn (London: John Murray, 1858).

Bronfen, Elisabeth, *Dorothy Richardson's Art of Memory: Space, Identity, Text*, translated by Victoria Appelbe (Manchester: Manchester University Press, 1999).

Brown, Sterling A., *The Collected Poems of Sterling A. Brown*, selected by Michael S. Harper (New York: Harper and Row, 1980).

Browne, Andrew J., 'Aspects of Stravinsky's Work', *Music and Letters* 11:4 (1930), pp. 360–6.

Bruccoli, Matthew J. with Judith S. Baughman, *Reader's Companion to F. Scott Fitzgerald's 'Tender is the Night'* (Columbia: University of South Carolina Press, 1997).

Bryher, *Development* (London: Constable, 1920).

Bryher, *Two Selves* (Paris: Contact Publishing, 1923).

Bryher, *The Days of Mars: A Memoir, 1940–1946* (London: Calder and Boyars, 1977).

Bucknell, Brad, *Literary Modernism and Musical Aesthetics: Pater, Pound, Joyce and Stein* (Cambridge: Cambridge University Press, 2002).

Budgen, Frank, *James Joyce and the Making of Ulysses* (London: Grayson and Grayson, 1934).

Busoni, Ferruccio, *Sketch of a New Esthetic of Music*, translated by Th. Baker (New York: G. Schirmer, [1907] 1911).

Butler, Christopher, *Early Modernism: Literature, Music and Painting in Europe, 1900–1916* (Oxford: Oxford University Press, 1994).

Cahan, Abraham, *The Rise of David Levinsky*, with an introduction by John Higham (New York: Harper Torchbook, [1917] 1960).

Cahan, Abraham, *Yekl, and The Imported Bridegroom, and Other Stories of the New York Ghetto*, with an introduction by Bernard G. Richards (New York: Dover Books, 1970).

Cantril, Hadley and Gordon W. Allport, *The Psychology of Radio* (New York: Harper and Brothers, 1935).

Cantril, Hadley, Hazel Gaudet and Herta Herzog, *The Invasion from Mars: A Study in the Psychology of Panic* (Princeton: Princeton University Press, [1940] 1982).

Carse, Adam, *The History of Orchestration* (New York: Dover, [1925] 1964).

Chanan, Michael, *Musica Practica: The Social Practice of Western Music from Gregorian Chant to Postmodernism* (London: Verso, 1994).

Chanan, Michael, *Repeated Takes: A Short History of Recording and its Effects on Music* (London: Verso, 1995).

Chávez, Carlos, *Toward a New Music: Music and Electricity*, translated by Herbert Weinstock (New York: De Capo, [1937] 1975).

Chopin, Kate, *The Awakening, and Other Stories*, edited with an introduction and notes by Pamela Knights (Oxford: Oxford University Press, 2000).

Connor, Steven, *Dumbstruck: A Cultural History of Ventriloquism* (Oxford: Oxford University Press, 2000).

Conrad, Joseph, *The Mirror of the Sea: Memories and Impressions; A Personal Record: Some Reminiscences* (London: J. M. Dent, 1923).

Conrad, Joseph, 'Preface' to *Youth: A Narrative, and Two Other Stories* (1902), in *Conrad's Prefaces to His Works*, with an introductory essay by Edward Garnett, and a biographical note by David Garnett (London: J. M. Dent, 1937), pp. 71–4.

Conrad, Joseph, 'Preface', in *The Nigger of the 'Narcissus'*, edited with an introduction by Jacques Berthoud (Oxford: Oxford University Press, [1897] 1984).

Conrad, Joseph, *Heart of Darkness, and Other Tales*, edited with an introduction by Cedric Watts (Oxford: Oxford University Press, 1990).

Cowell, Henry, *New Musical Resources* (New York: Alfred A. Knopf, 1930).

Crane, Hart, *The Letters of Hart Crane, 1916–1932*, edited by Brom Weber (New York: Heritage House, 1952).

Crane, Hart, *The Complete Poems of Hart Crane*, edited by Marc Simon, with a new introduction by Harold Bloom (New York: Liveright, 2001).

Crary, Jonathan, *Suspensions of Perception: Attention, Spectacle, and Modern Culture* (Cambridge, MA: MIT Press, 2001).

Dahlhaus, Carl, *The Idea of Absolute Music*, translated by Roger Lustig (Chicago: University of Chicago Press, 1989).

Dahlhaus, Carl, *Studies on the Origin of Harmonic Tonality*, translated by Robert O. Gjerdingen (Princeton: Princeton University Press, 1990).

Danius, Sara, *The Senses of Modernism: Technology, Perception, and Aesthetics* (Ithaca, NY: Cornell University Press, 2002).

Dann, Kevin T., *Bright Colors Falsely Seen: Synaesthesia and the Search for Transcendental Knowledge* (New Haven: Yale University Press, 1998).

Darwin, Charles, *The Descent of Man, and Selection in Relation to Sex*, with an introduction by James Moore and Adrian Desmond (Harmondsworth: Penguin, [1873] 2004).

de la Mare, Walter, *The Listeners, and Other Poems* (London: Constable, 1912).

Dehnert, Edmund, 'The Consciousness of Music Wrought by Musical Notation', in Joseph W. Slade and Judith Yaross Lee (eds), *Beyond the Two Cultures: Essays on Science, Technology, and Literature* (Ames: Iowa State University Press, 1990), pp. 99–116.

Delaunay, Robert, 'Notes on the Development of Robert Delaunay's Painting' (1939–40), in *The New Art of Color: The Writings of Robert and Sonia Delaunay*, edited with an introduction by Arthur A. Cohen, translated by David Shapiro and Arthur A. Cohen (New York: Viking Press, 1978), pp. 16–19.

Dolar, Mladen, *A Voice and Nothing More* (Cambridge, MA: MIT Press, 2006).

Dos Passos, John, *Manhattan Transfer* (Boston: Houghton Mifflin, [1925] 1953).

Drucker, Johanna, *The Visible Word: Experimental Typography and Modern Art, 1909–1923* (Chicago: University of Chicago Press, 1994).

Du Bois, W. E. B., *The Souls of Black Folk* (New York: Dover, [1903] 1994).

Eagleton, Terry, *The Ideology of the Aesthetic* (Oxford: Blackwell, 1990).

Ehrenfels, Christian von, 'On "Gestalt Qualities"' (1890), translated by Barry Smith, in B. Smith (ed.), *Foundations of Gestalt Theory* (Munich: Philosophia Verlag, 1988), pp. 82–177.

Eisenstein, S. M., W. I. Pudowkin [Pudovkin] and G. V. Alexandroff [Alexandrov], 'The Sound Film: A Statement from the USSR' (1928), in James Donald, Anne Friedberg and Laura Marcus (eds), *Close Up, 1927–1933: Cinema and Modernism* (London: Cassell, 1998), pp. 83–6.

Eliot, T. S., *The Use of Poetry and the Use of Criticism: Studies in the Relation of Criticism to Poetry in England* (Cambridge, MA: Harvard University Press, 1933).

Eliot, T. S., *Collected Poems, 1909–1962* (London: Faber and Faber, 1974).

Eliot, T. S., *The Letters of T. S. Eliot, Volume 1: 1898–1922*, edited by Valerie Eliot (London: Faber and Faber, 1988).

Ellington, Duke, *The Duke Ellington Reader*, edited by Mark Tucker (New York: Oxford University Press, 1993).

Ellison, Ralph, *Shadow and Act* (New York: Vintage, 1972).

Ellmann, Richard, *James Joyce*, new and revised edn (New York: Oxford University Press, 1982).

Enzensberger, Hans Magnus, 'Constituents of a Theory of the Media', translated by Stuart Hood, in *Dreamers of the Absolute: Essays on Ecology, Media and Power* (London: Radius, 1988), pp. 20–53.

Epperson, Gordon, *The Mind of Edmund Gurney* (Madison: Fairleigh Dickson University Press, 1997).

Faulkner, Anne Shaw, 'Does Jazz put the Sin in Syncopation?' (1921), in Karl Koenig (ed.), *Jazz in Print (1856–1929): An Anthology of Selected Early Readings in Jazz History* (Hillsdale: Pendragon Press, 2002), pp. 152–4.

Faulkner, William, *As I Lay Dying: The Corrected Text* (New York: Vintage Books, [1930] 1987).

Faulkner, William, *Pylon: The Corrected Text* (New York: Vintage, [1935] 1987).

Fechner, Gustav, *Elements of Psychophysics*, vol. 1, edited by David H. Howes and Edwin G. Boring, translated by Helmut E. Adler (New York: Holt, Rinehart and Winston, [1860] 1966).

Fernando Pessoa, *Selected Poems*, 2nd edn, translated by Jonathan Griffin (Harmondsworth: Penguin, 2000).

Filreis, Alan, 'Stevens in the 1930s', in John Serio (ed.), *The Cambridge Companion to Wallace Stevens* (Cambridge: Cambridge University Press, 2007), pp. 37–47.

Fitzgerald, F. Scott, *The Great Gatsby*, edited with an introduction and notes by Ruth Prigozy (Oxford: Oxford University Press, [1925] 1998).

Fitzgerald, F. Scott, *Tender is the Night*, edited by Arnold Goldman, with an introduction and notes by Richard Godden (Harmondsworth: Penguin, [1934] 1998).

Ford, Ford Madox, *The Soul of London*, edited by Alan G. Hill (London: J. M. Dent, [1905] 1995).

Forster, E. M., *Howard's End*, with an introduction and notes by David Lodge (Harmondsworth: Penguin, [1910] 2000).

Frazer, Persifor, Jr, 'Some Microscopical Observations of the Phonograph Record', *Proceedings of the American Philosophical Society* 17:101 (1878), pp. 531–6.

Freud, Sigmund, *The Standard Edition of the Complete Psychological Works of Sigmund Freud*, 24 vols, translated and edited by James Strachey, in collaboration with Anna Freud, assisted by Alix Strachey and Alan Tyson (London: Hogarth Press, 1948–74).

Frisch, Walter, *German Modernism: Music and the Arts* (Berkeley: University of California Press, 2005).

Gage, John, *Colour and Culture: Practice and Meaning from Antiquity to Abstraction* (London: Thames and Hudson, 1995).

Gates, W. F., 'Ethiopian Syncopation – The Decline of Ragtime' (1902), in Karl Koenig (ed.), *Jazz in Print (1856–1929): An Anthology of Selected Early Readings in Jazz History* (Hillsdale: Pendragon Press, 2002), pp. 68–9.

Gendron, Bernard, *Between Montmartre and the Mudd Club: Popular Music and the Avant-Garde* (Chicago: University of Chicago Press, 2002).

Gitelman, Lisa, *Scripts, Grooves, and Writing Machines: Representing Technology in the Edison Era* (Stanford: Stanford University Press, 1999).

Goffin, Robert, 'Hot Jazz', in Nancy Cunard (ed.), *Negro: Anthology* (London: Wishart, 1934), pp. 378–9.

Gold, Michael, *Jews Without Money*, with woodcuts by Howard Simon (London: Noel Douglas, 1930).

Graham, Stephen, *London Nights* (London: Hurst and Blackett, 1925).

Graham, Stephen, *New York Nights*, illustrated by Kurt Wiese (New York: George H. Doran, 1927).

Graham, T. Austin, 'The Literary Soundtrack: Or, F. Scott Fitzgerald's Heard and Unheard Melodies', *American Literary History* 21:3 (2009), pp. 518–49.

Green, Henry, *Nothing, Doting, Blindness*, with an introduction by D. J. Taylor (London: Vintage, 2008).

Greenberg, Clement, 'Towards a Newer Laocoon' (1940), in *The Collected*

Essays and Criticism, Volume 1: Perceptions and Judgements, 1939–1944, edited by John O'Brian (Chicago: University of Chicago Press, 1986), pp. 23–38.

Griffiths, Paul, *Modern Music: A Concise History*, revised edn (London: Thames and Hudson, 1994).

Gurney, Edmund, *The Power of Sound*, with an introductory essay by Edward T. Cone (New York: Basic Books, [1880] 1966).

H. D., *Collected Poems, 1912–1944*, ed. Louis L. Martz (New York: New Directions, 1982).

H. D., 'The Cinema and the Classics, III: The Mask and the Movietone' (1927), in James Donald, Anne Friedberg and Laura Marcus (eds), *Close Up, 1927–1933: Cinema and Modernism* (London: Cassell, 1998), pp. 114–20.

Habermas, Jürgen, 'Modernity: An Unfinished Project' (1981), in Maurizio Passerin D'Entrèves and Seyla Benhabib (eds), *Habermas and the Unfinished Project of Modernity* (Cambridge: Polity, 1996), pp. 38–55.

Halliday, Sam, 'Weather, Sound Technology, and Space in Wallace Stevens', *Wallace Stevens Journal* 33:1 (2009), pp. 83–96.

Hamilton, Marybeth, *In Search of the Blues: Black Voices, White Visions* (London: Jonathan Cape, 2007).

Hamilton, Patrick, *Hangover Square*, with an introduction by J. B. Priestley (Harmondsworth: Penguin, [1941] 2001).

Hanslick, Eduard, *Vom Musikalisch-Schönen* (1854) [excerpts], translated by Martin Cooper, in Bojan Bujić (ed.), *Music in European Thought, 1851–1912* (Cambridge: Cambridge University Press, 1988), pp. 11–39.

Hartford, Robert (ed.), *Bayreuth: The Early Years; An Account of the Early Decades of the Wagner Festival as seen by the Celebrated Visitors and Participants* (London: Victor Gollancz, 1980).

Hecht, Ben and Charles MacArthur, *The Front Page* (New York: Covici Friede, 1928).

Hegel, G. W. F., *Hegel's Philosophy of Nature: Being Part Two of the Encyclopaedia of the Philosophical Sciences, 1830. Translated from Nicolin and Poggeler's Edition, 1959, and from the Zusatz in Michelet's Text, 1847*, translated by A. V. Miller (Oxford: Clarendon Press, 1970).

Hegel, G. W. F., *Aesthetics: Lectures on Fine Art*, 2 vols, translated by T. M. Knox (Oxford: Clarendon Press, [1835] 1975).

Heidegger, Martin, *Being and Time*, translated by John Macquarrie and Edward Robinson (Oxford: Blackwell, [1927] 1962).

Helmholtz, Hermann von, *On the Sensations of Tone, As a Physiological Basis for the Theory of Music*, 3rd edn, translated by Alexander J. Ellis (Bristol: Thoemmes, [1870; 1875] 1998).

Herring, Robert, 'Delayed Action (A Diary of Recent Events)', *Life and Letters To-day* 27:39 (1940), pp. 89–107.

Herring, Robert, 'Sheffield (Diary at a Distance)', *Life and Letters To-day* 27:41 (1941), pp. 211–35.

Hershey, Burnet, 'Jazz Latitude' (1922), in Karl Koenig (ed.), *Jazz in Print (1856–1929): An Anthology of Selected Early Readings in Jazz History* (Hillsdale: Pendragon Press, 2002), pp. 191–4.

Hertz, David Michael, *The Tuning of the Word: The Musico-Literary Poetics of the Symbolist Movement* (Carbondale: Southern Illinois University Press, 1987).

Hocker, Jürgen, 'My Soul is in the Machine – Conlon Nancarrow – Composer for the Player Piano – Precursor of Computer Music', in Hans-Joachim Braun (ed.), *'I Sing the Body Electric': Music and Technology in the 20th Century* (Hofheim: Wolke, 2000), pp. 84–96.

Hoffmann, E. T. A., 'Review of Beethoven's Fifth Symphony' (1810), in *E.T.A. Hoffmann's Musical Writings: 'Kreisleriana', 'The Poet and the Composer', Music Criticism*, edited annotated and introduced by David Charlton, translated by Martyn Clarke (Cambridge: Cambridge University Press, 1989), pp. 234–51.

Hoffmann, E. T. A., 'Master Flea' (1822), in *The Golden Pot, and Other Tales*, translated with an introduction and notes by Ritchie Robertson (Oxford: Oxford University Press, 2000).

Hollander, John, *The Untuning of the Sky: Ideas of Music in English Poetry, 1500–1700* (Princeton: Princeton University Press, 1961).

Hornbostel, Erich M. von, 'The Unity of the Senses' (1927), in Willis D. Ellis (ed.), *A Source Book of Gestalt Psychology*, with an introduction by Kurt Koffka (London: Kegan Paul, Trench, Trubner, 1938), pp. 210–16.

Hosler, Bellamy, *Changing Aesthetic Views of Instrumental Music in Eighteenth-Century Germany* (Ann Arbor: UMI Research Press, 1981).

Howells, W. D. and S. L. Clemens [Mark Twain], *Colonel Sellers as a Scientist* (1883), in *The Complete Plays of W. D. Howells*, edited by Walter J. Meserve (New York: New York University Press, 1960).

Hughes, Langston, *The Collected Poems of Langston Hughes*, edited by Arnold Rampersad, with David Roessel (New York: Vintage, 1994).

Huneker, James, *Melomaniacs* (London: T. Werner Laurie, [1902] 1906).

Huneker, James, *Visionaries* (London: T. Werner Laurie, [1905] 1906).

Hunt, Frederick Vinton, *Origins in Acoustics: The Science of Sound from Antiquity to the Age of Newton* (New Haven: Yale University Press, 1978).

Huxley, Aldous, *Point Counter Point*, with an introduction by David Bradshaw (London: Vintage Books, [1928] 2004).

Irwin, John T., *Hart Crane's Poetry: 'Apollinaire Lived in Paris, I Live in Cleveland, Ohio'* (Baltimore: Johns Hopkins University Press, 2011).

Jackson, Myles W., *Harmonious Triads: Physicists, Musicians, and Instrument Makers in Nineteenth-Century Germany* (Cambridge, MA: MIT Press, 2006).

James, Henry, *The Question of Our Speech, The Lesson of Balzac: Two Lectures* (Boston: Houghton Mifflin, 1905).

James, Henry, *The American Scene*, edited with an introduction by John F. Sears (Harmondsworth: Penguin, [1907] 1994).

James, William, *The Principles of Psychology*, 2 vols (New York: Dover, [1890] 1950).

Jones, Gavin, *Strange Talk: The Politics of Dialect Literature in Gilded Age America* (Berkeley: University of California Press, 1999).

Joyce, James, *Poems and Shorter Writings*, edited by Richard Ellmann, A. Walton Litz and John Whittier-Ferguson (London: Faber and Faber, 1991).

Joyce, James, *Ulysses: The 1922 Text*, edited with an introduction by Jeri Johnson (Oxford: Oxford University Press, 1993).

Kahn, Douglas, *Noise, Water, Meat: A History of Sound in the Arts* (Cambridge, MA: MIT Press, 1999).

Kandinsky, Wassily, *Concerning the Spiritual in Art*, translated by Michael T. H. Sadler, with an introduction by Adrian Glew (London: Tate Publishing, [1912] 2006).

Kandinsky, Wassily and Franz Marc (eds), *The Blaue Reiter Almanac*, edited with an introduction by Klaus Lankheit, translated by Henning Falkenstein with Manug Terzian and Gertrude Hinderlie (London: Tate Publishing, [1912] 2006).

Kant, Immanuel, *Anthropology from a Pragmatic Point of View*, revised and edited by Hans H. Rudnick, translated by Victor Lyle Dowdell (Carbondale and Edwardsville: Southern Illinois University Press, [1798] 1996).

Kargon, Jeremy, 'Harmonizing These Two Arts: Edmund Lind's *The Music of Colour*', *Journal of Design History* 21:1 (2010), pp. 1–14.

Katz, Mark, *Capturing Sound: How Technology has Changed Music* (Berkeley: University of California Press, 2004).

Kaufmann, Michael, *Textual Bodies: Modernism, Postmodernism, and Print* (London: Associated University Presses, 1994).

Kendrick, Baynard H., *The Odour of Violets* (London: Methuen, 1941).

Kennaway, James. 'Singing the Body Electric: Nervous Music and Sexuality in *Fin-de-Siècle* Literature', in Anne Stiles (ed.), *Neurology and Literature, 1860–1920* (Houndmills: Palgrave, 2007), pp. 141–62.

Kennedy, R. Emmet, *Mellows: A Chronicle of Unknown Singers* (New York: Albert and Charles Boni, 1925).

Kierkegaard, Søren, *Either/Or*, part 1, edited, translated, and with an introduction and notes by Howard V. Hong and Edna H. Hong (Princeton: Princeton University Press, [1843] 1987).

Kittler, Friedrich, *Discourse Networks, 1800/1900*, translated by Michael Metteer with Chris Cullens, with a foreword by David E. Wellbery (Stanford: Stanford University Press, 1990).

Kittler, Friedrich, *Gramophone, Film, Typewriter*, translated and with an introduction by Geoffrey Winthrop-Young and Michael Wutz (Stanford: Stanford University Press, 1999).

Kivy, Peter, 'Charles Darwin on Music', *Journal of the American Musicological Society* 12:1 (1959), pp. 42–8.

Klein, Adrian Bernard, *Colour-Music: The Art of Light* (London: Crosby Lockwood and Son, 1926).

Klein, Adrian Bernard, *Colour Cinematography* (London: Chapman and Hall, 1936).

Knowles, Sebastian, 'Death by Gramophone', *Journal of Modern Literature* 27: 1 (2003), pp. 1–13.

Koenig, Karl (ed.), *Jazz in Print (1856–1929): An Anthology of Selected Early Readings in Jazz History* (Hillsdale: Pendragon Press, 2002).

Koss, Juliet, *Modernism After Wagner* (Minneapolis: University of Minnesota Press, 2010).

Kracauer, Siegfried, *The Mass Ornament: Weimar Essays*, translated, edited and with an Introduction by Thomas Y. Levin (Cambridge, MA: Harvard University Press, 1995), pp. 323–8.

Krehbiel, Henry E., 'Lafcadio Hearn and Congo Music' (1906), in Karl Koenig (ed.), *Jazz in Print (1856–1929): An Anthology of Selected Early Readings in Jazz History* (Hillsdale: Pendragon Press, 2002), pp. 78–9.

Kreilkamp, Ivan, *Voice and the Victorian Storyteller* (Cambridge: Cambridge University Press, 2005).

Krohn, William O., 'Pseudo-Chromesthesia, or the Association of Colors with Words, Letters and Sounds', *American Journal of Psychology* 5:1 (1892), pp. 20–41.

Kubin, Alfred, *The Other Side*, translated by Mike Mitchell (Sawtry: Dedalus, [1908] 2000).

Lachenbruch, Jerome, 'Jazz and the Motion Picture' (1922), in Karl Koenig (ed.), *Jazz in Print (1856–1929): An Anthology of Selected Early Readings in Jazz History* (Hillsdale: Pendragon Press, 2002), pp. 179–80.

Laplanche, Jean and Jean-Bertrand Pontalis, *The Language of Psychoanalysis*, translated by Donald Nicholson-Smith, with an introduction by Daniel Lagache (London: Karnac Books, 1973).

Last, Rex W., *German Dadaist Literature: Kurt Schwitters, Hugo Ball, Hans Arp* (New York: Twayne, 1973).

Lastra, James, *Sound Technology and the American Cinema: Perception, Representation, Modernity* (New York: Columbia University Press, 2000).

Lawder, Standish D., *The Cubist Cinema* (New York: New York University Press, 1975).

Lawrence, D. H., *Aaron's Rod* (Harmondsworth: Penguin, [1922] 1950).

Lawrence, D. H., *The Trespasser* (Harmondsworth: Penguin, [1912] 1960).

Lawrence, D. H., *Fantasia of the Unconscious and Psychoanalysis and the Unconscious* (Harmondsworth: Penguin, 1971).

Lee, Vernon, *Music and its Lovers: An Empirical Study of Emotion and Imaginative Responses to Music* (London: George Allen and Unwin, 1932).

Lees, Heath, *Mallarmé and Wagner: Music and Poetic Language*, with extracts from the French translated by Rosemary Lloyd (Aldershot: Ashgate, 2007).

Lefebrve, Henri, *Rhythmanalysis: Space, Time and Everyday Life*, translated by Stuart Elden and Gerald Moore, with an introduction by Stuart Elden (London: Continuum, 2004).

Leppert, Richard, *The Sight of Sound: Music, Representation, and the History of the Body* (Berkeley: University of California Press, 1993).

Lessing, Gotthold Ephraim, *Laocoon: An Essay upon the Limits of Painting and Poetry*, translated by Ellen Frothingham (Mineola: Dover Publications, [1766] 2005).

Lippman, Edward, *A History of Western Musical Aesthetics* (Lincoln, NE: University of Nebraska Press, 1992).

Lock, Graham and David Murray, 'Introduction: The Hearing Eye', in G. Lock and D. Murray (eds), *The Hearing Eye: Jazz and Blues Influences in African American Visual Art* (Oxford: Oxford University Press, 2009), pp. 1–18.

Locke, Alain, *The Negro and his Music* (Port Washington, NY: Kennikat Press, [1936] 1968).

Loesser, Arthur, *Men, Women and Pianos: A Social History* (London: Victor Gollancz, 1955).

Loy, Mina, *The Lost Lunar Baedeker*, edited by Roger L. Conover (Manchester: Carcanet, 1997).

Luhmann, Niklas, *Love as Passion: The Codification of Intimacy*, translated by Jeremy Gaines and Doris L. Jones (Stanford: Stanford University Press, 1998).

Lutz, Tom, *American Nervousness, 1903: An Anecdotal History* (Ithaca, NY: Cornell University Press, 1991).

Lutz, Tom, 'Claude McKay: Music, Sexuality, and Literary Cosmopolitanism', in Saadi Simawe (ed.), *Black Orpheus: Music in African American Fiction from the Harlem Renaissance to Toni Morrison* (New York: Garland, 2000), pp. 41–64.

Mach, Ernst, *Contributions to the Analysis of the Sensations*, translated by C. M. Williams (Bristol: Thoemmes, [1885; 1896] 1998).

McKay, Claude, *Home to Harlem* (New York: Harper and Brothers, 1928).

Mackenzie, Compton, *Sinister Street*, 2 vols (London: Martin Secker, 1913).

McShane, Clay and Joel A. Tarr, *The Horse in the City: Living Machines in the Nineteenth Century* (Baltimore: Johns Hopkins University Press, 2007).

Mallarmé, Stéphane, *Collected Poems*, translated and with a commentary by Henry Weinfield (Berkeley: University of California Press, 1994).

Mann, Thomas, *Doctor Faustus*, translated by H. T. Lowe-Porter (Harmondsworth: Penguin, [1947] 1968).

Mann, Thomas, *Death in Venice, and Other Stories*, translated and with an introduction by David Luke (London: Vintage, 1998).

Mann, Thomas, *Buddenbrooks*, translated by H. T. Lowe-Porter (London: Vintage, [1902] 1999).

Marcus, Laura, *The Tenth Muse: Writing about Cinema in the Modernist Period* (Oxford: Oxford University Press, 2007).

Marks, Lawrence E., 'On Coloured-Hearing Synaesthesia: Cross-Modal Translation of Sensory Dimensions', in Simon Baron Cohen and John E. Harrison (eds), *Synaesthesia: Classic and Contemporary Readings* (Oxford: Blackwell, 1997), pp. 49–98.

Martin, Paul, '"Mr Bloom and the Cyclops": Joyce and Antheil's Unfinished "Opéra Mécanique"', in Sebastian D. G. Knowles (ed.), *Bronze by Gold: The Music of Joyce* (New York: Garland, 1999).

Martin, Timothy, *Joyce and Wagner: A Study of Influence* (Cambridge: Cambridge University Press, 1991).

Marx, Karl, *Economic and Philosophic Manuscripts of 1844*, translated by Martin Milligan, in Robert C. Tucker (ed.), *The Marx–Engels Reader*, 2nd edn (New York: Norton, 1978).

Mason, Daniel Gregory, 'Concerning Ragtime', in Karl Koenig (ed.), *Jazz in Print (1856–1929): An Anthology of Selected Early Readings in Jazz History* (Hillsdale: Pendragon Press, 2002), pp. 121–4.

Menand, Louis, *The Metaphysical Club* (London: Flamingo for HarperCollins, 2002).

Metfessel, Milton, *Phonophotography in Folk Music: American Negro Folk Songs in New Notation*, with an introduction by Carl E. Seashore (Chapel Hill: University of North Carolina Press, 1928).

Millard, Andre, *America on Record: A History of Recorded Sound* (Cambridge: Cambridge University Press, 1995).

Miner, Margaret, *Resonant Gaps: Between Baudelaire and Wagner* (Athens: University of Georgia Press, 1995).

Moderwell, Hiram K., 'Ragtime' (1915), in Karl Koenig (ed.), *Jazz in Print (1856–1929): An Anthology of Selected Early Readings in Jazz History* (Hillsdale: Pendragon Press, 2002), pp. 102–4.

Moderwell, Kelly, 'A Modest Proposal' (1917), in Karl Koenig (ed.), *Jazz in Print (1856–1929): An Anthology of Selected Early Readings in Jazz History* (Hillsdale: Pendragon Press, 2002), pp. 116–19.

Moholy-Nagy, László, 'Production – Reproduction: Potentialities of the Phonograph' (1922–23), in Christoph Cox and Daniel Warner (eds), *Audio Culture: Readings in Modern Music* (New York: Continuum, 2006), pp. 331–3.

Morris, Adalaide, *How to Live/What to Do: H. D.'s Cultural Poetics* (Urbana: University of Illinois Press, 2003).

Münsterberg, Hugo, *The Film: A Psychological Study* [first published as *The Photoplay: A Psychological Study*], with a foreword by Richard Griffin (Mineola: Dover, [1916] 1970).

Musil, Robert, *The Man Without Qualities*, translated by Sophie Wilkins and Burton Pike (London: Picador, [1930–42] 1997).

Neubauer, John, *The Emancipation of Music from Language: Departure from Mimesis in Eighteenth-Century Aesthetics* (New Haven: Yale University Press, 1986).

Nietzsche, Friedrich, *Beyond Good and Evil: Prelude to a Philosophy of the Future*, translated and with an introduction and commentary by R. J. Hollingdale (Harmondsworth: Penguin, [1886] 1972).

Nietzsche, Friedrich, 'On Music and Words' (c. 1871), translated by Walter Kaufmann; reprinted as an appendix to Carl Dahlhuas, *Between Romanticism and Modernism*, translated by Mary Whittall (Berkeley: University of California Press, 1980), pp. 103–19.

Nietzsche, Friedrich, *Untimely Meditations*, translated by R. J. Hollingdale, with an introduction by J. P. Stern (Cambridge: Cambridge University Press, 1983).

Nietzsche, Friedrich, *The Birth of Tragedy, Out of the Spirit of Music*, edited with an introduction by Michael Tanner, translated by Shaun Whiteside (Harmondsworth: Penguin, [1872] 1993).

Paget, Richard, *Human Speech: Some Observations, Experiments, and Conclusions as to the Nature, Origin, Purpose and Possible Improvement of Human Speech* (London: Kegan Paul, Trench, Trubner, 1930).

Partch, Harry, *Genesis of a Music* (1949) [excerpt], in Daniel Albright (ed.), *Modernism and Music: An Anthology of Sources* (Chicago: University of Chicago Press, 2004).

Pater, Walter, *The Renaissance*, edited with an introduction and notes by Adam Phillips (Oxford: Oxford University Press, [1873] 1998).

Patterson, William Morrison, *The Rhythm of Prose: An Experimental Investigation of Individual Difference in the Sense of Rhythm*, 2nd edn (New York: Columbia University Press, [1916] 1917).

Perloff, Marjorie, *The Futurist Moment: Avant-Garde, Avant Guerre, and the Language of Rupture*, with a new preface (Chicago: University of Chicago Press, 2003).

Picker, John M., *Victorian Soundscapes* (New York: Oxford University Press, 2003).

Pickering, Ruth, 'The Economic Interpretation of Jazz' (1921), in Karl Koenig (ed.), *Jazz in Print (1856–1929): An Anthology of Selected Early Readings in Jazz History* (Hillsdale: Pendragon Press, 2002), pp. 151–2.

Pirandello, Luigi, 'Will Talkies Abolish the Theatre?' (1929), translated by Nina Davinci Nicols, in *Shoot!: The Notebooks of Serafino Gubbio, Cinematograph Operator*, translated by C. K. Scott Moncrieff, with an introduction by Tom Gunning (Chicago: University of Chicago Press, [1915] 2005), pp. 215–22.

Plummer, Harry Chapin, 'Color Music – A New Art created with the Aid of Science', *Scientific American* 15:112 (10 April 1915), pp. 343–51.

Pollock, Isabel A., *Lip-Reading, What it Is, and What it Does for the Partially Deaf* (London: J. J. Perfitt, 1901).

Potter, Ralph K., George A. Kopp and Harriet C. Green, *Visible Speech* (New York: D. Van Nostrand, 1947).

Pound, Ezra, *Antheil, and the Treatise on Harmony* (Chicago: Pascal Covici, [1924] 1927).

Pound, Ezra, *Machine Art, and Other Writings: The Last Thought of the Italian Years*, selected and edited with an introduction by Maria Luisa Ardizzone (Durham, NC: Duke University Press, 1996).

Powell, Richard J. and David A. Bailey, *Rhapsodies in Black: Art of the Harlem Renaissance* (Berkeley: University of California Press, 1997).

Prince, Morton, *The Unconscious: The Fundamentals of Human Personality Normal and Abnormal*, 2nd revised edn (New York: Macmillan, [1914] 1921).

Proust, Marcel, *In Search of Lost Time*, 6 vols, translated by C. K. Scott Moncrieff and Terence Kilmartin, revised by D. J. Enright (London: Vintage, [1913–27] 1996).

Reed, Brian, *Hart Crane: After His Lights* (Tuscaloosa: University of Alabama Press, 2006).

Richardson, Dorothy, 'Data for Spanish Publisher' (1943), *London Magazine* 6 (June 1959), pp. 14–19.

Richardson, Dorothy, 'A Thousand Pities' (1927), in James Donald, Anne

Friedberg and Laura Marcus (eds), *Close Up, 1927–1933: Cinema and Modernism* (London: Cassell, 1998), pp. 166–8.

Richardson, Dorothy, 'Continuous Performance: A Tear for Lycidas' (1930), in James Donald, Anne Friedberg and Laura Marcus (eds), *Close Up, 1927–1933: Cinema and Modernism* (London: Cassell, 1998), pp. 196–201.

Richardson, Dorothy, 'Continuous Performance, II: Musical Accompaniment' (1927), in James Donald, Anne Friedberg and Laura Marcus (eds), *Close Up, 1927–1933: Cinema and Modernism* (London: Cassell, 1998), pp. 162–3.

Richardson, Dorothy, *Pilgrimage*, 4 vols (London: Virago, [1915–67] 2002).

Richter, Hans, 'My Experience with Movement in Painting and in Film', in Gyorgy Kepes (ed.), *The Nature and Art of Motion* (London: Studio Vista, 1965), pp. 142–57.

Richter, Simon, 'Intimate Relations: Music in and Around Lessing's "Laokoon"', *Poetics Today* 20:2 (1999), pp. 155–73.

Rilke, Rainer Maria, *Rodin and Other Prose Pieces*, translated by G. Craig Houston, with an introduction by William Tucker (London: Quartet Encounters, 1986), pp. 127–32.

Rimbaud, Arthur, *Collected Poems*, translated and with an introduction and notes by Martin Sorrell (Oxford: Oxford University Press, 2001).

Rimington, A. Wallace, *Colour Music: The Art of Mobile Colour*, with prefatory notes by Hubert von Herkomer and W. Brown (London: Hutchinson, 1912).

Ross, Alex, *The Rest is Noise: Listening to the Twentieth Century* (New York: Farrar, Straus and Giroux, 2007).

Roth, Henry, *Call it Sleep* (Harmondsworth: Penguin, [1934] 1977).

Rousseau, Jean-Jacques, *Essay on the Origin of Languages, and Writings Related to Music*, edited and translated by John T. Scott (Hanover, NH: University Press of New England, 1998).

Russel, Myra T., '*Chamber Music*: Words and Music Lovingly Coupled', in Sebastian D. G. Knowles (ed.), *Bronze by Gold: The Music of Joyce* (New York: Garland, 1999).

Russolo, Luigi, *The Art of Noises*, translated and with an introduction by Barclay Brown (Hillsdale: Pendragon Press, [1913–16] 1986).

Ryan, Judith, *The Vanishing Subject: Early Psychology and Literary Modernism* (Chicago: University of Chicago Press, 1991).

Samson, Jim, *Music in Transition: A Study of Tonal Expansion and Atonality, 1900–1920* (London: J. M. Dent, 1977).

Scarborough, Dorothy assisted by Ola Lee Gulledge, *On the Trail of Negro Folk Songs* (Cambridge, MA: Harvard University Press, 1925).

Schaeffer, Pierre, 'Acousmatics' (1966), translated by Daniel W. Smith, in

Christoph Cox and Daniel Warner (eds), *Audio Culture: Readings in Modern Music* (New York: Continuum, 2006).

Schaefer, R. Murray, *The Tuning of the World* (New York: Alfred A. Knopf, 1977).

Schmidt, Leigh Eric, *Hearing Things: Religion, Illusion, and the American Enlightenment* (Cambridge, MA: Harvard University Press, 2000).

Schoenberg, Arnold, *Style and Idea: Selected Writings of Arnold Schoenberg*, edited by Leonard Stein, translated by Leo Black (London: Faber and Faber, 1975).

Schoenberg, Arnold, *Theory of Harmony [Harmonielehre]*, translated by Roy E. Carter (London: Faber and Faber, [1911; 3rd edn 1922] 1978).

Schopenhauer, Arthur, *The World as Will and as Representation*, vol. 1, translated by E. F. J. Payne (New York: Dover, [1819] 1969).

Sears, Elizabeth, 'The Iconography of Auditory Perception in the Early Middle Ages: On Psalm Illustration and Psalm Exegesis', in Charles Burnett, Michael Fend and Penelope Gouk (eds), *The Second Sense: Studies in Hearing and Musical Judgement from Antiquity to the Seventeenth Century* (London: Warburg Institute, 1991), pp. 19–42.

Semon, Richard, *Mnemic Psychology*, translated by Bella Duffy, with an introduction by Vernon Lee (London: George Allen and Unwin, [1909] 1923).

Shattuck, Roger, *The Innocent Eye: On Modern Literature and the Arts* (New York: Farrar, Straus and Giroux, 1984).

Shaw-Miller, Simon, *Visible Deeds of Music: Art and Music from Wagner to Cage* (New Haven: Yale University Press, 2002).

Simmel, Georg, *The Sociology of Georg Simmel*, edited, translated and with an introduction by Kurt H. Wolff (New York: Free Press, 1964).

Spender, Stephen, *World Within World* (London: Hamish Hamilton, 1951).

Spiller, Gustav, 'The Dynamics of Attention', *Mind* 10:40 (1901), pp. 498–524.

Spotts, Frederic, *Bayreuth: A History of the Wagner Festival* (New Haven: Yale University Press, 1994).

Stamm, David, *A Pathway to Reality: Visual and Aural Concepts in Dorothy Richardson's 'Pilgrimage'* (Tübingen: Francke Verlag, 2000).

Stansky, Peter and William Abrahams, *London's Burning: Life, Death and Art in the Second World War* (London: Constable, 1994).

Sterne, Jonathan, *The Audible Past: Cultural Origins of Sound Reproduction* (Durham, NC: Duke University Press, 2003).

Stevens, Wallace, *Collected Poetry and Prose*, edited by Frank Kermode and Joan Richardson (New York: Library of America, 1997).

Stewart, Garrett, *Literature and the Phonotext* (Berkeley: University of California Press, 1990).

Stewart, Susan, *Poetry and the Fate of the Senses* (Chicago: University of Chicago Press, 2002).

Stravinsky, Igor, *Chronicle of My Life* [translated anonymously from the French] (London: Victor Gollancz, 1936).

Stuckenschmidt, H. H., 'The Mechanization of Music' (1925), translated by Michael Gilbert, in Jost Herman and Michael Gilbert (eds), *German Essays on Music* (New York: Continuum, 1994), pp. 149–56.

Synnott, Anthony, 'Puzzling over the Senses: From Plato to Marx', in David Howes (ed.), *The Varieties of Sensory Experience: A Sourcebook in the Anthropology of the Senses* (Toronto: University of Toronto Press, 1991), pp. 61–76.

Taussig, Michael, *Mimesis and Alterity: A Particular History of the Senses* (New York: Routledge, 1993).

Thompson, Emily, *The Soundscape of Modernity: Architectural Acoustics and the Culture of Listening, 1900–1933* (Cambridge, MA: MIT Press, 2002).

Thoreau, Henry David, *Walden*, edited with an introduction and notes by Stephen Fender (Oxford: Oxford University Press, [1854] 1999).

Tolmer, A., *Mise en Page: The Theory and Practice of Lay-Out* (London: The Studio, 1931).

Tolstoy, Leo, *The Kreutzer Sonata and Other Stories*, translated and with an introduction by David McDuff (Harmondsworth: Penguin, 2004).

Tovey, Donald Francis, *Musical Articles from the 'Encyclopaedia Britannica'*, with an editorial preface by Hubert J. Foss (London: Oxford University Press, 1944).

Toye, Francis, 'Ragtime: The New Tarantism' (1913), in Karl Koenig (ed.), *Jazz in Print (1856–1929): An Anthology of Selected Early Readings in Jazz History* (Hillsdale: Pendragon Press, 2002), pp. 94–6.

Tyndall, John, *Sound: A Course of Eight Lectures* (London: Longmans, Green and Co., 1867).

Vechten, Carl Van, *Nigger Heaven* (New York: Alfred A. Knopf, 1926).

Vernon, P. E., 'Synaesthesia in Music', *Psyche* 10:4 (1930), pp. 22–40.

Vertov, Dziga, *Kino-Eye: The Writings of Dziga Vertov*, edited with an introduction by Annette Michelson, translated by Kevin O'Brien (Berkeley: University of California Press, 1984).

Villey, Pierre, *The World of the Blind: A Psychological Study*, translated by Alys Hallard (London: Duckworth, [1914; 1922] 1930).

Vinge, Louise, *The Five Senses: Studies in a Literary Tradition* (Lund: C. W. K. Gleerup, 1975).

Vološinov, V. N., *Marxism and the Philosophy of Language,* translated by Ladislav Matejka and I. R. Titunik (Cambridge, MA: Harvard University Press, 1986).

Wagner, Richard, *Richard Wagner's Prose Works*, 8 vols, translated by William Ashton Ellis (London: Kegan Paul, Trench, Trübner, 1892–99).

Watt, Ian, *Conrad in the Nineteenth Century* (London: Chatto and Windus, 1980).

Waugh, Evelyn, *Vile Bodies* (Harmondsworth: Penguin, [1930] 1938).

Weber, Max, *The Rational and Social Foundations of Music*, edited and translated by Don Martindale, Johannes Riedel and Gertrude Neuwirth (Carbondale: Southern Illinois University Press, [1921] 1958).

Webern, Anton, *The Path to the New Music*, edited by Willi Reich, translated by Leo Black (Bryn Mawr: Theodore Presser, [1932–3] 1963).

Wheeler, Raymond H. and Thomas D. Cutsforth, 'Synaesthesia, A Form of Perception', *Psychological Review* 29:3 (1922), pp. 212–20.

Wittgenstein, Ludwig, *Tractatus Logico-Philosophicus*, translated by C. K. Ogden, with an introduction by Bertrand Russell (Mineola: Dover, [1921] 1999).

Woolf, Virginia, *The Waves* (Harmondsworth: Penguin, [1931] 1964).

Woolf, Virginia, *Collected Essays*, 4 vols (London: Hogarth Press, 1967).

Woolf, Virginia, *Mrs Dalloway*, edited by Stella McNichol, with an introduction and notes by Elaine Showalter (Harmondsworth: Penguin, [1925] 1992).

Woolf, Virginia, *To the Lighthouse*, edited by Stella McNichol, with an introduction and notes by Hermione Lee (Harmondsworth: Penguin, [1927] 1992).

Woolf, Virginia, *Flush*, edited with an introduction and notes by Kate Flint (Oxford: Oxford University Press, [1933] 1998).

Woolf, Virginia, *Jacob's Room*, edited with an introduction by Kate Flint (Oxford: Oxford University Press, [1922] 1999).

Woolf, Virginia, *Between the Acts*, edited by Stella McNichol, with an introduction and notes by Gillian Beer (Harmondsworth: Penguin, [1941] 2000).

Woolf, Virginia, *The Voyage Out*, edited with an introduction and notes by Lorna Sage (Oxford: Oxford University Press, [1915] 2001).

Yaffe, David, *Fascinating Rhythm: Reading Jazz in American Writing* (Princeton: Princeton University Press, 2006).

Films

Double Indemnity (dir. Billy Wilder, 1944, USA)

The House of Darkness (dir. W. D. Griffith, 1913, USA)

L'Inhumaine (dir. Marcel L'Herbier, 1924, France)

Listen to Britain (dir. Humphrey Jennings, 1942, UK)

Man with a Movie Camera (dir. Dziga Vertov, 1929, USSR)

The Merry Widow (dir. Erich von Stroheim, 1925, USA)

The Play House (dir. Buster Keaton and Edward F. Cline, 1921, USA)
Rhythmus 21 (dir. Hans Richter, 1921, Germany)
Symphonie Diagonale (dir. Viking Eggerling, 1921–4, Germany)

INDEX

Accents, 53, 64–5, 87n
Acousmatic sound, 13–14, 80, 100–1, 137
Acoustic science, 14, 104–5, 128, 135
Adams, Henry, 28
Adorno, Theodor, 6, 9, 24, 44–6, 79, 81, 126, 151, 160
  Composing for the Films (written with Hanns Eisler), 6–7, 13, 58–9, 77, 106, 112, 170
  'The Form of the Phonograph Record', 117
  'Music, Language, and Composition', 44–6
African American spiritual, 117, 141, 146
Albright, Daniel, 111, 129
Alexandrov, G. V., 169–70
'all sound' *see* Kahn, Douglas
Antcliff, Herbert, 128, 130
Antheil, George, 3–4, 17, 145
  Bad Boy of Music, 4
  Ballet Mécanique, 137
Apollinaire, Guillaume, 149
  'Lettre-Océan', 93–6, 97, 107
Aristotle, 22, 29, 34
  De Anima, 21
Arnheim, Rudolf, 67
Attali, Jacques, 14, 165
Attention, 158, 159–63, 167, 171–3
  voluntary and involuntary, 163
Augustine, St, *Confessions*, 21

Babbitt, Irving, 112
  The New Laokoon, 40
Bach, Johann Sebastian, 77, 99, 128
Bakhtin, Mikhail, 52–3
Balázs, Béla, 169, 170–1, 173
Barnes, Djuna, 62, 63
Bartók, Béla, 138, 140–2, 143, 145
Baudelaire, Charles, 102
  'Correspondances', 90
  'The Painter of Modern Life', 29, 111
  on Wagner, 89–91, 107
Beard, George Miller, 144

Beckett, Samuel
  'German Letter of 1937', 165–6
  Krapp's Last Tape, 163–5
  Proust, 163
Beer, Gillian, 103
Beethoven, Ludwig van, 41, 46, 77, 130, 133–4, 137, 143
  Fifth Symphony, 41–2, 161
  Ninth Symphony, 44, 46, 59, 77, 78, 83
  Seventh Symphony, 166
Bell, Clive, 144, 147
Benjamin, Walter, 6, 7, 9, 21, 24, 45–6, 117
  'The Work of Art in the Age of Mechanical Reproduction', 28
Berg, Alban
  Lulu, 133
  Wozzeck, 133
Berger, Karol, 130
Bergson, Henri, 30, 82, 160
  Laughter, 26
  Matter and Memory, 159
  Time and Free Will, 26
Berlewi, Henryk, *Mechano-Faktura, Contrasting Elements*, 106
Bernstein, Leonard, 144
Blindness, 9, 171–4, 175
Blues, 136, 141, 150
Boulanger, Nadia, 130
  'Lectures on Modern Music', 129
Brancusi, Constantin, 91, 107
Brewster, Sir David, 109
Brown, Sterling A., 'Cabaret', 149
Bryher (Winifred Ellerman), 175–6
  Development, 114
  Two Selves, 114
Bucknell, Brad, 20
Budgen, Frank, 26–7
Busoni, Ferruccio, 136, 137
  Sketch of a New Esthetic of Music, 135

Cage, John, 'Imaginary Landscape No. 1', 137
Cahan, Abraham
  The Rise of David Levinsky, 65
  Yekl, 65

Cahill, Thaddheus, 136, 137
Cantril, Hadley, *The Invasion from Mars*, 69–70
Cantril, Hadley and Gordon W. Allport, 67–9
Carse, Adam, 129–30
Castel, Louis Betrand, 109
Cendrars, Blaise, 111
Chanan, Michael, 142
Chávez, Carlos, 118–19
  Toward a New Music, 138–9
Chladni, E. F. F., 14, 83, 104, 117
Chopin, Frédéric, 74–5, 76
Chopin, Kate, *The Awakening*, 74–5
Cinema, 67, 79–80, 104, 109–10, 148
  as 'music', 101, 106–7
  music in, 99–101, 112, 167–8, 170
  'silent', 2, 91, 99–101, 102, 106, 110, 159, 167–71
  sound, 2, 99, 102, 110, 159, 167–71, 173
  see also individual film-makers
Close Up (journal), 114, 168–70, 175
Colour, 107–12
  'colour music', 92, 108–10, 112
Connor, Steven, 97
Conrad, Joseph
  Heart of Darkness, 33–8
  A Mirror of the Sea, 35–6
  'Preface' to *The Nigger of the 'Narcissus'*, 31, 38–9
  A Personal Record, 30–1, 38
  The Secret Agent, 138
Cooper, James Fenimore, 49n
Copeland, Aaron, 129
Coriat, Isador, 112
Courbet, Gustave, 26, 40
Cowell, Henry, 136, 137
  New Musical Resources, 135
Crane, Hart
  The Bridge, 102–3
  'Chaplinesque', 92
  'For the Marriage of Faustus and Helen', 148–9
Crary, Jonathan, 25, 159, 162
'crooning', 142

Crosland, Alan, *The Jazz Singer*, 2, 80, 168
Cryssipus, 103

da Vinci, Leonardo, 39
Danius, Sara, 18n
Davy, Charles, 120n
Darwin, Charles, 29, 31, 42, 75, 78
    The Descent of Man, 24–5
de la Mare, Walter, *The Listeners, and Other Poems*, 166–7
Debussy, Claude, 145
    Prélude à l'après-midi d-un faune, 126–7
Dehnert, Edmund, 119
Delaunay, Robert, 111
Delaunay, Sonia, 111
Derrida, Jacques, 166
Diaghilev, Sergie, 4
Dissonance, 131–3, 170; *see also* Harmony; Schoenberg, Arnold: serial technique of; Tonality
Dolar, Mladen, *A Voice and Nothing More*, 37–8
Dos Passos, John, *Manhattan Transfer*, 61, 66, 71
Douglas, Aaron, 148
Drucker, Joanna, 93
Du Bois, W. E. B., *The Souls of Black Folk*, 117–18

Eagleton, Terry, 42
Edison, Thomas, 70, 71, 116
Eggerling, Viking, *Symphonie Diagonale*, 106–7
Ehrenfels, Christian von, 160
Eisenstein, Sergey, 169–70
Eisler, Hanns *see* Adorno, Theodor: *Composing for the Films*
Eliot, T. S., 35, 62–3, 147, 166
    'Burnt Norton', 150–1
    'The Dry Salvages', 166, 167
    'The Hollow Men', 49n
    'Portrait of a Lady', 138
    The Use of Poetry and the Use of Criticism, 31
Ellington, Duke, 147, 148
Ellison, Ralph, 156n
Ethnomusicology *see* 'Folk' music
Europe, James Reese, 145

Faulkner, Anne Shaw, 147
    'Does Jazz put the Sin in Syncopation?', 144–5
Faulkner, William
    As I Lay Dying, 14, 64, 96–7, 98
    Pylon, 67
Fechner, Gustav, 25
Film *see* Cinema
First World War, 145
Fischinger, Oskar, 109–10
Fitzgerald, F. Scott, 147
    The Great Gatsby, 61

Tender is the Night, 71–3, 117
'Folk' music, 127, 140–2
Ford, Ford Madox, 4
    The Soul of London, 29
Forster, E. M., *Howard's End*, 161–2
Frazer Jr, Persifor, 104–5
Freud, Sigmund, 162
    'Civilization and its Discontents', 28
    see also Psychoanalysis
Futurism, 93, 135

Gaye, Marvin, *What's Going On*, 16
Gershwin, George, 144
Gesamtkunstwerk ('Total Work of Art'), 9–11, 12, 40, 77–8, 79–80, 81–3, 90, 106–7, 108, 110–12, 170; *see also* Wagner, Richard
Gitelman, Lisa, 116
Goethe, Johann Wolfgang von, 128
Goffin, Robert, 142
Gold, Michael, *Jews Without Money*, 61
Grab, Herman, 'The Moonlit Night', 60, 67
Graham, Stephen, 63–4, 70–1
    London Nights, 64, 178–9
    New York Nights, 64
Gramophone, 2, 13, 14, 27, 53, 65, 66, 70, 96, 102, 127, 138, 139–43, 177; *see also* Phonograph
Graphophone, 14, 96
Greek tragedy, 9, 110, 132
Green, Henry, *Blindness*, 172–3
Greenberg, Clement, 26, 42, 101, 110, 169, 172
    'Towards a Newer Laocoon', 40–1
Griffith, W. D., *The House of Darkness*, 99
Gurney, Edmund, 42, 50n, 126
    The Power of Sound, 25, 160

Habermas, Jürgen, 30
Hamilton, Patrick, *Hangover Square*, 67, 167–8
Hanert, John, 136
Hanslick, Eduard, 45, 46, 78–9, 81
    Vom Musikalisch-Schönen, 44
Harlem Renaissance, 148
Harmony, 12, 32, 39, 42, 58, 59, 60, 102–3, 125, 126, 128, 129, 131, 135, 137; *see also* Dissonance; Schoenberg, Arnold: serial technique of; Tonality
Hartley, David, 103, 104, 109
Haydn, Franz Joseph, 41

H. D. (Hilda Doolittle), 114, 168, 175, 176
    'The Walls Do Not Fall', 176–7
Hecht, Ben and Charles MacArthur, *The Front Page*, 66–7
Hegel, G. W. F., 22–3, 24, 32, 40, 42, 82, 101, 110, 128, 150, 159–60, 163
Heidegger, Martin, on 'Being-with' and 'Being-among-one-another', 55–7, 64, 65, 78
Helmholtz, Hermann von, 46–7n, 104
Herring, Robert, 175–6
Hershey, Burnet, 143
Hess, Myra, 157
Hoffmann, E. T. A.
    'Master Flea', 116
    'Review of Beethoven's Fifth Symphony', 41–2
Hornbostel, Erich von, 105–6
Hosler, Bellamy, 41
Hughes, Langston
    'The Big Timer', 149
    'Blues Fantasy', 150
    'Gal's Cry for a Dying Lover', 150
    'Harlem Night Club', 149
    'The Weary Blues', 150
Huneker, James, 113–14
Huxley, Aldous, *Point Counter Point*, 61
Huysman, Joris-Karl, *A Rebours*, 113

Inter-titles, 2, 168

James, Henry, 29, 65
    The Question of Our Speech, 85n
James, William, 159, 172
Jazz, 3, 72, 73, 111, 127, 136, 142–50
    as American, 143–4, 145, 147
    and economic processes, 144–5
    and the extra-musical, 145, 147, 148–9
    and 'race', 145–7, 148, 149
Jennings, Humphrey, 170, 179n
    Listen to Britain, 157–8
Joyce, James, 4, 12, 17, 26–7
    Chamber Music, 4, 11
    A Portrait of the Artist as a Young Man, 27
    Ulysses, 4, 15, 26, 52–3, 70, 103, 117, 138, 146–7

Kahn, Douglas, 13, 14–15, 27, 52, 162
Kandinsky, Wassily
    Composition IV, 110
    Concerning the Spiritual in Art, 111
    'On the Question of Form', 110–11
    The Yellow Sound, 111

Kandinsky, Wassily and Franz Marc *Der Blaue Reiter Almanac*, 110–11
Kant, Immanuel, 27, 58, 77, 82
    Anthropology from the Pragmatic Point of View, 22
    Critique of Pure Reason, 25
Katz, Mark, 142
Keaton, Buster and Edward F. Cline, *The Play House*, 99
Kendrick, Baynard H., *The Odour of Violets*, 172
Kennedy, R. Emmet, 141, 146
Kierkegaard, Søren, 40, 43, 44
Kittler, Friedrich, 37, 44
Klein, Adrian Bernard, *Colour-Music*, 109
Kodály, Zoltán, 145
Koenig, Karl, *Jazz in Print*, 144
Koss, Juliet, 77–8, 81
Kracauer, Siegfried, 79–80
Kreilkamp, Ivan, 37
Kubin, Alfred, *The Other Side*, 106

Lachenbruch, James, 'Jazz and the Motion Picture', 148
Language, 20–1, 26, 37–8, 40, 41, 43–6, 53, 57, 64–5, 102, 103, 114–15, 117, 150; *see also* Musical notation; Typography; Writing
Lastra, James, 13, 14
Lawrence, D. H., 35, 147
    Aaron's Rod, 60, 107–8
    Fantasia of the Unconscious, 31
    The Trespasser, 108
le Traz, Robert, *Silent Hours*, 167
Lee, Vernon, *Music and its Lovers*, 160–1
Lefebrve, Henri, 63
L'Herbier, Marcel, 17
    L'Inhumaine, 1–3, 7, 12, 14, 99, 148
Leppert, Richard, 99
Lessing, Gotthold Ephraim, 41, 110, 169
    Laocoon, 39–40
Lind, Edmund George, 109
Lip-reading, 92
Liszt, Franz, 89–90, 152n
Locke, Alain, 145–6, 147, 148
Lomax, John, 141
London, 28–9, 34, 35–6, 53, 61, 62–4, 178–9
Loy, Mina
    'Brancusi's Golden Bird', 91–2, 107
    on modern poetry, 91–2

Mach, Ernst, 31, 169
    Contributions to the Analysis of the Sensations, 82, 159
McKay, Claude, 147, 148
    Home to Harlem, 146

Mackenzie, Compton, *Sinister Street*, 62, 173–4
McLuhan, Marshall, 69
Mallarmé, Stéphane, 90, 97–8, 166
    'Un Coup de Dés Jamais N'Abolira Le Hasard', 93–5, 96
    L'après-midi d-un faune, 126
Mann, Thomas
    Buddenbrooks, 76
    Doctor Faustus, 40, 118, 130
    'Tristan', 76
Mansfield, Katherine, 'Miss Brill', 60
Marinetti, F. T., 97
Marx, Karl, 23–4, 27, 31, 128
Melody, 25, 32, 33, 42, 131, 135, 141, 160
Memory, 159, 160, 164–5
    voluntary and involuntary, 163, 165
Messiaen, Oliver, 129
Milhaud, Darius, 145
Modernity, 16–17, 24, 77, 141
Moholy-Nagy, László, 139–40
Morrison, Toni, *Beloved*, 118
Mozart, Wolfgang Amadeus, 41, 118
Munch, Edvard, *The Scream*, 97, 98, 104
Münsterberg, Hugo, 169
    The Photoplay, 101
Music, 2, 3, 4, 5, 11, 12, 20, 23, 30, 31–2, 33, 38–46, 53, 90, 91, 93, 99–101, 102, 108, 124–51, 157, 158, 159–62, 177, 178
    and the body, 25, 42, 160
    historicity of, 127–34
    as immaterial, 30, 31–2, 101
    as non-representational, 41–2, 74, 101, 38, 161
    and sexuality, 24, 71–7, 126
    and sociality, 58–60, 73
    see also individual genres and musicians
Musical notation, 102, 116–19, 135, 139, 140
Musil, Robert, *The Man Without Qualities*, 63

Nancarrow, Conlon, 138
National Socialism, German, 69, 81
Neubauer, John, 41
Neurasthenia, 144
Neurophysiology, 91, 112, 115–16
Newton, Isaac, 104, 109
    Opticks, 103
New York, 29, 53, 61–5
Nietzsche, Friedrich, 26, 30, 44, 76–7, 78, 81–3
    The Birth of Tragedy, 59, 79, 132
Nijinsky, Vaslav, 126, 136

Origen, 21

Painting, 26, 39, 40–1, 83, 91, 97–9, 106, 109, 111, 147
Partch, Harry, 135
Pater, Walter, 41, 42, 44, 178, 179
    'The School of Giorgione', 39
Patterson, William Morrison
    The Rhythm of Prose, 162–3
Perloff, Marjorie, 111
Pessoa, Fernando, 92
Phonograph, 14, 15, 27–8, 37, 64, 65, 70–2, 73, 96–7, 104–5, 116–17, 127, 138, 139–43, 149, 162, 177; *see also* Gramophone
Physiology, 25
Piano, 72–6, 99, 100, 107, 146, 150, 157
Picasso, Pablo, 4
Picker, John M., *Victorian Soundscapes*, 5
Pickering, Ruth, 'The Economic Interpretation of Jazz', 144
Pirandello, Luigi, 169
Pitch, 134–6, 140, 141
Plato, 72, 102–3
Player piano, 138
Pound, Ezra, 4, 137
    'Machine Art', 137
    Treatise on Harmony, 135–6
Primitivism, 29–30, 31, 34–5, 61, 127, 140–2, 146
Prince, Morton
    The Unconscious, 115–16
    The Dissociation of a Personality, 116
Proust, Marcel, 17, 38, 41, 44, 59, 101, 163
    In Search of Lost Time, 7–9, 14, 29, 31–2, 33, 76, 163
Psychoanalysis, 37, 80, 162
Pudovkin, W. I., 169–70
Pythagoras, 11, 103, 110–11

'Race', 104, 117–18, 141, 163; *see also* Jazz: and 'race'
Radio, 1, 2, 13, 14, 28, 53, 66, 67–70, 96, 100, 138, 141, 166
Ragtime, 136, 144, 147
Recording, 13, 14, 27, 59, 70; *see also individual technologies*
Rhythm, 25, 31, 39, 106, 134, 135–6, 137, 143, 145, 149, 159–60, 162–3
Richardson, Dorothy, 17, 62, 64, 82, 167, 168–9
    Pilgrimage, 12–13, 30–1, 48n, 53–8, 61, 77, 81, 167, 68, 169
Richter, Hans, *Rhythmus 21*, 106–7
Rilke, Rainer Maria, 140
    'Primal Sound', 27–8, 70
Rimbaud, Arthur, 'Voyelles', 90, 113

Rimmington, Alexander Wallace, 109
Romanticism, 22, 73–4
Roth, Henry, *Call it Sleep*, 61–2, 65, 173–4
Rousseau, Jean-Jacques, 77
    Essay on the Origin of Languages, 58
Russolo, Luigi, 135
    The Art of Noises, 137
Ryan, Judith, 31

Sabaniev, Leonid, 110
Samson, Jim, 131
Satie, Erik, 145
Scarborough, Dorothy, *On the Trail of Negro Folk Songs*, 141
Schaefer, R. Murray, *The Tuning of the World*, 5
Schaeffer, Pierre, 13–14, 80, 100, 137
Schiller, Friedrich, 44, 47n
Schoenberg, Arnold, 118–19, 124, 127, 129, 131, 136
    Erwartung, 132
    Harmonielehre, 124–6, 128–9, 132
    serial technique of, 133–4
Schopenhauer, Arthur
    The World as Will and Representation, 42–3
Schumann, Robert, 74
Schwitters, Kurt, 37
Scriabin, Alexsandr, *Prometheus – The Poem of Fire*, 110
Second World War, 157–8, 159
    the Blitz, 175–8
Senses
    critique of, as 'prejudiced', 26, 113, 162
    hierarchically related, 22, 82
    'inner' and 'outer', 11–12, 21–2, 25, 82, 88n, 111, 161
    integrated and apart, 6–10, 23–4, 39, 81–3, 100–1, 105–6, 158–9, 169, 171–3, 178
Severini, Gino, *Cannoni in Azione*, 97–8
Silence, 11–12, 21, 34–5, 56–7, 92, 96, 118, 159, 165–8
Simmel, Georg, 'The Metropolis and Mental Life', 29
Smith, Lee Orean, 143
Sociality, 69, 84n; *see also* Music: and sociality
Sonata form, 130, 153n
Sound
    'depth' approach to, 30, 31, 33, 61, 147
    'shock' approach to, 30–1, 33
    as writing, 115–17

'sound-space', 53–7, 58–9, 172–3
'sound-world', 5, 10, 12, 15, 33, 52
Spender, Stephen, 157–8, 179n
Spiller, Gustav, 'The Dynamics of Attention', 159
Sterne, Jonathan, *The Audible Past*, 5
Stevens, Wallace, 'The Man with the Blue Guitar', 60
Stockhausen, Karl-Heinz, *Kontakte*, 135–6
Stoker, Bram, *Dracula*, 116
Strauss, Richard, *Salome*, 133
Stravinsky, Igor, 4, 118, 136, 138–9, 140, 143, 145, 151
    The Rite of Spring, 4, 136
    Sérénade en la, 140
Stroheim, Erich von, *The Merry Widow*, 99
Stuckenschmidt, H. H., 'The Mechanization of Music', 139
Symbolism, 90, 106
Synaesthesia, 91, 112–14

Tape recording, 135–6, 159, 164–5
Tchaikovsky, Piotr Ilyich, 78
Telephone, 2, 8–9, 12, 13, 14, 65, 66–7, 73, 162
Television, 1
Theology, 21, 45–6, 151, 166, 177
Theosophy, 110
Thompson, Emily, *The Soundscape of Modernity*, 5
Thoreau, Henry David, *Walden*, 15
Timbre, 134, 136–7
Time, 14, 23, 24, 31, 32, 33, 39–40, 43, 96–7, 101, 130, 136, 146, 150–1, 159, 160, 165
Tolmer, Alfred, *Mise en Page*, 118
Tolstoy, Leo, *The Kreutzer Sonata*, 37, 75
Tonality, 125–6, 128–9, 132, 133–4, 135 152n; *see also* Dissonance; Harmony; Schoenberg, Arnold: serial technique of
Twain, Mark and William Dean Howells, *Colonel Sellers as a Scientist*, 70
Tyndall, John, 108
    Sound, 104
Typography, 93–8, 115, 149

Udaltsova, Nadezhda
    At the Piano, 99

Van Vechten, Carl, *Nigger Heaven*, 71

Varèse, Edgar, *Intégrales*, 140
Vertov, Dziga, 120n
    Man with a Movie Camera, 99–101
Villey, Pierre, 174
    The World of the Blind, 171–2
Voice, 2, 8–9, 11–12, 21, 31, 34, 36–8, 61, 67, 70, 81, 145, 168, 176–7
Vološinov, V. N., 53
Vorticism, 93

Wagner, Richard, 4–5, 6, 9, 10–11, 12, 33–4, 40, 42, 44, 46, 52, 77–83, 89–91, 106, 108, 110, 118, 137, 169, 170, 178
    Anti-semitism of, 81
    'The Art-Work of the Future', 10, 88n
    Bayreuth Festival, 78–79, 80–1, 90, 178
    'Beethoven', 5
    Lohengrin, 89–90
    Parsifal, 76
    The Ring of the Nibelung, 78, 108
    Tristan and Isolde, 75–7, 78, 131–2
Waugh, Evelyn, *Vile Bodies*, 67
Weber, Max, *The Rational and Social Foundations of Music*, 118, 131
Webern, Anton, *The Path to the New Music*, 128, 133–4
Welles, Orson, *The War of the Worlds*, 69–70
Wells, H.G., 69
Wheeler, Raymond H. and Thomas Cutsforth, 'Synaesthesia: A Form of Perception', 112–13
Wieck, Clara, 74
Wilder, Billy, *Double Indemnity*, 116
Wittgenstein, Ludwig, 116–17
    Tractatus, 102
Woolf, Virginia, 17, 21, 22, 103, 177–8
    Between the Acts, 11–12, 178
    Flush, 61
    Jacob's Room, 114–15
    Mrs Dalloway, 92
    'The String Quartet', 59–60
    To the Lighthouse, 92, 114–15
    The Voyage Out, 75–6, 166
    The Waves, 15, 28–9, 61, 66–7
Writing, 92–7, 99, 139, 140, 176; *see also* Language; Musical Notation; Sound: as writing; Typography

Yeats, W. B., 35, 147
    'Hound Voice', 31